INTERNATIONAL BUSINESS TRANSACTIONS
IN A NUTSHELL

NINTH EDITION

By

RALPH H. FOLSOM
Professor of Law
University of San Diego

MICHAEL WALLACE GORDON
John H. & Mary Lou Dasburg Professor of Law Emeritus
University of Florida

JOHN A. SPANOGLE
William Wallace Kirkpatrick Professor of Law
The George Washington University

MICHAEL P. VAN ALSTINE
Professor of Law
University of Maryland Francis King Carey School of Law

WEST®
A Thomson Reuters business

Mat #41326202

COPYRIGHT © 1981, 1984, 1988, 1992, 1996 WEST PUBLISHING CO.
COPYRIGHT © West, a Thomson business, 2000, 2004
© 2009 Thomson Reuters
© 2012 Thomson Reuters

       610 Opperman Drive
       St. Paul, MN 55123
       1-800-313-9378

Printed in the United States of America
ISBN: 978-0-314-28436-5

DEDICATION

We dedicate this book:

to Paris and the University of San Diego Institute of International and Comparative Law, and

to all those who work to promote the harmonization of international commercial, trade, and investment law

PREFACE TO NINTH EDITION

This ninth edition of International Business Transactions in a Nutshell follows the first two editions authored by the late Professor Donald T. Wilson and published in 1981 and 1984. Because of the size of our fourth edition, further expansion to cover developments between 1991 and 1995 could be accomplished only if we split the nutshell in two. Thus was born what is now the second Nutshell: International Trade and Economic Relations in a Nutshell.

The authors have completed both this ninth edition of International Business Transactions in a Nutshell, and the fifth edition of International Trade and Economic Relations in a Nutshell. Together, these Nutshells cover all significant areas of international business, from selling goods across borders to foreign direct investments abroad, plus the role of nations in regulating trade and economic relations, both unilaterally and by participation in bilateral and multilateral agreements.

International Business Transactions in a Nutshell commences with a general introduction to international business, followed by a chapter on international business negotiations, and thereafter focuses on documentary international sales and letters of credit, E-commerce, transfers of technology, foreign investment, expropriations, extraterritorial antitrust, and international business litigation and arbitration. International Trade and Economic Relations in a Nutshell focuses principally on government controls on imports and exports, customs unions and free trade agreements, trade remedies, and the law and economic relations of the World Trade Organization, the European Union, and NAFTA

The two Nutshells are intended to provide our readers with a broad introduction to the people and institutions who practice international business law, and the government and multilateral organizations which both encourage and restrict trade and economic relations. The allocation of chapters between the two Nutshells reflects our value judgments as to what ought to be included in introductory volumes on a very broad subject which is constantly affected by change. These judgments will be familiar to those who have read or adopted our International Business Transactions: A Problem-Oriented Coursebook, originally published in 1986, with many new editions since then. We have also produced a West's Concise Hornbook on Principles of International Business Transactions (2d ed. 2010).

We have been aided by colleagues at our own law schools and others both in this country and abroad, by student research assistants and by persons in practice. We welcome continued suggestions for the next edition.

RALPH. H. FOLSOM
rfolsom@sandiego.edu

MICHAEL WALLACE GORDON
Gordon@law.ufl.edu

JOHN A. SPANOGLE
aspanogle@law.gwu.edu

MICHAEL P. VAN ALSTINE
MVanAlst@law.umaryland.edu

September 2012

OUTLINE

TABLE OF CASES

References are to Pages

INTERNATIONAL BUSINESS TRANSACTIONS

IN A NUTSHELL

NINTH EDITION

INTRODUCTION
FROM BROCKTON AND BURBANK
TO BANGKOK
AND BEIJING

Representing a Boston client who sells goods to a buyer in Burbank, California, creates relatively few issues that are not similarly present if the buyer is in the same state as the seller, for example Brockton, Massachusetts. Both sales are likely to constitute a standard, domestic documentary sale transaction. Unlike a face-to-face transaction, the seller will not meet the buyer and hand over the goods simultaneously as the buyer hands over the money. Payment is likely to be required upon presentation of the *documents* by the seller to the buyer, not upon an inspection of the goods by the buyer after the goods have arrived. A letter of credit may be used to reduce risks and avoid a situation where either the seller or the buyer has possession of both the goods and the money at the same time. Use of a letter of credit adds to the transaction an issuing bank, and perhaps a second confirming bank. The Boston seller may be willing to accept the letter of credit issued by a Brockton or Burbank bank, without confirmation by a bank in, or closer to, Boston. The sale to Brockton will be in dollars, just as will be the sale to Burbank. And the parties will correspond in English.

Perhaps the most significant features unique to the Burbank purchase involve which state's law will apply and which state's courts will be the appropriate forum if there is a conflict. But the rules of commercial law of Massachusetts and California are nearly identical. Both states have adopted the Uniform Commercial Code. The California lawyer representing the Burbank buyer passed a different bar exam than the Boston lawyer. But nearly all of the substantive law on each exam was the same, rooted in the common law tradition and expressed in state legal systems containing many common features. The two lawyers studied the common law in their respective law schools, and they may even have gone to the same law school, located in a third state such as Florida. Although a continent apart, the Massachusetts and California lawyers for the buyer and seller could exchange practices, and quickly function with little loss of efficiency and skill.

But what if the sale from Boston is not to either a buyer in Brockton or in Burbank, but to a buyer in Bangkok? This *international* transaction will involve two different business and social cultures, and two different legal systems. The economy of Thailand is less developed than the economy of the United States, and may present some problems unique to developing nations, such as a less efficient infrastructure at the port of entry for unloading the goods. Risk of damage thus is greater, and insurance rates will be higher. Customs officials might demand "unofficial" payments to admit the goods. As in the case of the sale to Brockton or Burbank, the sale to Bangkok probably will involve the use of a documentary sale and almost certainly involve a letter of credit. But the usage of documentary sales and letters of credit may differ in each nation. Commonly used commercial terms, such as c.i.f. or f.o.b., may have different meanings and place different risks on the parties in each nation. The parties may help resolve this by specifying the use of the Paris based International Chamber of Commerce Incoterms, which provide interpretations of commercial terms usually accepted by courts. Wanting assurance that the goods received are the same as the goods ordered, the Bangkok buyer may wish to have a third party inspect the shipment and certify that the goods shipped are the same as the goods ordered. Such certification would be required before the buyer would be obligated to pay the seller.

The letter of credit in an international transaction is also more complex. If the Bangkok buyer uses a Bangkok bank as the issuing bank of the letter of credit, the Boston seller is almost certain to require that a U.S. bank, very likely with an office in Boston, confirm the letter of credit. The Boston seller does not wish to have to go to Bangkok to challenge the Bangkok bank if a conflict over the letter of credit arises. The Boston seller will prefer to go to a Boston bank to present the documents for payment, thus avoiding having to send the documents to an agent in Bangkok for presentation to a Bangkok bank. Additionally, letters of credit may be irrevocable or revocable. The Boston seller will almost certainly insist on the irrevocable form, but practice in Bangkok might be to issue revocable letters. As in the case of rules applicable to the documentary sale, the parties may choose international rules generally accepted to govern letters of credit. They will likely be the Uniform Customs and Practice for Documentary Credits (UCP). Like the Incoterms, the UCP are a product of the International Chamber of Commerce.

Not only will the contract for sale differ in our international transaction, the bill of lading contract for shipping the goods to Bangkok will differ. The greater distance to Bangkok will involve greater risks of loss during transportation. But that is true of the greater distance to Burbank than to Brockton in the domestic sale. If ocean transportation is used, shipments to either Burbank or Bangkok will likely transit the Panama Canal. However, the Boston seller can avoid any international issues in the sale to Burbank, such as transiting the canal, by shipping the goods across the continental United States to California. Selling to Bangkok does not offer that option. The shipment to Bangkok might be on a vessel with stops in several foreign nations before reaching Bangkok, creating additional and different risks. Furthermore, the laws and rules applicable to the shipment may differ. The United States applies its Carriage of Goods at Sea Act, based on the Hague Rules, while some other nations base their shipping laws on the Hamburg Rules or the Hague-Visby Rules.

A major difference in many international transactions involves the choice of *currency*. The Boston seller probably will insist on being paid in U.S. dollars, not Thai bahts. If Thai bahts are received by the Boston seller, it cannot pay suppliers with them, nor give them to workers as salary. When the seller takes Thai bahts to a Boston bank, the bank may reject them because the bank is not familiar with them, and believes it might not be able to exchange bahts for U.S. dollars. If the bank is willing to accept the bahts, it may do so only with a substantial discount, causing a projected profit from the sale to become a loss. Even if the Thai currency is freely exchangeable, the rates of conversion from bahts to dollars might change between the time of the signing of the contract and the time of the exchange, causing either an unexpected gain or an unwelcome loss. And, if the Bangkok buyer agreed to pay in dollars, the Thai government might impose exchange restrictions prohibiting the removal of hard currency from Thailand.

Not only the currency but the *language* of the contract will have to be decided. Even if the contract terms are expressed in English, as preferred by the Boston seller, the Bangkok buyer may believe the contract terms say something quite different than the view of the Boston seller. While differences in the meaning of terms may also occur in the domestic transactions, the likelihood and magnitude of differences in the international transaction are likely to be more extensive.

If the sale from Boston is to Beijing rather than to Bangkok, the Boston seller will address most of the same issues as noted above with the sale to Bangkok, plus issues of dealing with an economy that possesses some *nonmarket* economy characteristics. There are fewer nonmarket economies today than a decade ago, and many nonmarket economies are in a stage of transition to various forms of a market economy, including China. Thus there may be a question regarding the character or nature of the buyer's economy. It may be a nonmarket economy and also a developing nation, such as Cuba. It may be an advanced developing country (ADC) or newly industrializing country (NIC), but still be a nonmarket economy, such as China (if it is fair to currently characterize the PRC as beyond a mere developing nation). It may be a nonmarket economy trying to become a market economy, but having difficulty overcoming decades of central planning and government involvement in the production and distribution of goods. This is true of some of the nations in Eastern Europe and the former USSR. Or it may be a nonmarket economy which prefers to remain a nonmarket economy, but which finds it necessary to do business with market economies and opens the door to market economy characteristics only enough to achieve specific goals. Such remains the policy of Cuba.

Where the buyer is located in a nonmarket economy, a major difference is that the purchaser may be the government rather than a private entity. Furthermore, the purchaser may not be the end user of the goods, but a centralized government agency, frequently called a foreign or state trading organization (FTO or STO). Most nonmarket economies have very strictly controlled currencies. The currencies tend to be nonexchangeable in international currency markets, and are usually artificial in value. They are sometimes so strictly controlled that they may not be removed from the country.

Unable to obtain scarce dollars from the buyer's nation, and unwilling to accept that nation's currency, the Boston seller may be asked to find local goods to accept in exchange. This is *countertrade,* a modern variation of barter. The Boston seller receives goods instead of currency, and may have to search the other country for goods of value. The Boston seller might find goods it may use in its own operations. But if it is unable to use those goods in its own operations, it will have to market those goods. This additional and often complex aspect of what was to be a simple sale to the foreign country now involves two sales, and probably three contracts. The first sale is from the Boston seller to the foreign buyer. The second sale is the purchase of the countertrade goods by the Boston party from that foreign nation. The presence of two sales probably means the use of two contracts and two letters of credit. Because the two contracts are *linked*, there will have to be a third contract establishing the interrelationships between the parties. Often called the protocol contract, it may include penalties against the Boston seller if it does not find foreign goods to purchase within a certain time period.

Countertrade has many faces. It includes the exchange outlined above, usually called "counterpurchase". More complex forms may appear if the Boston seller wants to establish a factory in the foreign nation, and in lieu of profits agrees to accept a percentage of the foreign production—a form called "compensation" or "buy-back". In whatever face it appears, it is usually involuntary on the part of the U.S. seller or investor. Countertrade adds costs to the transaction, which will be passed on to the foreign buyer. Often countertrade occurs because the foreign nation's products are not of sufficient quality to be competitive in international trade. But sometimes traditional trade patterns tend to lock-out such products even when they are very good quality, and countertrade may thus be a way of forcing open a market. Some countertrade is voluntary, especially the above noted compensation or buy-back forms. Whatever form countertrade assumes, it has been around for much longer than currency, and it will continue to play some role in international trade.

We have noted only a few differences in a commercial sale of goods where the seller and buyer are in different countries. There are many other new issues to confront. The differences noted above tend to be attributable to different legal and economic systems in the two nations. There also may be differences in the cultures of the two nations which affect the transaction. Misunderstandings of cultural norms may create minor embarrassments, or constitute serious improprieties that terminate negotiations. The result is lost business. If the Boston seller or its counsel has gone to Bangkok or to Beijing to negotiate or sign the contract, what conduct is expected? Do people greet each other by shaking hands, or is touching inappropriate? Is it proper to discuss business over breakfast? Should spouses be invited to a business dinner? Should one sit with legs crossed? Are nominal gifts appropriate or distasteful? What transpires during the negotiations may involve one of the nation's laws which attempts to govern moral conduct, such as the U.S. Foreign Corrupt Practices Act (FCPA), that prohibits many payments or gifts intended to influence foreign officials' decisions.

Our Boston seller may begin to sell sufficient products to Bangkok or Beijing that it decides to establish some form of agency or distributorship abroad. It may have experience with the use of agents or distributors in its sales to Brockton or Burbank. The buyer might have used an *agent* to represent it. The agent would not possess title to the goods; title would pass directly from the Boston seller to the buyer. The agent would be said to have had the goods "on consignment". Or the Boston seller might have used a *distributor*. The distributor takes title to the goods, and passes that title upon the sale to the buyer. The same decision between an agent or a distributor will have to be made when selling abroad, but the Boston seller may learn that there are quite different laws governing such sales. The foreign nation may have a special distributorship law, which reduces some of the seller's choices available in U.S. law. The foreign law is likely to favor the local distributor, especially regarding matters of the right to, and rights upon, termination. Even where there is no special distributorship law, the applicable laws may be different. Those laws may be included among the many provisions of the local civil or commercial code, if the foreign nation has a civil law legal system. Establishing a foreign distributorship also may raise issues of questionable trade restraints under the foreign law, when the distributor becomes the exclusive agent, or is limited to certain territory, or must sell at seller established prices.

Depending upon the form chosen for the sale of goods abroad, the Boston seller may become enough of an employer in the foreign country to be subject to the foreign nation's labor law. Labor law in many foreign nations differs dramatically from labor law in the United States. Nations are often protective of their workforce, and the Boston seller may encounter far stricter rules regulating the employment relationship, especially termination. A "once hired, can't be fired" rule is perhaps the most troublesome for employers. In addition to the foreign labor law, the Boston seller will have to deal with the movement of business persons across borders. Even a brief *business* visit to Bangkok or Beijing may require entry papers far more complex than a *tourist* visa. Much business is undertaken using tourist visas, but such use may create a risk if a contract is breached. As business persons cross borders for longer stays, visa requirements are likely to increase. But it is not only the immigration rules of Bangkok and Beijing which may appear to constitute an impenetrable maze to the Boston seller, it is also the U.S. immigration rules which create obstacles. The Boston seller may wish to bring Bangkok or Beijing business associates to Boston for training. That may require a business visa, or perhaps an education visa.

As our Boston client's trade evolves and increases, from an isolated sale, to occasional sales, and perhaps to the creation of a distributorship agreement, thought may be given to the manufacture of the products abroad. Manufacture abroad may follow the major step of creating a direct foreign investment, or perhaps by licensing a foreign producer in Bangkok or Beijing to manufacture the goods. Licensing production to a company in Brockton or Burbank would involve only the negotiation of the licensing agreement by the Boston licensor and the Brockton or Burbank licensee. But if the Boston seller licenses the production to a developing or nonmarket economy nation, the transfer of technology agreement may be subject to careful scrutiny by the host government. The Boston licensor will be most concerned with protecting its intellectual property, while the foreign government may be more concerned with regulation of the transfer of technology.

Even if the foreign licensee is a privately owned enterprise, the government may mandate that all technology agreements be registered, and sometimes subjected to review for approval to ensure that they do not include provisions considered detrimental to the economic development of the nation. Those concerns reach such issues as duration of the agreement, royalty amount, grant-back requirements, territory restrictions on sales, rejection of technology "adequately" available locally, and choice of law and forum. Not all developing nations and nonmarket economies have such requirements, which developed nations consider trade restrictive and which are generally inconsistent with contemporary rules on intellectual property, which focus more on protection of intellectual property than restrictions on its transfer.

The Boston licensor of the technology is very concerned about the existence and adequacy of laws protecting intellectual property in the foreign country. The Boston licensor has invested considerable time and money in developing its products, and wants the fullest protection offered by patent, trademark, copyright and trade secret laws. If the products are licensed to be manufactured by a Brockton or Burbank licensee, the Boston entity is protected by a scheme of mostly federal law protecting intellectual property. But if the license is to Bangkok or Beijing, the licensor may confront very different views about rights to intellectual property. Such rights may not be recognized at all, because they are considered not subject to private ownership, but to constitute part of the national patrimony or the property of mankind. Even if intellectual property is acknowledged to be private property, if the foreign nation's gross national product depends to a sufficient degree on counterfeit production and exports that loss of such production may cause economic dislocations, it may refuse to adopt or actively enforce laws protecting intellectual property rights.

The above business transactions illustrate some of the differences in selling to or licensing the production of goods in foreign nations. These differences occur every day in international business. The differences may create additional transaction costs. One transaction cost all business persons hope to avoid is the cost of resolving disputes. That is accomplished by avoiding them. But we are yet to find a way to assure that all transactions will occur without conflict, and thus must be prepared to assume some costs of dispute resolution, and to understand the nature of dispute settlement in international transactions.

If a conflict arises between the seller and the buyer, the choice of law and choice of forum issues are very possibly extremely important to each party. It should come as no surprise to the Boston lawyer and client that the contract law of Thailand differs from that of Massachusetts much more than did the contract law of California. Furthermore, the legal system of Thailand, including procedural law, may have very different characteristics than the legal system of Massachusetts. But as more nations become parties to the 1980 Convention on Contracts for the International Sale of Goods (CISG), the applicable contract rules will be nearly the same. While they may be the same, a Bangkok court will use a copy of the law in Thai, while a Boston court will use one in English. Different meanings to terms may result from different translations. Furthermore, the method of judicial interpretation in Bangkok will differ from that in Boston, far more so than judicial interpretation in Brockton or Burbank. The Bangkok court will interpret the statutory provision, with some assistance from scholarly treatises, but with less attention to Thai cases then the Boston lawyer may expect. The Boston court is likely to focus on past Massachusetts decisions, and, if none are found, decisions of other states which interpret the particular provision. Harmonization of law does not mean harmonization of the legal systems, and therefore of methods of judicial interpretation.

Because of the very different attitudes towards dispute resolution, the parties may choose to include a provision in their contract for mandatory arbitration. Considered essential when dealing with some nations because of inefficient or corrupt judicial systems, and the failure to enforce foreign judgments, arbitration is often chosen when judicial systems function honestly. Court back-logs, costs of litigation and more relaxed rules of evidence are often the reasons arbitration is used in a domestic setting, for example for disputes arising in the sale from Boston to Brockton, or Boston to Burbank. Those same reasons exist in the international setting, plus a sense of fairness provided by third party arbitration.

International litigation and arbitration add many new dimensions to the same issues when part of domestic litigation. Choosing Burbank (meaning California) law rather than Boston (meaning Massachusetts) law is a much less significant decision than choosing Bangkok (meaning Thailand) law or Beijing (meaning PRC) law, rather than Boston law. The same is true in choosing a forum. Initiating a suit in a foreign country is likely to introduce us to different rules of jurisdiction, including not recognizing the distinction between subject matter and personal jurisdiction. Service of process in many foreign nations is a more formal process than in the United States, and is unlikely to be linked to personal jurisdiction so as to allow jurisdiction based on service. The extensive process of discovery in the United States is essentially nonexistent abroad, and has few admirers sitting on the bench in foreign courts and asked to honor a U.S. court order for discovery in their nations. If the Boston seller is able to obtain jurisdiction over the Bangkok or Beijing buyer in a Boston court, and obtains a judgment, it may have little value unless the courts in Bangkok or Beijing will recognize and enforce the Boston judgment. Recognition and enforcement rules vary throughout the world. In the United States recognition and enforcement varies state-to-state, often confusing to foreign lawyers. But that variance from state-to-state in the United States is with respect to recognition of a judgment granted in a foreign *nation* rather than in a sister foreign state. Full faith and credit mandates recognition of sister state judgments. Thus the Boston judgment creditor will have an easier time enforcing a judgment in a Brockton or Burbank court, than in a Bangkok or Beijing court.

The participation of foreign officials in the transaction adds new dimensions beyond the possible questionable payments which may violate the Foreign Corrupt Practices Act. If the buyer is the foreign government, or an instrumentality of the government, special problems may arise if litigation over the contract ensues. What if the sale is canceled by the Bangkok or Beijing government agency, and the Boston seller sues, only to be confronted with a defense of sovereign immunity? The foreign government would be saying that it is sovereign and is immune to suit anywhere. But that immunity is increasingly limited to *government* actions, rather than to *commercial* actions conducted by a government. Drawing the line between what is a government act and what is a commercial act is not easy. The United States, after decades of following the *absolute* theory of foreign state immunity, enacted the Foreign Sovereign Immunities Act (FSIA) in 1976, which adopts the *restrictive* theory—that foreign states are not immune when the transaction is commercial. That may help our Boston seller if the sales are commercial sales to foreign states, or to their agencies or instrumentalities.

A second defense our Boston seller may encounter when suing a foreign state is that the foreign act was an "act of state". The courts of one nation tend not to want to sit in judgment of acts of a foreign government which took place in the territory of that foreign government. This theory developed in case law, and unlike the above noted codification of state immunity theory in the FSIA, the act of state doctrine remains based in U.S. case law. That law has yet to clearly conclude whether or not a commercial action exception exists to the act of state doctrine. The doctrine as a whole has been partly restricted by the Supreme Court. Whatever the outcome of the commercial exception is, our Boston seller might be wise to insist on arbitration, or an express waiver of these defenses, in any contract to sell to the government in Bangkok or Beijing.

Even if the sale is to a private buyer, the government may interfere with the sale for such reasons as the scarcity of reserves which limits access to foreign currency, or the prohibition or limitation of entry of the products of the Boston seller into the nation. Would these reasons constitute *force majeure* and allow the buyer to avoid performance because of a frustration of performance? What if the buyer is an agency of the government and the purchase is canceled by order of the executive? Is the agency sufficiently separate from the executive to be entitled to present a *force majeure* defense?

Our Boston client has entered the world of international business transactions, and has learned quickly of the complexities of dealing with Bangkok or Beijing rather than Brockton or Burbank. It might decide not to deal with developing nations or nonmarket economies, but to sell to, or license or establish a direct foreign investment in, only those nations which are more developed and which are market economies. For example it may sell to buyers in Brussels. In selling goods to a Brussels buyer it will not confront import licenses; it will receive a strong, convertible currency; and it will not be asked to accept countertrade. But it may have to deal in another language and, depending on the nature of the product, it may confront European Union tariff and nontariff barriers absent in domestic U.S. sales. If the Boston company licenses a Brussels firm to make its products, it will have its intellectual property protected, but with some variations from the form of protection received in the United States. If it creates a subsidiary in Belgium it will not have to adopt a joint venture. But it will face civil law tradition corporate concepts and possibly some workers' rights not present in the United States. The company will have to learn something about dealing in an economically integrated market, in this case the European Union. The similarities with dealing in Brockton or Burbank are as prevalent as the disparities in dealing with Bangkok or Beijing. That is partly why a very large part of U.S. trade and investment abroad is with developed, market economy nations.

What follows in the chapters ahead is an introduction to some of the laws and policies, the organizations and entities, and the people that are involved in some of the activities that we believe are included in the term "international business transactions". Because that term includes, as noted above, the trade of goods across borders, licensing, foreign investment, the role of governments in the use of tariff and non-tariff barriers, as well as such other areas as controls on exports, the taking of foreign property by governments, insuring foreign investment, the increasing implementation of bilateral and multilateral trade agreements, and forms and procedures of dispute resolution in all of these international business transactions, this 9th edition of the International Business Transactions Nutshell will share some of these areas with its companion volume by the same authors—the International Trade and Economic Relations Nutshell, 5th edition. This Nutshell focuses on the documentary sale and use of letters of credit, E-commerce, technology transfers, foreign investment transactions, expropriations and remedies, EU business competition law, extraterritorial antitrust, and international business dispute settlement. The International Trade and Economic Relations Nutshell covers the government imposed restrictions on imports and exports, the GATT/WTO, free trade agreements and customs unions, and economic integration with an emphasis on the European Union and the North American Free Trade Agreement. The two Nutshells are intended to provide a broad introduction to the people and institutions who practice international business transactions, and the government and multilateral organizations which both encourage and restrict trade.

CHAPTER 1

NEGOTIATING INTERNATIONAL BUSINESS TRANSACTIONS

Sensitivity to negotiating in an international context is a valuable skill. An international business negotiation involves style and timing, as well as procedure and substance. Each of these features is discussed below. Procedure is the ingredient which is frequently underplanned, but is most often outcome determinative.

Negotiating styles differ from culture to culture and person to person. But at least two general styles may be observed in international settings: the adversarial-standoff style and the consensus building style. Each style can be effective in its own context.

NEGOTIATING BY CONTEST

The adversarial standoff style may be illustrated by reverting to medieval Europe and imagining two opposing armies drawn up in battle array. Although their common purpose is to secure agreement about who is to have what, they will bludgeon each other to achieve that agreement while parrying, shouting provocations, and carrying out diverting sorties along the way. This style is often counterproductive when negotiating an international business transaction. Its emphasis upon pressing maximum advantage to the point of conquest is frequently inappropriate when measured against other, more important factors. These factors include the efficient use of time, political and cultural differences, the volatility of international markets, currency exchange fluctuations, and expenses that must be paid by a client along the way to shaping a satisfactory international agreement. Moreover, the bad will engendered by this style may prejudicially color the opponent's judgment, in some cases killing the deal. In short, the adversarial-standoff style can have too high a cost for the "winner."

The adversarial-standoff style was used by representatives from the former Soviet Union in diplomatic and international commercial negotiations. Soviet negotiators attempted and sometimes successfully extracted the most from their negotiating opposite at the least cost to themselves. It should not be a surprise that this style involves the use of bluffs, threats, the ultimatum, rapid changes in previously "irrevocable" positions, procedural manipulations, purposeful ambiguity, repetitive demands, little or no desire for friendly interpersonal relations, and the impugning of a negotiating opposite's motivations. All of this occurs in the broader context of attempts to extract as much information as can be gained while revealing no information before agreement is reached on any point. For example, Soviet negotiators were known to enter a room with a large negotiating team that asks a seemingly endless stream of questions in exhausting detail, usually with multiple requests that answers be "clarified" with further information. The team then leaves the room, and an entirely new team arrives to ask further, and often the same, questions.

BUILDING A ROLLING CONSENSUS TOWARD AGREEMENT

The experienced, U.S. negotiator, W. Averell Harriman, suggested that "You have to put yourself in the other fellow's shoes . . . You also have to consider how to make it possible for him to make a concession . . . But the idea that you can whip your negotiating opposite into agreeing with you is nonsense. . . If you call a hand, you must recognize that you may lose it."

The consensus building style places an emphasis upon negotiators rapidly finding some kernels of agreement and expanding upon those areas with a view to building a momentum toward complete agreement. This momentum may overcome differences about how to resolve difficult issues. Because of each negotiator's underlying, often long-held and usually unexpressed images about the political, social and personal views held by a negotiating opposite, momentum stopped is not restarted easily in an international commercial setting. For example, in Europe, Americans are sometimes thought of as either spoiled, self-indulgent children or as gunslingers ready to start a war. Conversely, Churchill reportedly said that "The Germans are either at your throat or at your feet." The consensus building style's emphasis upon common ground helps to finesse such stereotypes as a "hidden dimension" in a negotiation.

One problem is that there may be no initial consensus about the reasons for negotiating at all. The United States went to the Paris Peace Talks to negotiate an end to the military conflict in Vietnam. The North Vietnamese went to the Talks to negotiate while the military conflict was being ended. Understanding why negotiating opposites are meeting with you is not always possible by considering only the explanation that is offered. In some countries, such as Japan, it is considered courteous to tell people what they want to hear. The key to the consensus building style is an advance determination of: (a) what your negotiating opposites really want; (b) what they really must have; (c) what they may offer in return; and (d) what they really cannot offer either because they lack authority to do so or because it would be unacceptable for enterprise, national or international reasons.

Because the consensus building style requires an advance strategy for moving toward complete agreement, the strategy must yield to negotiating opposites that which they absolutely must have in order to join in any agreement. For example, the Chinese require sufficient time and opportunity to adequately inspect and test purchased goods. Several Latin American countries require that foreign investments be structured as joint ventures and have regulated the level of royalty payments under licensing agreements. Some Islamic states cannot politically, and perhaps legally, countenance an agreement with persons doing business in Israel. Some nations cannot accommodate politically, and perhaps economically, an agreement that will have a negative effect upon the country's balance of payments. Unless these minimum requirements are acceptable beforehand, a consensus agreement is unlikely. Therefore, good practice demands that you research your opponents' goals, as well as the limits of their cultural, political, legal and business milieu. The timing of the indication of willingness to agree to such terms, however, should be carefully planned to facilitate the building of a consensus.

NEGOTIATING TEAMS

Negotiating teams are most often used with direct foreign investments, joint ventures and large licensing or sales transactions. Knowing in advance what minimum quid pro quo a negotiating opposite really must have in order to join in an international business agreement makes it easier to decide upon the persons who are necessary members of the negotiating team. Anyone who negotiates alone in an international setting runs a high risk of not appreciating all of the personal, cultural and linguistic meanings in any conversation, quite apart from the substance of whatever subject matter is under discussion. A team too large can be intimidating and suggest "imperialist" overtones; a team too small can be insulting and suggest "imperialist" overtones. The team, often of three people, should have one member with enough status or importance to convey a sufficient impression of sincerity of purpose and of respect for the dignity of those who will be the negotiating opposites. Specialists should be added as needed, perhaps in a capacity as part of an informal subcommittee. This is especially helpful when technical engineering or scientific issues are anticipated. A savvy technical person is a must, and should give a briefing to the lawyer on technical issues before the negotiations commence.

People who comprise the negotiating opposites may come from different, and perhaps unanticipated, quarters. In Japan, officials from a government ministry may participate in negotiations between a United States investor and a Japanese national, and the national's banker may also join the talks. A lawyer may well not be a part of the Japanese negotiating team. In the early days of Western trade with the People's Republic of China, lawyers were not welcome. They sometimes participated as "consultants" or "assistant vice-presidents." Negotiators in the former Soviet Union were often drawn from various Ministry of Trade Foreign Trade Organizations. Such people were experienced in negotiating and often were specialists in various subject matter areas, e.g., petroleum exploration.

It is always essential to understand the cultural background of negotiating opposites and the potential for cross-cultural misunderstandings. Most cultures and foreign enterprises involve hierarchies which must be understood so as to properly evaluate the rank and power of negotiating opposites. Disclosure duties, for example, may vary as between cultures and within hierarchies. Also, past catastrophes of foreign companies or governments must be discovered and considered in advance. Large institutions will tend to over-compensate to avoid making the same disastrous mistakes twice.

Foreigners negotiating with U.S. lawyers would do well to review the empirical findings of Prof. Gerald R. Williams on American legal negotiating styles. See Legal Negotiation and Settlement (West Publishing Co. 1983). Prof. Williams analyzes the attributes of U.S. attorneys using two fundamentally different styles: cooperative versus competitive. These attributes are broadly similar to the two international negotiating styles described in this chapter: consensus building versus adversarial. Prof. Williams indicates that both the competitive and cooperative styles can be effective, but that cooperative U.S. legal negotiators are much more common and noticeably more likely to be effective in domestic negotiations.

ROLE PLAYING

All team members must know about and agree upon the negotiating strategy. However, it is inevitable that at some point in the negotiations an unplanned decision will have to be taken extemporaneously. Team members should agree in advance upon the person who will be the team's "voice" to make that decision. Other roles, such as the "coinpromiser" or the "diplomat", may be preassigned. A team which assigns the role of "hatchet man" to one of its members should remember the Chinese saying: "The nail which sticks up gets hit." Roles may be changed intentionally during a negotiation. One of the most interesting parts of any negotiation is an accurate assessment of the role being played by each negotiating opposite at any given moment.

TIMING

Understanding the overall timing framework for a successful negotiation is sometimes difficult for the U.S. attorneys and business executives. The phrase, "Life is long," may help to explain why it took the Vietnamese two years to agree about the shape of the negotiating table at the Paris Peace Talks. The Chinese and people from many other countries negotiate with a recognition that what cannot be settled today perhaps can be settled tomorrow or next week. Japanese are reluctant to do business with someone in whom they do not have sufficient trust and with whom they do not sense reciprocal feelings of friendship. (Remember this if considering the adoption of the adversarial standoff style of negotiations.) It may take weeks spent together on a golf course before such trust is engendered. People in other countries prefer not to negotiate during certain times of the year, e.g., Ramadan in Islamic nations. In some countries the "weekend" is on days other than Saturday and Sunday, those days being normal business days. Some hours which in the United States are considered the normal business day (9:00 A.M.-5:00 P.M.) are not considered appropriate for doing business in other countries. In parts of Africa "noon" may be any time between 10 a.m. and 2 p.m. The hours between 2 p.m. and 5 p.m. are inappropriate for doing business in Saudi Arabia.

IMPORTANCE OF PROCEDURE

It may be, and often is, that the procedure employed in international business negotiations is the single most important cause of their success or failure. The careful lawyer or executive will make advance inquiry about whether contacts preliminary to the negotiation are advisable and about which locations may be preferable for conducting negotiations. Procedures calculated to facilitate the building of personal relationships increase prospects for a successful negotiation, especially in Asia. In tough moments during a negotiation, courtesy alone may keep a consensus momentum going. Enduring courtesy is the essential lubricant of international negotiations.

A negotiating opposite may not want to admit that an apparent unwillingness to agree to a suggested point is caused by bureaucratic foot dragging, lack of coordination, lack of technical understanding or simple confusion on its side. Procedures that are flexible enough to allow time to work out such problems may cultivate ego, avoid a loss of "face" and continue participation in the negotiations. For example, a negotiating opposite may be unwilling to let you know that failure to reach quick agreement is due to the fact that he or she, despite having a lofty sounding title or other credentials, does not have authority to make a final agreement or will not assume personal responsibility for the consequences of an agreement. The latter case occurs frequently in Japan. Some nations find it prudent to advertise publicly that only certain government agencies are authorized to carry out sales or purchases.

Procedures which cause surprise are intimidating and can engender hostility and distrust. Obvious examples include emotional displays used as smoke screens, changing the agreed agenda for negotiation, unannounced or late arrivals and departures of negotiating personnel, and retreating from agreements already made. The surprise introduction of a written document (such as an investor's initial proposal), the contents of which a negotiating opposite is asked to consider or even to read on the spur of the moment, often causes similar reactions. Taking minutes of a negotiation and preparing written summaries of points of agreement often speeds the consensus building process, but the surprise transmission of such documents to a negotiating opposite can work a greater and opposite effect. Of course, these procedures may be useful if negotiating by contest rather than consensus. Because the intimidating nature of a written document increases with its thickness, a one page summary of the contents stands a better chance of being read, especially by someone who need not consider the document.

IMPORTANCE OF CULTURE

Cultural and language differences between negotiating opposites accentuate the importance attached to procedure in international negotiations. Self-praise is deprecated in virtually all cultures. A story is told of one multinational investor in Africa who inserted certain "whereas" clauses into a negotiated agreement to the effect that the local government was unable to perform a task and that the investor possessed worldwide management and technical success at the same task. An African newspaper published those "whereas" clauses as evidence of "imperialist attitudes."

Although giving gifts of modest value is appreciated in virtually all cultures, it is an expected occurrence between negotiating opposites in some countries. Certain gifts, such as books depicting the natural beauty of the investor's home area, are generally appreciated while more specialized gifts may be preferred in a particular country. For example, Johnny Walker Black Label Scotch is appreciated in Japan, but Red Label is valued in Thailand and Burma.

There is an almost universal cultural importance attached to sharing a meal with a negotiating opposite. Meal time affords a good opportunity for an investor to show an interest in and sensitivity about the host's culture. Unlike the United States, where business luncheons and dinners are common, in many cultures talking about business matters during a meal is considered impolite and is counterproductive.

There is considerable cultural diversity about the meaning of silence and delay in international negotiations. The common law rule that, under appropriate circumstances, "silence is acceptance" is not shared widely in many countries. In some countries silence may mean "no", while in other countries periods of silence are an acceptable and common occasion during which thoughts are arranged and rearranged. For example, an investor in Indonesia brought the final draft of a completely negotiated agreement to a counterpart for signature and, following some pleasant conversation, placed the agreement on the desk. In complete silence, the counterpart simply returned the document, unsigned, to the investor. The investor later learned that this day was not considered propitious in Indonesia for signing one's name. The agreement was signed the next day. Delays of days or even of months may not be signs that a negotiation is in difficulty, nor represent an attempt at increasing the costs of negotiating. Such delays may simply be the minimum time period in which a necessary consensus or authority is being achieved within a negotiating team.

An excellent analysis of cultural variables affecting international negotiations, known as LESCANT, has been prepared by David A. Victor. See International Business Communication (1992). LESCANT involves identification of the following cultural variables: Language; environment and technology; social organization; contexting (a measurement of explicit and implicit communications); authority conception; non-verbal behavior; and temporal conception. U.S. lawyers and business persons should consult the American Bar Association Guide to International Business Negotiations: A Comparison of Cross-Cultural Issues and Successful Approaches (1994). This Guide covers cultural aspects of international business negotiations generally, and specifically with reference to 17 nations.

THE LANGUAGE OF NEGOTIATIONS

Differences in language skills between negotiating opposites raise some peril in every international business transaction. Each negotiating party prefers quite naturally to use the language whose nuances are best known. Words that have a clear and culturally acceptable meaning in one language may be unclear or culturally offensive in another tongue. The converse may be true as well. For example, the French word "detent" does not translate easily into the English language. The consequences of this translation difficulty have worldwide importance. Because some hand gestures and body movements are acceptable in one culture yet deeply offensive in another culture, they are rarely an appropriate communications aid in international negotiations.

For example, raising an open hand in the direction of another party can mean in North Africa that you hope that person will lose all five senses.

The use of interpreters substantially slows the pace of negotiations and may spawn further difficulties because the interpreter is one more fallible person taking part in the negotiations. Interpreting is exhausting work and rarely exact. During an international commercial arbitration in Los Angeles, a witness testified in German alongside a skilled interpreter whose job it was to translate the testimony into English. While the arbitrators waited, it required the interpreter's efforts, the efforts of a U.S. lawyer fluent in German, and the efforts of a German lawyer fluent in English, to produce an oral translation which all agreed was sufficiently accurate. Even assuming the availability of an accurate literal translation, a Japanese person saying "yes" in answer to a question may not be signifying agreement but may only mean, "Yes, I understand the question."

The peril of language difficulty can be equally acute in negotiations between a lawyer from the United States and a negotiating opposite who speaks the English language. Each party may be embarrassed to raise a language question. For example, in the middle of a telephone conversation between a lawyer from the United States and a negotiator in England, a London operator interrupted to ask if the lawyer was "through." Not wishing to terminate the conversation, the American answered, "No, I am not through". The operator disconnected the circuit, apologized, and once again dialed to get the call "through." A few minutes later the London operator came on the line again, interrupting the parties' conversation, to ask again if the U.S. caller was "through." Desiring to continue the conversation without further interruption, the American lawyer this time said "Yes, thank you", and the operator left the line connected.

Certain foreign enterprises require their negotiators to speak English when negotiating with Americans. The problem is that their English seldom tracks American English, and embarrassing moments occur when U.S. negotiators must delicately seek clarification of the opponent's words. Such clarifications must be undertaken with the utmost politeness and goodwill in order not to insult or intimidate the foreign party.

Even exceptionally able interpreters may have difficulty if a U.S. lawyer or executive uses American slang in communicating during an international negotiation. The American penchant for using "ball park" figures may not be shared or understood in countries where baseball is not a popular sport. Slow and distinct patterns of speech combined with simple declarative sentences will always facilitate international business negotiations.

LANGUAGE IN THE AGREEMENT

The person who controls the drafting of an international business agreement often drives the negotiations. U.S. lawyers will almost always seek to perform this leading role. The careful language normally used by American lawyers in commercial contracts may prove controversial. While legally trained persons in some countries share an affinity for written contracts that set out the full extent of every right and duty of each party, the practice in many other countries tends toward more generally worded agreements that leave it to the parties (e.g., in Japan) or to the courts (e.g., in Germany) to supply any necessary details. A detailed, exhaustively worded, draft contract which is introduced during negotiations with Japanese or Chinese persons may arouse distrust. To them, a contract relationship is perceived as something that is shaped mutually as understanding develops. A German negotiating opposite may not be willing to sign an exhaustively worded contract because German courts dislike such agreements. The German courts take the position that they know the law and do not need a contract to state what is known already.

This attitude may trap unwary parties. Chinese negotiators, for example, will resist bargaining on the details of a contract or joint venture, saying "All that is of course understood" or "a part of our law." They may even show resentment at attempts to detail business agreements. However, during performance at a later date, other representatives of a

Chinese entity may not hesitate to say: "That is not written expressly in the contract and is not our duty." If a detail is important to the transaction, spell it out in the agreement. Many attorneys involved with Chinese business transactions have learned the hard way.

Permissible contract clauses in one country may be impermissible in another country and vice versa. For example, penalty clauses which are not legally enforceable in the United States are enforced routinely by French and, to a lesser extent, Italian courts. One-sided (adhesion) contracts may be fun for lawyers to draft, but they may serve only to raise suspicion by identifying the drafter as an adversary or to generate hostility and ill will. Draft adhesion contracts do not promote the consensus building style of international business negotiations. German courts will eviscerate an unfair adhesion contract without mercy.

One of the most frustrating features of international business agreements is the presence of texts in different languages, each of which is considered authoritative. Counsel to a U.S. enterprise will always seek to make English the sole language of the agreement, and sometimes succeed since English has become the predominant language of international business. Especially when negotiations have been conducted exclusively in English, time, expense, clarity and mutual understanding favor such a result. Even parties who do not natively speak

English may use it as the language of agreement for these reasons. Agreements between Japanese and Indonesian businesses, for example, are often in English. But cultural pride (especially with French speaking negotiators) or fear of unfair dealing (especially with Chinese negotiators) may leave multiple texts in different languages the only acceptable solution once "agreement" is reached.

Another important linguistic feature of international transactions, particularly of concern to lawyers, is the existence of different language texts of relevant laws. In the European Union, for example, there are over 20 official, authoritative texts for every treaty, regulation, directive, parliamentary report, etc. The NAFTA agreement is authoritative in English, French and Spanish. The nuances of languages can significantly affect the legality of any business transaction. Those same nuances can undermine any carefully constructed "consensus" international negotiators have worked hard to create.

PLANNING FOR RENEGOTIATION

An international business agreement, once achieved, must be monitored and maintained in good order. An agreement, particularly one spanning ten or twenty years, should be negotiated and written with a recognition that it may be renegotiated and rewritten after a few years. People live with unbalanced agreements only until such agreements can be changed. The foreign party may perform carefully and faithfully in accordance with a negotiated agreement, but other things may work to change a host country's attitude. For example, OPEC's rapid revision of the price of oil affected economic parameters of contract arrangements worldwide. The People's Republic of China has been known to cancel or slow payment under contracts with foreign investors when currency exchanges or market prices fluctuate.

Marked shifts in the political climate of a host country may bring marked changes in its government's attitude toward international business transactions. Marked change in the home country government attitude toward the host country may invite retaliation. Media discovery of contract terms unfavorable to a host country may focus local attention upon a foreign business. A foreign enterprise which is highly visible in a host country becomes an easy vehicle for venting local resentment against foreign investors.

Where plant, machinery and other assets are already "in place," renegotiation is one of several, relatively unattractive alternatives. One alternative may be expropriation. The unattractiveness of that choice, for example, led Occidental Petroleum Company and Belco Petroleum Company to renegotiate certain oil concession arrangements with the Peruvian government. The pressure of a suggested expropriation has prompted similar renegotiations in other countries, notably Venezuela under Hugo Chavez. If the initial, negotiated agreement contemplates and institutionalizes a series of periodic (e.g., once yearly) discussions about "readjustments" of certain parts of the investment agreement in light of the parties' accumulated experiences, the prospect of an unanticipated and traumatic renegotiation may be lessened and the consensus continued.

CHAPTER 2

INTERNATIONAL SALES OF GOODS

Most students who have taken a first-year Contracts course believe that Article 2 of the Uniform Commercial Code (UCC) is the United States law that governs all contracts for the sale of goods, both domestic and international. The UCC may indeed apply to international sales of goods, provided that the transaction in dispute bears an "appropriate relation" to a UCC state. *See* UCC Rev. § 1-301 (former § 1-105). And other countries have their own choice-of-law rules to determine which body of domestic law applies to a particular transaction. One prominent example is the European Union's Regulation on the Law Applicable to Contractual Obligations (2009), which applies in all EU member states. For sale of goods transactions, this so-called "Rome I" Regulation chooses "the law of the country where the seller has his habitual residence." *See* Article 4(1).

Since 1988, however, there is also U.S. federal law governing contracts for the international sale of goods in the form of an international treaty, the United Nations Convention on Contracts for the International Sale of Goods (1980). This federal law came into force through the U.S.'s formal ratification of the treaty and, pursuant to the Supremacy Clause of the U.S. Constitution, it preempts state laws like the UCC. The parties to a contract may "opt out" of the treaty, but it must be the starting point for any analysis of international sales transactions.

THE U.N. SALES CONVENTION (CISG) AND OTHER EFFORTS TO UNIFY INTERNATIONAL COMMERCIAL LAW

The United Nations Convention on Contracts for the International Sale of Goods (which is commonly known, even internationally, by the acronym "CISG") governs the sale of goods between parties in the United States and those in nearly eighty other countries. The CISG entered into force on January 1, 1988, thirteen months after the ratifications of the United States, China, and Italy exceeded the Convention's prescribed threshold of ten Contracting States. Under U.S. law, the CISG operates as a so-called "self-executing treaty," which means that it functions as directly applicable federal law without implementing legislation by Congress. And because ratified international treaties function as supreme federal law under Article VI of the Constitution, the CISG preempts all state law within its scope, including Article 2 of the UCC. The CISG also creates a cause of action in favor of aggrieved buyers and sellers in ordinary commercial litigation before federal courts in the United States. Thus, for example, a sale of goods contract between a private party in the United States and one in Canada would be governed by the CISG, and not by the UCC.

As of August 1, 2012, seventy-eight countries are "Contracting States" to the CISG, representing three-quarters of the world's trade in goods. The list of Contracting states include countries from all parts of the world and from all legal traditions, as well as nearly every major trading partner of the United States, from Canada and Mexico, to Japan and China, to Germany and France, and to South Korea and Singapore. (Notable exceptions include the United Kingdom, India, and Brazil.) In addition to the United States, the Contracting States of the CISG are: Albania, Argentina, Armenia, Australia, Austria, Belarus, Belgium, Benin, Bosnia and Herzegovina, Bulgaria, Burundi, Canada, Chile, China, Columbia, Croatia, Cuba, Cyprus, Czech Republic, Denmark, Dominican Republic, Ecuador, Egypt, El Salvador, Estonia, Finland, France, Gabon, Georgia, Germany, Greece, Guinea, Honduras, Hungary, Iceland, Iraq, Israel, Italy, Japan, Kyrgyzstan, Latvia, Lesotho, Liberia, Lithuania, Luxembourg, Macedonia, Mauritania, Mexico, Mongolia, Montenegro, the Netherlands, New Zealand, Norway, Paraguay, Peru, Poland, Republic of Korea, Romania, the Russian Federation, Saint Vincent and Grenadines, Serbia, Singapore, Slovakia, Slovenia, Spain, Sweden, Switzerland, Syria, Uganda, Ukraine, Uruguay, Uzbekistan, and Zambia. As a result of this broad acceptance, courts and arbitral tribunals have already generated thousands of opinions interpreting the CISG.

Other countries are expected to ratify or otherwise accept the CISG in the near future. This will increase the impact and effectiveness of the CISG in unifying international sales law. A current and complete list of Contracting States to the Convention is available at www.uncitral.org.

The CISG was adopted and opened for signature and ratification by a U.N.-sponsored diplomatic conference held at Vienna in 1980. The Convention resulted from the work of a specialized body of the United Nations, the United Nations Commission on International Trade Law (UNCITRAL), whose mandate is the unification and harmonization of international trade law. The purpose of such unification is to reduce legal obstacles to international trade, decrease transaction costs, enhance predictability and certainty, and promote the orderly development of new legal concepts as international commerce evolves in the future.

In addition to the CISG, UNCITRAL is responsible for a series of further treaties in the field of international commercial law. The most significant of these for present purposes is the 1974 Convention on the Limitation Period in the International Sale of Goods (as amended by Protocol in 1980). This Convention, which the United States and two dozen other countries have ratified as of 2012, provides special rules for what American lawyers would call the "statute of limitations" for international sale of goods transactions. (For more detail on this treaty, *see* below.) Other such UNCITRAL treaties—thus far, substantially less successful—include the Convention on the Use of Electronic Communications in International Contracts (2005); the Convention on the Assignment of Receivables in International Trade (2001); the Convention on Independent Guarantees and Stand-by Letters of Credit (1995); and the Convention on International Bills of Exchange and International Promissory Notes (1988).

Separately, UNCITRAL has prepared "model laws" for consideration by individual countries as domestic legislation. Prominent among these are the Model Law on International Commercial Arbitration (1985, as amended in 2006), which has served as a model for legislation in over sixty countries and seven states of the United States; the Model Law on Electronic Commerce (1996), which has influenced more than forty national laws, uniform acts in nearly every state of the U.S. and nearly every province of Canada, and various European Union directives; a Model Law on Cross-Border Insolvency (1997), which the United States implemented through a new Chapter 15 of the Bankruptcy Code; a new Model Law on Public Procurement (2011); and a Legal Guide on Drawing Up International Contracts for Construction of Industrial Works (1987). UNCITRAL is continuing its work on promoting international uniformity in other areas of commercial law, with present projects on international security interests and on online dispute resolution.

UNCITRAL is not the only international organization involved in proposing legal instruments for the unification and harmonization of international commercial law. Another prominent body, the International Institute for the Unification of Private Law (UNIDROIT), has prepared a variety of formal treaties in the field, including a Convention on International Factoring (1988), a Convention on International Financial Leasing (1988), and a promising (and as of 2012 already quite successful) framework Convention on International Interests in Mobile Equipment (2001). The Organization of American States (OAS) also has been active in this field on a hemisphere-wide basis.

In addition, UNIDROIT has prepared and issued the Principles of International Commercial Contracts (1994, as revised in 2004 and again in 2010). The Principles provide rules for all types of international commercial contracts, not just sales of goods, and their provisions are set forth in more general terms. If the CISG is the international analog to UCC Article 2 in United States law, then the Principles are the international analog to the Restatement of Contracts in U.S. law. They are not intended to be adopted as a convention or enacted as formal domestic law. Instead, they are designed for use principally by international commercial arbitrators, and even by judges where local law is ambiguous (and so permits). Some of the specific concepts are discussed later in this chapter. The substantive rules of the Principles are often different from those of the CISG, because the Principles were drafted by independent experts (not official delegations of governments), and the drafters could thus adopt what they considered to be "best practices" in international commercial contracts.

THE CISG's STRUCTURE AND SPHERE OF APPLICATION

The goal of the U.N. Sales Convention is to promote legal certainty in international sales transactions by creating a uniform set of legal rules to operate in the place of the diverse domestic legal systems of its Contracting States. The Convention does not even permit Contracting States to declare reservations to limit the effect of any of its substantive provisions (but for a short list of expressly stated exceptions). In addition to rules governing its scope, the CISG contains provisions on contract formation; the respective rights and performance obligations of sellers and buyers; the rights and remedies upon breach; the passing of the risk of loss from the seller to the buyer; as well as most other significant subjects in international sales transactions. The CISG is structured in four principal parts: Part I on scope and general principles; Part II on contract formation; Part III on the substantive rights and obligations of the buyer and the seller; and Part IV on the non-substantive "diplomatic" provisions relating to ratification, permitted reservations, withdrawal, etc. As noted, in the United States the CISG operates as a "self-executing treaty," with the result that as of 1988 it has functioned as directly applicable, preemptive federal law without any need for separate implementing legislation.

To achieve its goal of certainty and predictability, it is important that the CISG's scope of application be clear, both as to the circumstances where it applies, and those where it does not. The first six articles of the CISG define its sphere of application, but the principal rules are found in Article 1. That Article provides that the CISG will apply if a transaction (1) involves a sale of goods; (2) is "international"; and (3) bears a stated relation to at least one Contracting State.

(1) On the first requirement, the CISG unfortunately does not define "contract," "sale," or "goods." Nonetheless, it is generally understood that the subject matter of the transaction must involve an actual "sale"—that is, the passing of title for a price (and thus not a bailment, gift, or lease)—of a moveable thing.

(2) In contrast, the CISG clearly defines its "internationality" requirement. This is determined not by whether the goods cross a national border, but rather by the "places of business" of the persons involved in the transaction. Specifically, under Article 1(1) the transaction must be "between parties whose places of business are in different states" (with "states" being sovereign countries, not the states of the United States).

This "place of business" criterion may cause difficulty where a party has more than one business location. Although the Convention does not define the term, its drafting history suggests that a "place of business" is a location with at least some permanence and the authority to make independent business decisions. Thus, neither a simple warehouse nor the office of a seller's agent qualifies as a "place of business." Interpretive case law has established, on the other hand, that a branch office may suffice as long as it has some level of independent decision-making authority. For emphasis, Article 1(3) also declares that neither the nationality of the parties (*e.g.*, where a business is incorporated) nor their "civil or commercial character" (*e.g.*, whether or not domestic law would consider a party a "merchant") is to be taken into consideration in determining whether the CISG applies. The fact that the parties are from different states will be disregarded, however, if this does not appear from information available to them upon the conclusion of the contract. Article 1(2).

If a party has more than one location that qualifies as a "place of business," CISG Article 10 provides that the relevant place is the one with the "closest relationship" to the transaction. This provision is subject to some ambiguity, because it chooses the place of business that has the closest relationship "to the contract *and* its performance" (emphasis added). Thus, where one office is more closely associated with the formation of the contract and a second office is more closely associated with a party's performance of its contractual obligations, courts will need to weigh the relative significance of both of the considerations to determine which office is the relevant "place of business." Nonetheless, Article 10(a) limits the usable facts in such cases to those circumstances known to "the parties" at or before the conclusion of the contract. This should permit well-advised parties to resolve possible ambiguities by stating in the contract which office of each party they believe to have the "closest relationship" as contemplated by Article 10.

(3) Finally, the CISG governs only those contracts for the international sale of goods that have a substantial relation to one or more Contracting States—that is, the countries that have ratified, accepted, or otherwise acceded to the Convention before the relevant transaction (or, if contract formation is at issue, the making of the offer, *see* Article 100). The CISG defines two different ways to satisfy this requirement. First, under Article 1(1)(a) the Convention will apply if the parties have their places of business in different states and *both* of these states are CISG Contracting States. Under this option, therefore, the CISG will govern a contract of sale (unless the parties expressly "opt out" under Article 6, see below), where one party has its place of business in the United States and the other has its place of business in France, China, Mexico, or any other CISG Contracting State.

Under Article 1(1)(b), the CISG could also apply if the applicable domestic conflict of law rules (known by the civil law term "the rules of private international law") lead to the application of the law of a Contracting State. This possibility does not apply, however, for courts in the United States. When it ratified the CISG, the United States declared an allowed reservation under Article 95 that it would not be bound by Article 1(1)(b). The effect of this reservation is that courts in the United States will apply the CISG only when the parties' respective places of business are in different states and both of those states are CISG Contracting States. Thus, for example, the CISG will not apply to a sale contract between a party located in the United States and one located in the United Kingdom (a non-Contracting State to the CISG), even if under appropriate choice-of-law rules a U.S. court would apply U.S. law. What law should the court then apply? Instead of the CISG, United States law for domestic sales transactions would govern, which means the UCC as applicable in forty-nine states (all but Louisiana).

The Article 95 reservation was included at the insistence of the United States delegation, because it was believed that the UCC is a superior approach to sales law as compared to the CISG. At the time, the CISG was considered helpful to United States interests only where it provided uniform law as between two countries that had adopted the CISG. It was believed that if a court first had to resolve choice-of-law issues and then determined that domestic United States law applied, it might as well apply the "best" United States law—the UCC. The drafting history of the reservation also indicates that even a foreign court should not consider the United States as a CISG "Contracting State" for purposes of Article 1(1)(b). Thus, in our U.S.-U.K. example above, even if the litigation somehow were brought in France (a CISG Contracting State that has not made an Article 95 reservation), the French court should apply the UCC (not the CISG), if French choice-of-law rules point to United States law. Nonetheless, with the growing world-wide acceptance of the Convention (and thus the increasing application of Article 1(1)(a)), the Article 95 reservation of the United States is rapidly decreasing in significance.

PARTY AUTOMOMY AND CHOICE OF LAW CLAUSES

One of the most important provisions for understanding the basic philosophy and scope of the CISG is Article 6. That provision states the core principle of "party autonomy," that is, the power of the parties to "exclude application of th[e] Convention" and to "derogate from or vary the effect of any of its provisions." The agreements of the parties, in other words, take precedence over the provisions of the CISG. In its most fundamental sense, this includes the power of the parties to declare that the CISG will not govern their transaction (the power to "opt out" of the Convention). Special care is required, however, in the exercise of this power. First, and most important, CISG Article 6 grants the power to the parties (in the plural). As a result, an international trader cannot be assured that a unilateral choice of law clause in its standard business terms will be effective. The recent case of *Hanwha Corp. v. Cedar Petrochemicals, Inc.*, 760 F. Supp. 2d 426 (S.D.N.Y. 2011), illustrates this point. There, a South Korea-based buyer and a New York-based seller exchanged standard business forms that had conflicting choice-of-law clauses. Even though both parties tried to choose domestic law (and not the CISG), the absence of an agreement between them on one choice meant that the court applied the CISG, and especially its contract formation rules.

Moreover, a simple statement that, for example, a contract "shall be governed by New York law" will not effectively exclude the CISG. Indeed, courts addressing such clauses have commonly held that a choice of the law of a CISG Contracting State means, for international sale of goods transactions, merely a choice of the CISG, with the result that the CISG nonetheless applies. As a federal Court of Appeals has declared in a case where the parties had agreed on the application of Ecuadorian law, "[g]iven that the CISG *is* Ecuadorian law, a choice of law provision designating Ecuadorian law merely confirms that the treaty governs the transaction." *BP Oil Int'l, Ltd. v. Empresa Estatal Petroleos*, 332 F.3d 333 (5th Cir. 2003)(emphasis in original). The same rule applies, under preemption doctrines, if a party attempts to choose the law of a state of the United States.

As a result, if the parties wish to exercise their Article 6 "opt out" power, they must do so through express language that excludes the Convention by name and they should also agree on the applicable domestic law. (*E.g.*: "The law of the State of New York, including as applicable the New York Uniform Commercial Code, shall govern all disputes relating to this transaction. The parties hereby exclude application of the United Nations Convention on Contracts for the International Sale of Goods (CISG)"). Note also that, even if the parties do not wish to exclude the CISG, they are well advised to designate a default domestic law, because the CISG, like any other single legal instrument, does not represent a complete legal regime for all issues that may arise between the parties.

Many attorneys seek to "opt out" of the CISG for all contracts under all conditions, simply because they do not understand it as well as they understand the UCC. Such an action may work a disservice to their client's interests. If an attorney represents the seller in an international transaction, for example, the UCC and its "perfect tender" and "implied warranty" rules may be less favorable than the corresponding rules under the CISG (*see* below). In such cases, automatic rejection of the CISG may prejudice the client's interests, unless the attorney can be assured that comparable seller-friendly rules will make it into the express terms of the contract. One prominent author has observed in this vein that routinely opting out of the CISG, or even simply negotiating an international sales contract without understanding how the treaty affects the client's interests, may constitute malpractice.

OTHER SCOPE ISSUES

A variety of other issues may arise concerning the CISG's sphere of application. A prominent example is so-called "mixed" (or "hybrid") transactions, under which the seller both sells goods and provides services to the buyer as part of the same contract. CISG Article 3(2) states that the Convention will not apply to such transactions if "the preponderant part" of the seller's obligations concerns "labour or other services." For goods not yet produced, the Convention also will not apply if the buyer undertakes to supply a "substantial part" of the materials necessary for the seller's subsequent manufacture or production of the goods. Article 3(1).

In addition, CISG Article 2 expressly excludes a variety of transactions that otherwise might fall within the definition of a "sale of goods." It thus provides that the Convention does not apply to contracts for the sale of investment securities or negotiable instruments; of ships, vessels, hovercraft, or aircraft; or of electricity. Unfortunately, these express exclusions leave some ambiguity about the proper understanding of the term "goods" for the rest of the Convention. Under the UCC, negotiable instruments clearly would not be "goods" that would be subject to a statute on sales of goods in any event. But by expressly referring to negotiable instruments, CISG Article 2 may leave ambiguity over its application to other documents or intangibles not expressly excluded. In addition, the exclusion of ships, etc., arose because such vessels are usually subject to registration and regulatory legislation. But timber to be cut, growing crops, and railroad rolling stock may be subject to the same conceptual and regulatory difficulties, and CISG Article 2 does not expressly exclude these forms of potential goods. Thus, the term "goods" leaves some ambiguity, and CISG Article 2 does not seem to help clarify it. The most important ambiguity may concern software. The cases under the CISG have indicated that discs bought off the shelf from a store may be "goods," but there is a conflict over whether a contract to develop software is a contract for the sale of "goods" or not. The status of pure software, especially that bought and downloaded over the internet, remains unclear.

The most important exclusion under CISG Article 2 is sales of goods to consumers (unless the seller neither knew nor ought to have known of the buyer's consumer status). *See* Article 2(a)(referring to sales of goods "bought for personal, family, or household use"). As a result, the Convention should not conflict with consumer protection laws, which are often "mandatory law." Articles 2(b) and 2(c) also exclude auctions and goods sold on execution "or otherwise by authority of law." Further, CISG

Article 5 provides that the Convention does not govern causes of action against the seller "for death or personal injury," even if they arise out of a sales transaction, because of concerns over conflicting with core public policy values of domestic law.

One further limitation on the application of the CISG is that it expressly does not address all issues that may arise even under a contract otherwise within its scope. Under CISG Article 4, the Convention governs "only the formation of the contract" and the "rights and obligations" of the parties to the contract. Thus, the CISG will preempt state law claims based on the contract law notion of promissory estoppel, but not any related business tort claims.

Under the same provision, the CISG does not govern the "validity" of the contract, or its effect on title to ("property in") the goods, including presumably most rights and obligations of third parties to the contract. The restriction concerning "validity" arose because the CISG was not designed to police sales contracts for fairness or otherwise address core defenses to contract enforcement. Originally created to avoid conflicts with regulatory law, the case law indicates that Article 4 also excludes at least issues arising out of fraud, negligent misrepresentation, duress, illegality, incapacity, mistake, and similar basic contract defenses.

As noted, the Convention does not define "contract of sale," so its application to some types of transactions is unclear. Known problems include pure "consignments," in which the "buyer" may not assume ownership of the goods and may freely return them to the seller; barter transactions or "countertrade," in which goods are exchanged for other goods and not for money; and "conditional sales," in which the seller retains title to secure payment. For transactions denominated as a "consignment," the application of the CISG should depend on whether the buyer at any time assumes legal ownership of the goods. For barter transactions, in contrast, the weight of authority clearly holds that the CISG does not apply. With respect to conditional sales, the authorities seem clear that the CISG may govern the sale of goods issues, but not their secured transaction aspects. Finally, most courts have concluded that the CISG does not apply to framework distribution contracts (which merely define the parties' basic relationship, but do not (yet) involve a sale of goods), to franchise contracts, or to "turnkey project" contracts.

THE GENERAL PROVISIONS OF THE CISG

CISG Articles 7 through 13 contain its "general provisions." These articles deal with interpretation of the Convention and filling gaps in its provisions (Article 7); interpretation of party expressions and conduct as well as usages of trade (Articles 8 and 9); a few definitions (Articles 10 and 13); and a general removal of form requirements (Articles 11 and 12). Article 7 is designed to assist in interpretation of the Convention itself, while Articles 8 and 9 provide rules on interpretation of party intent, both pre-formation and as reflected in their contract. In turn, Article 8 concentrates on the parties' own statements and conduct, while Article 9 concentrates on customs and usages external to the parties.

Article 7(1) is designed to inhibit local courts from applying local norms and rules, rather than the Convention, to international sales disputes governed by the CISG. It first directs that interpretation of the Convention must heed its "international character." The purpose of this provision is to ensure that local courts respect the fact that the Convention reflects a broad international compromise among domestic legal systems. Courts must thus interpret the CISG on its own ("autonomously"), without resort to domestic interpretive norms or substantive rules. Unfortunately, some courts in the United States have missed this essential message when they have turned to the domestic UCC to assist in interpreting the CISG.

The requirement of an international perspective is stressed further by a second directive in Article 7(1)—that interpretation of the CISG must "promote uniformity of its application." This directive serves both to highlight the persuasive authority of foreign decisions interpreting the CISG and to emphasize (again) that local decisions on domestic sales law should not be relevant. Even the doctrine of "good faith" under the CISG is muted. Although UCC Rev. § 1–304 (former § 1-203) imposes an obligation of good faith on the parties to sales (and other) transactions, CISG Article 7(1) only refers to good faith in the interpretation of the Convention, not of the parties' contract (although some courts have shown recent flexibility on this score via Article 7(2), *see* immediately below).

Article 7(2) continues this approach with respect to apparent gaps in the express provisions of the Convention. Reflective of a civil code interpretive approach, this provision states as a primary rule that gaps in the CISG "are to be settled in conformity with the general principles on which it is based." This approach (unlike that of the domestic UCC) thus again mandates that courts first attempt to fill regulatory gaps on an "autonomous" basis—that is, with reference to the broader principles reflected in the *Convention itself* (such as notions of reasonableness and timeliness). It is only if this effort fails that Article 7(2) permits resort to domestic law principles determined under applicable choice-of-law rules. The danger to uniform application is that local courts will discover many "gaps" and no usable "general principles" derivable from the Convention, and then easily fall back on their own familiar supplementary principles of law. The fundamental philosophy of the CISG is that local courts must assiduously resist this impulse.

Article 8 establishes rules for interpreting party expressions and conduct as well as any final contract between them. It establishes a three-tier hierarchy: (1) Where the parties have a common understanding concerning their intent or the meaning of a provision, that common understanding will prevail. (2) Where the parties do not have a common understanding or intent, but one party "knew or could not have been unaware" of the other party's (subjective) intent, under Article 8(1) the latter party's interpretation prevails. The idea here is that a party's *actual* intent should prevail where the other party knows of that *actual* intent. And (3) in all other cases, and especially where the meaning of a disputed term is ambiguous, under Article 8(2) the parties' statements and conduct are determined by the traditional "reasonable person" standard. In evaluating party conduct and statements, Article 8(3) instructs courts to look to "all relevant circumstances," including the negotiating history of the contract (contrary to the American parol evidence rule) and the parties' prior practices and subsequent conduct.

Fortunately, United States courts seem to have taken this hierarchy to heart. In *MCC-Marble Ceramic Center, Inc. v. Ceramica Nuova d'Agostino, S.p.A.*, 144 F.3d 1384 (11th Cir. 1998), for example, a federal Court of Appeals interpreted Article 8(1) to require consideration of a party's subjective intent in interpreting the statements and conduct of the parties in the formation of a contract. Article 8(3) also can direct a court to a very different approach to contract interpretation than is usual in other U.S. contract cases. Its requirement that a court give consideration to all relevant circumstances is a clear direction to consider parol evidence, even in interpreting a subsequent and final written agreement (as the *MCC-Marble* court also held). Some courts and scholars likewise have relied on the interpretive rules in Article 8 to promote the actual intent of the parties in "battle of the forms" situations and thus to avoid mechanical application of the traditional "last shot" doctrine (*see* "Contract Formation" below).

CISG Article 9 addresses express and implied acceptance of usages of trade. Article 9(1) first gives effect to "any usage" on which the parties have agreed or which they have otherwise "established" through their practices. The drafting history indicates that this paragraph focuses on express agreements to include a trade usage, although the express agreement need not be written. Further, "any" usage may be so incorporated, including local ones, not just an international usage. If so incorporated, the usage is considered to be part of the express contract items. This is significant, for under Article 6 the express terms of the contract will prevail even over the provisions of the Convention. The one exception to the last statement—just as with Article 6 as a whole—is Article 12, which limits the power of party agreements where a Contracting State has declared a reservation relating to writing requirements under domestic law (*see* below).

Article 9(2) concerns the incorporation of usages by implication. In the drafting of the CISG, both less

developed countries (LDCs) and nonmarket economies (NMEs) demanded a limit on the application of
trade usages by implication. The result was a rule
that, if the parties do not expressly agree to incorporate a usage, it may apply in the parties' contractual
relationship only if (a) "the parties knew or ought to
have known" of it; (b) it is international (not merely
local) in nature; and (c) it is both "widely known to"
and "regularly observed by" others in that particular
international trade. This seems to set a very high
standard for a party seeking to rely on an implied
trade usage, and in particular with regard to the
identification of the specific "international trade"
involved.

Article 11 provides that a contract for the international sale of goods need not be evidenced by any
writing and may be proven by any means. Thus,
there is no equivalent in the Convention of the
common law Statute of Frauds. Nonetheless, Articles 12 and 96 allow a Contracting State to declare a
reservation that the local law of that Contracting
State will govern the form requirements for a sale
contract "where any party has his place of business
in that State." Such a reservation may be declared
at any time, but it is applicable only to the extent
that the domestic law of the State making the reservation "requires contracts of sale to be concluded
in or evidence by writing." Article 96. The United
States has not made this declaration, so its Statute
of Frauds provisions in UCC § 2-201 are not applicable to contracts under the Convention. In fact,

only eight Contracting States have declared an Article 96 reservation; but prominently included among these are Russia, China, Chile, and Argentina, with the result that their domestic law on writing requirements would continue to apply for CISG contracts.

If a Contracting State has declared an Article 96 reservation, the parties may not agree otherwise under Article 6. *See* Article 12. This gives the local law the effect of "mandatory law" under the Convention. However, one should note that under Article 13 a telex or telegram may satisfy the "writing" requirement and Articles 12 and 96 only make unenforceable those contracts that are "other than in writing." Nonetheless, the telex and telegram of course long ago yielded to electronic communication, so the effect of Article 13 will be limited.

CONTRACT FORMATION

The CISG has a separate "Part" (Part II) for its contract formation provisions. *See* Articles 14-24. Under Article 92, a Contracting State may declare a reservation at the time of ratification that it will not be bound by Part II, even though it is bound by the rest of the CISG. Only the Scandinavian countries, however, have declared such a reservation.

Every first-year American law student studies about "offer, acceptance and consideration," but these three elements of contract formation are not present in other legal systems. Civil law emphasizes the agreement process, and does not include a "consideration" requirement. Nonetheless, an examination of the consideration cases will show that few such disputes arise in true commercial transactions. Rather, they tend to involve family members arguing over failed promises (uncles attempting to induce nephews not to smoke and the like). Thus, it should not be surprising to learn that the CISG has no requirement of "consideration" in its contract formation provisions.

As was discussed in the previous section, writing requirements such as in the Statute of Frauds also do not apply for CISG contracts, unless one of the parties has a place of business in a Contracting State that has declared an Article 96 reservation. Further, the "integration" concepts of the parol evidence rule are not applicable pursuant to Articles 8(1) and 8(3).

Offer and Acceptance. Part II of the CISG focuses on "offer" (Articles 14-17) and "acceptance" (Articles 18–22). In Convention terminology, a contract "is concluded at the moment when an acceptance of an offer becomes effective." Article 23. There is no need for consideration, and no similar requirements of form.

Article 14 defines three requirements for an "offer." First, it must be "a proposal for concluding a contract," which is a standard notion. Second, it must indicate "an intention to be bound in case of acceptance," which will distinguish an offer from a general sales catalogue, an advertisement, or a purchase inquiry. Article 14(2) elaborates on this concept by making proposals addressed to the general public presumptively not offers "unless the contrary is clearly indicated." Third, an offer must be "sufficiently definite." A proposal satisfies this definiteness requirement if it "indicates the goods" and "expressly or impliedly fixes or makes provision for determining the quantity and the price." By implication, other terms can be left open, but not those three.

The requirement that an offer at least "make[] provision for determining" the price seems more restrictive than the comparable UCC provision on open, or flexible, price contracts (§ 2-305), and was so intended because many civil law states do not recognize such contracts. Article 55—which permits reference to the price "generally charged ... under comparable circumstances"—might seem to be helpful; but this provision only applies where a contract has already been "validly concluded," which assumes a valid offer. The Convention language is flexible enough, however, to authorize most forms of flexible pricing. Thus, a contract will sufficiently "make provision for determining the price" where the price is to follow a specified index, or is subject to an escalator clause, or is to be set by a third party. Arguably, the latter would include "lowest price to others" clauses. The only serious problem not resolved under this analysis may be an order for a replacement part in which no price is stated. It is here that Article 55 is certainly useful. The offeror may have "implicitly" agreed to pay the seller's current price for such goods, and Article 55 fixes the price as that generally charged at the time the contract was "concluded." One court thus enforced a seemingly price-less contract, but it did so because the parties had established a payment practice under prior contracts.

Open quantity contracts, such as those for requirements, output, or exclusive dealings, should cause less difficulty. In each such contract, a "provision for determining the quantity" likely will arise through party performance, even if the precise number cannot be fixed in advance. However, in view of the requirements of CISG Article 14, the parties should include either estimated quantity amounts or minimum quantity amounts, in order to set a reference point for a "fixed or determinable" quantity.

Assortment, under which one party has discretion over the choice of goods from among an assortment, is a final problem concerning "definiteness." Compare UCC § 2-311. However, a clause that permits either the buyer or the seller to specify the assortment of goods during the performance of the contract would seem to make a provision for determining both quantity and type of goods. The major hurdle in such cases is the requirement that the offer "indicate the goods." But Article 14(1) does not require that the offer "specify" the goods, and so clauses that allow later selection of assortment are presumably authorized, if the parties take care in describing the type of goods from which the assortment will be selected. In a case involving the sale of an airplane, for example, a Hungarian court held that a seller's proposal was an offer under CISG Article 14, even though it gave a choice to the buyer as between two types of engines and two types of airplanes. The court reasoned that the offer sufficiently indicated the goods and fixed the quantity under Article 14(1) because it gave the buyer a choice between only two specific engines for each of only two specific airplanes (one manufactured by Boeing and one by Airbus). Thus, the parties concluded a contract when the buyer indicated its acceptance.

One of the consequences of the abandonment of the "consideration" requirement is that there is no foundation for the strict common law approach to the revocability of an unaccepted offer. Traditional common law doctrine makes an offer revocable at will until accepted, unless the parties had an agreement supported by consideration to keep it open (such as an option). In German law, an offer is binding unless the offeror states that it is revocable. These two approaches are opposites, and the compromise adopted by the CISG uses neither.

Under Article 16, an offer governed by the Convention is revocable unless it "indicates" that it is not revocable. In adopting this position, the Convention rejects both the common law rule that an offer is always revocable and the German civil law rule that an offer is not revocable unless it is expressly stated to be revocable. This basic concept is similar to that used in creating a "firm offer" under UCC § 2-205, but no "signed writing" is required. Article 16 identifies two ways in which an offer can become irrevocable: (a) through an indication in the offer itself; or (b) through reasonable reliance by the offeree.

Under Article 16(2), an offer can indicate that it is irrevocable "by stating a fixed time for acceptance or otherwise." The first reference seems relatively clear, and would include a statement that an offer will be held open for a specified period and no longer. The "or otherwise" language should embrace any other aspects of the offer (as interpreted under Article 8), including those that permit reference to the circumstances surrounding the negotiation of the contract or the nature of the parties' relationship.

The possibility of irrevocability through reasonable and actual offeree reliance is similar in concept to (but should not be influenced by) the notion of an "option contract" created through reasonable reliance by an offeree under Section 87(2) of the Second Restatement of Contracts. For emphasis, however, the § 87(2) requirements are idiosyncratic to U.S. domestic law and courts should not consult them for guidance in developing the autonomous law required by the CISG (for no gap exists as contemplated by CISG Article 7(2)). Finally, in either of the two means for irrevocability under Article 16, the offer must also meet the Article 14 requirements, including an indication of the goods and a fixed or determinable price and quantity.

Article 18(1) defines "acceptance" as a statement or "other conduct" by an offeree "indicating assent to an offer." Silence or inactivity is not alone acceptance, but the negotiations and other prior conduct of the parties may establish an implicit understanding that lengthy silence followed by an absence of an affirmative objection indicates an acceptance. *See also* CISG Article 8(3).

Article 18(2) determines when an "indication of acceptance" is effective in order to "conclude" a contract. Thus, along with Articles 16(1) and 22 (on the withdrawal of an acceptance), it forms the Convention's analog to "the mailbox rule"—except that the CISG rules are different. At U.S. common law, "the mailbox rule" passed the risk of loss or delay in transmission of an acceptance to the offeror once the offeree has dispatched the acceptance. It also chose that point in time to define the moment of contract formation, and thus to terminate the offeror's power to revoke the offer and to terminate the offeree's power to withdraw the acceptance. Under CISG Article 18(2), in contrast, an acceptance is not effective until it "reaches" (*i.e.*, is delivered to) the offeror. The same Article also provides, however, that an acceptance is not effective if it does not reach the offeror "within the time he has fixed or, if no time is fixed, within a reasonable time" under the circumstances. Thus, risk of loss or delay in transmission generally is on the offeree, who must now inquire should the offeror not timely acknowledge receipt of the acceptance.

Nonetheless, this rule is balanced by CISG Article 16(1), which provides that the offeror's power to revoke is terminated upon dispatch of the acceptance—which is the common law rule. However, the offeree's power to withdraw the acceptance terminates only when the acceptance reaches the offeror. Thus, an acceptance sent by a slow transmission method allows the offeree to speculate for a day or two while the offeror is bound. An email message will release the offeree from the not-yet-received acceptance.

Even though Article 18(1) states that acceptance by conduct alone is possible, the remaining paragraphs of Article 18 seem to imply that in the usual case the offeree must notify the offeror that acceptance by conduct is forthcoming. Notification of the acceptance may reach the offeror indirectly through third parties, such as banks or carriers. Article 18(3) indicates that acceptance by conduct without notice is possible only when that procedure is allowed by the offer, by usage, or by the parties' prior course of dealing. If so allowed, the acceptance by conduct without notice—such as shipment of the goods—is effective upon the performance of the act, rather than upon the delivery of the goods to the offeror (when knowledge of the acceptance would otherwise reach the offeror).

Battle of the Forms. One of the most vexing of modern contract formation issues is the "battle of the forms." This "battle" arises when the respective lawyers of the buyer and the seller prepare carefully crafted forms, but the parties themselves pay little attention to the forms when they actually negotiate their contract. The parties focus on the business terms (price, specification and quantity of goods, performance time); it is only if and when a dispute arises that the parties pull out the forms and review them carefully. The CISG's approach to the "battle of the forms" differs markedly from that of the UCC (the infamous § 2-207).

To begin the battle, the CISG, although in a circular fashion, generally follows the traditional "mirror-image" analysis. Under Article 19(1), if the buyer's purchase order form and the seller's reply order acknowledgment form—the typical arrangement—differ in any respect, the reply functions not as an acceptance, but instead as a rejection and counteroffer. Article 19(2) seems to inject some flexibility, for it states that a reply may operate as an acceptance—and thus form a contract—even with additional or different terms as long as they do not "materially alter" the terms of the offer (and the offeror does not timely object to them). What Article 19(2) gives, however, Article 19(3) takes away almost entirely. The latter defines as "material" nearly every term of interest to the parties, including "among other things," those relating to "price, payment, quality and quantity of the goods, place and time of delivery, extent of one party's liability to the other or the settlement of disputes."

In the great run of "battle of the forms" cases under the CISG, therefore, the reply document (again, usually the seller's order acknowledgement form) will not function as a legal acceptance of the buyer's offer. Instead, it operates as a rejection of the offer and a counteroffer. The rejection also terminates the original offer under CISG Article 17. Thus, the parties do not "conclude" a contract by exchanging forms, and if one party reneges on its promises, before performance, it likely will not be liable for breach.

Nonetheless, in the vast majority of transactions involving exchanges of such forms, the parties fail to notice, or disregard, the technical conflicts and perform the contemplated transaction. Once the seller ships the goods and the buyer accepts and pays for them, there is little doubt that the parties have formed a contract governing their transaction—but what are its terms? To put the same question in a different way, is the seller's shipment of the goods "conduct" by the seller that accepts the terms in the buyer's purchase order? Or, is the buyer's acceptance of and payment for the goods "conduct" that accepts the terms in the seller's order acknowledgement form? The common law analysis would give effect to the terms of the last form sent by either party, since that last form (usually the seller's) would be a rejection and counteroffer and terminate all prior unaccepted offers. The only offer left to accept through conduct, therefore, is this last counteroffer. This is the "last shot" principle, and, on the surface, CISG Articles 17, 18(3), and 19 seem to follow it. The drafting history of the CISG, however, is at best ambiguous, and shows instead that the drafters simply were unable to come to an agreement and consciously left the matter unresolved. (By general consensus of courts and scholars, this does not, however, represent a gap in the CISG that would permit resort to domestic law.)

The cases interpreting the CISG indicate a reluctance by judges to follow the mirror image—last shot legal reasoning of the 19th Century. Some French and several German court decisions—including one from the Federal Court of Justice of Germany (*Bundesgerichtshof*)—expressly adopt instead an "overlap" rule, under which the boilerplate provisions in the parties' respective forms become part of the contract only to the extent the provisions agree in substance. The CISG's provisions fill the resulting gaps in the contract. The courts have reached this result based on the principle in CISG Article 6 that the parties' actual agreement prevails over the terms of the Convention and on the flexible interpretive rules for determining that agreement in CISG Article 8. Other courts have disregarded the formal words of Article 19(3) and stretched the concept of "non-materiality" to find a mirror-image acceptance. A few courts, however, have hewn closely to the limited language of Articles 17, 18, and 19, and applied the mirror-image and last-shot doctrines. These courts have thus ignored the more sophisticated analytical tools available for resolving the battle of forms under the CISG.

In summary, and in comparison to the UCC, the CISG generally follows the traditional offer-acceptance scheme. But it reduces the flexibility of the parties by prohibiting some open price terms, and it expands the "firm offer" concept to more offers. On the battle of the forms, the CISG also may delay the formation of a contract through the "mirror image" rule, and may use the "last shot" principle to make the offeree's (usually the seller's) terms control the transaction. However, on the last point, both the courts and the authors who have analyzed the subject have suggested ways of avoiding this traditional analysis in a manner consistent with deeper principles in the Convention.

SELLER'S PERFORMANCE OBLIGATIONS

Part III of the CISG sets forth the basic performance obligations of the seller and the buyer. After some initial general provisions (such as on the core notion of "fundamental breach" in Article 25), Part III contains separate chapters for the obligations of the seller (Articles 30–52) and of the buyer (Articles 53–65).

CISG Article 30 defines the fundamental obligations of the seller. Under that provision, the seller is obligated to deliver the goods and any related documents as provided in the parties' contract and to transfer to the buyer "the property in the goods." In addition, the seller is obligated to deliver goods that conform to the contract as to quantity, quality, description, and freedom from third-party claims.

Domestic law may influence the content of some of these obligations, because under Article 4(b) the Convention "is not concerned with" the effect of the contract on "the property in the goods sold." Domestic law, therefore, determines whether "the property" passes from the seller to the buyer at the "conclusion" (formation) of the contract, upon delivery, or at some other time; whether a certificate of title is required; and whether the seller may retain title as security for the purchase price or other debts.

"Delivery" under the CISG is a limited concept, and relates only to transfer of possession of or control over the goods. The CISG's drafters did not attempt to consolidate all incidents of sale—physical delivery, passing of risk of loss, passing of title, liability for the price, and ability to obtain specific performance, etc.—into a single concept or make them turn on a single event, as has been done in many sales statutes. Instead, they followed the format of the UCC in providing separate provisions for each of these incidents.

As to the place of delivery, the CISG recognizes four distinct types of delivery terms: (1) delivery contracts, under which the seller must deliver the goods at a specified distant place; (2) shipment contracts, which "involve carriage of the goods," but do not require delivery at any particular distant place; (3) sales contracts where the goods are at a known location and are not expected to be transported; and (4) sales contracts without a specified place of delivery and where goods not expected to be transported. CISG Article 31.

In a delivery contract, the seller may be obligated to deliver the goods at the buyer's place, or at a sub-buyer's place, or at any other specified distant location. However, the CISG has no provisions directly describing the seller's duties in delivery contracts, for Article 31 expressly addresses only those contracts under which the seller "is not bound to deliver the goods at any other particular place." As a result, the identification of the seller's specific delivery obligations is left to interpretation of the contract terms only. A common practice in international sales transactions is to define such obligations through commercial terms such as "DAP," "DAT," or specific forms of "FOB." *See* "Commercial Terms" below.

In a shipment contract, the seller has no obligation to deliver the goods at any particular place, but it is clear that transportation of the goods by an independent third party carrier is involved. Subject (as always) to the parties' contractual agreements, a shipment contract may require the seller to take more than one action to accomplish its obligation of "delivery." First, Article 31(a) requires that the seller transfer ("hand over") the goods to a carrier—the first independent carrier. (Because the seller must "hand over" the goods to the carrier and not to the buyer, transactions requiring the buyer to assume responsibility for carriage seem excluded from this provision.) Second, Article 32(1) provides that if the goods are not "clearly identified to the contract" by the shipping documents or by their own markings, the seller must "give notice to the buyer of the consignment specifying the goods." Third, Article 32(2) states that if the seller is bound to arrange for carriage of the goods, it must make such carriage contracts as are "appropriate in the circumstances" and according to the "usual terms" for such transportation. Finally, Article 32(3) requires, depending upon the contract's terms, that the seller either "effect insurance" coverage of the goods during transit or, at the buyer's request, give the buyer the information necessary to effect insurance.

CISG Article 31 has different rules for transactions where carriage of the goods is not "involved." Absent a contrary agreement, if the parties knew at the time of the conclusion of the contract where the goods were or were to be produced, the buyer is expected to pick them up at that location; in all other cases, delivery is required only at the seller's place of business. Under Article 31(b) and (c), in such transactions the seller's obligation under the CISG is merely to put the goods "at the buyer's disposal" at the appropriate place. The Convention is not clear on whether this requires notification to the buyer, but it would require notification to any third party bailees to allow the buyer to take possession.

Where the delivery of the goods is to be accomplished by tender or delivery of documents, Article 34 requires only that the seller adhere to the terms of the contract. The second and third sentences of Article 34 also establish the principle that a seller who delivers defective documents early may cure the defects until the date due under the contract, if possible, and the buyer must take the cured documents, even though the original tender and cure has caused damage to the buyer. Of course, in the latter case the buyer nonetheless will retain any right to recover damages from the seller.

CISG Article 33 defines the time requirements for the seller's performance. That Article focuses again on the contract terms: the seller must deliver the goods or any documents (a) on or before a fixed or determinable date as set in the contract, (b) within a fixed or determinable time period as set in the contract (unless the buyer has a power to choose a date), or (c) if no date or time period is set, within a "reasonable time." "Reasonable time" is not defined, and will depend on the surrounding circumstances and trade usage, but at least it should preclude a demand for immediate delivery.

The Convention has no provisions concerning the seller's duties regarding export and import licenses and taxes, and thus leaves the determination of these incidents of delivery to the contract terms, or usage. Where these issues are not covered by the contract terms or usage, the authorities give conflicting analyses as to what rules may be derived from the general principles of the CISG. In any event, it is quite common in international transactions for the parties to agree on an incorporation of international "commercial terms" (FOB, CIF, etc.), and in particular the so-called Incoterms©, which expressly address export and import licenses and related issues. *See* "Commercial Terms" below.

With respect to the goods themselves, CISG Article 35 obligates the seller to deliver goods of the quantity, quality, description, and packaging required by the contract. In determining whether the quality of the goods conforms to the contract, the Convention eschews such separate and independent doctrines as "warranty" and "strict product liability" from U.S. law, as well as the doctrines of "fault" or "negligence" from civil law. Instead, the CISG focuses on the simpler concept that the seller is obligated to deliver the goods as "required by" the contract. Article 35(1). It then defines certain default obligations of the seller and creates certain related presumptions in Article 35(2).

Thus, Article 35(2)(a) and (d) require that the goods be fit for "the purposes for which goods of the same description would ordinarily be used" and be properly packaged (compare UCC § 2-314). Article 35(2)(b) also requires that the goods be fit for any particular use expressly or impliedly made known to the seller at contract formation (compare UCC § 2-315). Finally, Article 35(2)(c) requires that the goods conform to any goods the seller "has held out to the buyer as a sample or model" (compare UCC § 2-313(1)(c)). Each of these obligations, however, arises out of the contract, with the result that the parties may "agree otherwise" and limit the seller's obligations concerning quality (a more flexible concept than "disclaimer of warranties" under UCC § 2-316(2)). And as a federal Court of Appeals correctly held in *Chicago Prime Packers, Inc. v. Northam Food Trading Co.*, 408 F.3d 894 (7th Cir. 2005), the buyer has the burden to prove any such a nonconformity (although some foreign courts unfortunately have left some ambiguity on the point).

The CISG imposes no conditions on the seller's obligation relating to fitness for ordinary use. And because the CISG generally applies only to commercial contracts, there is no need for the UCC limitation to "merchant" sellers (compare UCC § 2-314). Nonetheless, this leaves one important unresolved issue—whether the "ordinary use" is defined by the seller's location or the buyer's location, if the "ordinary use" in the two is different. Although some scholars support a contrary position, an early decision of the German Federal Court of Justice has declared the prevailing view that the seller is liable for an "ordinary" use in the buyer's region only where the ordinary use at the seller's location was the same, the buyer had brought such use to the seller's attention, or the seller otherwise knew or should have known of the use because of the "special circumstances" of the case. A U.S. federal court subsequently endorsed this approach in *Medical Marketing Int'l, Inc. v. Internazionale Medico Scientifica, S.R.L.*, 1999 WL 311945 (E.D. La. 1999), as have courts of other jurisdictions. One might also add that the seller likewise should be liable where a use is "ordinary" in the international trade of the goods involved. To secure a broader obligation, the buyer must conclude an express contractual agreement under Article 35(1) or satisfy the criteria for fitness for a "particular purpose" under Article 35(2)(b).

The obligation of fitness for a particular purpose arises only if the buyer's particular purpose is expressly or impliedly made known to the seller at or before the "conclusion of the contract." *See* Article 35(2)(b). Moreover, this obligation does not apply if the seller can prove either that the buyer did not rely or it was unreasonable for the buyer to rely on the seller's skill and judgment (which switches the burden of proof on this element as compared to UCC § 2-315). Article 35(2)(b) states no express requirement that the buyer inform the seller of the buyer's reliance; the seller need only know of the buyer's particular purpose. More important, there is no requirement that the buyer inform the seller of any of the difficulties involved in designating or designing goods to accomplish the particular use. Courts may address abuse of this issue through a careful application of the "reasonable reliance" criterion.

The obligations of the seller under Article 35(2) relating to non-conformities of quality do not apply where the buyer is aware or "could not have been unaware" of a defect at the time the contract was "concluded." *See* Article 35(3). Thus, knowledge gained at the time of delivery or inspection of the goods will not affect the seller's obligation. The "could not have been unaware" language is the subject of much dispute among common law and civil law authorities. Most common law authorities consider it to be "subjective" and relate to the buyer's actual state of mind, rather than to impose "constructive knowledge" on the buyer for information he should have learned.

CISG Article 36(1) states that the relevant time for assessment of a nonconformity of the goods is "when the risk [of loss] passes to the buyer"—a concept explored in more detail below. Thus, any nonconformity concerning the goods that exists at the time the risk of loss passes is actionable, even if discovered long after delivery. The buyer must prove, however, that the defect actually was present at that point (typically, at delivery) and was not caused by third parties or the buyer's own use or lack of oversight of the goods. The buyer need not prove what caused the goods to be defective, only that they are, in fact, defective. Pursuant to CISG

Article 37, however, the seller may remedy any deficiencies in quantity, quality, and the like up to the agreed delivery date, provided this would not cause the buyer unreasonable inconvenience or expense.

The CISG also imposes certain obligations on the buyer in order to preserve its rights relating to nonconforming goods. The buyer may lose its right to rely on a nonconformity if it does not inspect the goods "within as short a time as is practicable" under the circumstances (*see* Article 38) or does not give notice to the seller "specifying the nature of the lack of conformity" within a reasonable time after the buyer discovered or "ought to have discovered it." CISG Article 39. The CISG also contains an interesting rule that requires such a notice by the buyer "at the latest within a period of two years from the date on which the goods were actually handed over to the buyer." Article 39(2). Under CISG Article 40, however, the seller may not rely on such failures of the buyer if the lack of conformity relates to facts known to the seller or of which it "could not have been unaware" and did not disclose to the buyer. Thus, if the seller knows of a defect and does not so notify, then it may not rely on the buyer's subsequent failure to inspect the goods in a timely manner or to give timely notice of any discovered defects.

May the seller exclude these obligations concerning the quality of the goods by terms in the contract—and, if so, how? As a basic rule, CISG Article

6 states that the parties may, by agreement, derogate from *any* provision of the Convention. But Article 35(2) also expressly affirms this point with specific reference to limitations on the seller's obligations concerning the quality of the goods and the like (*i.e.*, "except where the parties have agreed otherwise"). Nonetheless, it is also clear that the standard formulation under the UCC—"disclaimer of implied warranties"—will be inapposite, because the CISG describes the seller's obligations neither as "warranties" nor as "implied." Careful international sellers will need to employ different verbal formulations, ones that deal directly with the description of the goods and their expected use as defined in the CISG (not the UCC).

An issue once viewed as potentially controversial is the extent to which local law regulating disclaimers might apply for international contracts governed by the CISG. Such local law covers a spectrum, from prohibitions on "unconscionable" disclaimers (especially in printed standard terms) to the special linguistic and similar requirements set out in UCC § 2-316. Today, however, there seems to be agreement that the former raises a question of "validity" (*see* CISG Article 4), and thus relevant domestic law applies even for contracts governed by the CISG. The latter, in contrast, do not raise questions of "validity" as contemplated by CISG Article 4(a). As a result, the UCC's statutory requirements for an exclusion of warranties do not apply for CISG contracts. The distinction depends upon whether the local public policy prohibits conduct completely, as opposed to allowing the parties to limit the seller's obligations within certain specified conditions. Accordingly, the courts should draw a distinction between general contract defenses (such as unconscionability and fraud) and the specific UCC provisions that set requirements for exclusion of the express or implied warranties created by the UCC itself (*e.g.*, that the disclaimer be "conspicuous" or use particular words such "merchantability").

The seller's obligation under CISG Article 41 concerning title is to deliver goods not only free from any encumbrances on their title, but also free from any claim of a third party. Compare UCC § 2-312. Thus, the seller is obligated to transfer "quiet possession" of the goods. Although the obligation is very broad, it probably is not breached by claims that are frivolous on their face or by governmental restrictions on use of the goods. The parties may derogate from the terms of these provisions of the CISG by agreement, but the buyer's knowledge that the goods are subject to a bailee's lien does not necessarily imply such an agreement. Instead, the buyer may expect the seller to discharge the lien before tender of delivery.

In addition to good title, the seller is obligated to deliver the goods free from patent, trademark and copyright claims founded on the law of the "buyer's place of business" or the place where both parties expect the goods to be used or resold. This obligation is subject, however, to a number of qualifications. First, the seller's obligations arise only with respect to claims of which "the seller knew or could not have been unaware." Article 42(1). Second, the seller has no obligation with respect to intellectual property rights of which the buyer had knowledge when the contract was formed. Article 42(2)(a). Third, the seller is not liable for claims that arise out of its use of technical drawings, designs or other specifications furnished by the buyer, if the seller has acted in "compliance with" the buyer's specifications. Article 42(2)(b). It is clear that this provision applies when the seller is following specifications required by the contract; but its application is not clear when the seller is merely following "suggestions" of the buyer as to how best to meet more general contract requirements. Fourth, under Article 43 the seller is excused from these obligations if the buyer does not give timely notice of a related breach, unless the seller initially knew of the claim as contemplated by Article 42(1) in any event. Finally, some have argued that a mistake of law also will provide an excuse for the seller regarding intellectual property rights if it has relied on trustworthy legal advice that the buyer's use or resale of the goods will infringe on no such rights—because the seller then could not have "known" of the possible claims of infringement.

BUYER'S REMEDIES UPON
SELLER'S BREACH

CISG Articles 45 through 52 define the remedies available to the buyer upon a breach by the seller. As described below, if the seller breaches any of its obligations, the buyer has three basic types of remedies: (a) specific performance; (b) "avoidance" of the contract; and in any event (c) an action for damages. Separately, the CISG has a special remedy for the buyer that allows a "self-help" reduction in the price due. In general, the drafters of the remedy provisions of the CISG faced special challenges because of the divergent approaches of civil and common law legal systems. These challenges are illustrated by two facts: First, specific performance is the preferred remedy at civil law, while an action for damages is preferred at common law. Second, at civil law, a finding of "fault" is usually required for imposition of any recovery of damages, while under the common law an aggrieved party need show only breach of any nature. The CISG drafters attempted to bridge both gaps.

Specific Performance. CISG Article 46 gives a buyer a right to specific performance—such as delivery of the goods—subject to two important qualifications: First, the buyer must not have already resorted to an "inconsistent" remedy; and, second, a court (such as in a common law jurisdiction) need not grant such a remedy "unless the court would do so under its own law" for comparable contracts (*see* Article 28). Thus, the CISG gives the buyer the right to seek specific performance, rather than damages, but does not compel it to do so; and it permits a court to grant such a remedy, but does not compel it to do so. Even in civil law jurisdictions, buyers will often prefer damages and purchase of substitute goods, because of the expense and delays inherent in seeking formal court orders requiring performance.

If the remedy of specific performance is available, the buyer may require performance by seller of any of its breached obligations. Article 46(1). Where the goods have not been delivered, this would mean a requirement that the seller deliver the goods. If the seller has delivered, but the goods do not conform to the contract, the buyer may require delivery of conforming substitute goods if the nonconformity amounts to a "fundamental breach" (*see* below). Article 46(2). Likewise, the buyer may require the seller to repair nonconforming goods, unless this is "unreasonable having regard to all the circumstances." Article 46(3). In any event, the buyer will lose any right to specific performance if it has declared an "avoidance" of the contract (*see* below), which is an inconsistent remedy.

Avoidance. The CISG provides two separate grounds for the buyer to declare an "avoidance of the contract" upon a breach by the seller. (Compare "cancellation" under UCC § 2-106(4)). First, CISG Article 49(1)(a) permits the buyer to use this remedy in the event of a "fundamental breach," regardless of when the breach occurs. Thus, the CISG does not adopt the distinctions between "acceptance of the goods," "rejection," and "revocation of acceptance" contained in the UCC. The CISG's concept of "avoidance of the contract" also is quite different than the limited notion of "avoidance" under the UCC (*see* § 2-613). In addition, the drafting history of the CISG seems to indicate that "fundamental breach" imposes a stricter standard on the buyer than the "substantial impairment" test of the UCC (*see* § 2-608). Finally, after delivery of the goods the buyer loses the right to declare an avoidance if it does not give notice to the seller (*see* Article 26) within a reasonable time as defined in Article 49(2).

A "fundamental breach" is defined in Article 25 as a breach that "results in such detriment to [the aggrieved party] as substantially to deprive him of what he is entitled to expect under the contract," unless the results were both unforeseen and unforeseeable. Case law illustrations include a machine represented as "good-as-new" that in fact was rusty and did not operate when delivered, and goods that authorities ordered off the market after delivery. The concept clearly requires more than the common law "nonconformity."

For "instalment contracts," CISG Article 73(1) permits avoidance of a single installment for a "fundamental breach" with respect to that installment. Article 73(2) then permits avoidance of future installments if "good grounds" exist to conclude that a fundamental breach also will occur in the future installments. Separately, Article 73(3) grants an aggrieved buyer a right to avoid the whole contract (or affected portions) if the interdependence of deliveries means that future deliveries cannot be used for the purpose contemplated at time of contracting. This structure differs in important respects from the corresponding provisions in UCC § 2-612.

Given the inherent uncertainties of the "fundamental breach" test, it often will be very difficult for the buyer, or its attorney, to know how to react to a particular breach—and thus whether "avoidance" of the contract is permissible or not. Incorrect analysis could mean that the buyer has committed a fundamental breach through its response. CISG Articles 47 and 49(1)(b) attempt to address such uncertainties by offering the buyer a power to compel timely and conforming performance by the seller: Based on the German law notion of *Nachfrist*, the buyer may notify the seller that performance is due by a stated new date (after the contract date for performance); in such a case, the seller's failure to perform by the new date constitutes a fundamental breach. However, this *Nachfrist* provision seems to be available only for nondelivery by the seller, not for delivery of nonconforming goods, and avoidance is available only if the seller does not deliver during the additional period allowed by the notice. During the additional notice period, the buyer may not resort to any remedy for breach of contract. Article 47(2).

How long of an additional period must the buyer give the seller? Article 47 requires that it be "of reasonable length," but unless there is a custom on this issue the buyer will have no certainty that the period given in the *Nachfrist* notice is long enough, especially if long distances are involved. In one German decision, the court found that an additional period of eleven days fixed by an aggrieved buyer under CISG Article 47(1) was "too short to organize carriage by sea." The court nonetheless upheld the buyer's declaration of avoidance seven weeks later because the seller had offered only a partial delivery of conforming goods in the interim.

Even if the buyer seeks to avoid the contract after a "fundamental breach" by the seller, the latter has a right under CISG Article 48(1) to "cure" any defect in its performance. If the seller's nonconforming tender is early, the seller may cure by making a conforming tender up to the delivery date in the contract, whether the nonconformity would create a fundamental breach or not. *See also* Article 37. The seller's right to cure also survives the buyer's declaration of "avoidance of the contract," because it will be very difficult to sustain a finding of fundamental beach where the seller has made a timely offer of cure. If the seller's tender or offer of cure is made *after* the delivery date in the contract, it still has a right to cure through late performance, but only if it can do so "without unreasonable delay," and without causing the buyer unreasonable inconvenience or uncertainty of reimbursement of expenses. Article

48(1). Must performance offered as a cure meet a strict "nonconformity" test, or is it still subject to the "fundamental breach" test? The CISG has no provision on this issue. However, it has been held that, if the seller's offer of cure is defective, the buyer may procure cure on its own. In any event, the entire thrust of these CISG provisions on the buyer's remedies is to require cooperation between the parties in resolving disputes over timeliness of delivery and conformity of the goods. Moreover, as noted below, CISG Article 77 imposes an obligation on an aggrieved party to take reasonable steps to mitigate its damages.

The CISG's rules on avoidance and cure may leave the seller of goods in a significantly better position as compared to the UCC, if the buyer claims a relatively minor fault in the goods. First, under the UCC the buyer may reject the goods merely because a tender is not "perfect" (*see* § 2-601), but this is definitely not allowed under the CISG. In addition, although the seller has a right to cure defects under both regimes, the right under the UCC has either time limitations or knowledge requirements (*see* § 2-508) that do not exist under the CISG. Finally, under either the UCC or CISG the buyer will have a right to damages; but under the CISG, the buyer may return the goods only in the event of a "fundamental breach." Thus, the seller is less likely to find the goods rejected for an asserted minor nonconformity, and stranded an ocean or continent away.

Reduction in Price. Finally, in addition to the power of "avoidance," an aggrieved buyer has an informal remedy which appears to give it a power of self-help. Under CISG Article 50, a buyer who receives nonconforming goods "may reduce the price" it pays to the seller. There is no requirement of prior notice to the seller, and there is little guidance on how to determine the amount of the reduction, or what evidence of diminution in value the buyer must provide. If the buyer resells the defective goods, the resale price nonetheless should be strong evidence of their value at the time of delivery. In any event, the Article 50 remedy seems best suited to deliveries that are defective as to quantity, rather than quality, although at least one author has suggested that it should be available only for defective quality. A buyer attempting to use this self-help remedy must nonetheless allow the seller to attempt to cure, if the seller so requests. This type of self-help provision is familiar at civil law, and also appears in the UCC (§ 2-717), but seems not widely used by common law attorneys.

Requirements on the Buyer. To preserve any remedy for a delivery of nonconforming goods by the seller, the buyer must, as noted above, inspect the goods in "as short a period as is practicable" (Article 38); notify the seller of the nonconformity "within a reasonable time" (Articles 39, 49); and permit the seller to attempt to cure any nonconformity, if the cure does not cause "unreasonable delay" or "inconvenience" (*see* Article 48). In addition, for a fundamental breach permitting avoidance, the buyer must be able to prove that the result of the nonconformity is "substantially to deprive him of what he [was] entitled to expect under the contract" (*see* Article 25) and must give timely notice of the avoidance to the seller (*see* Article 26).

There has been more litigation over the requirement of timely notice by the buyer than over almost any other single issue. Although early German cases required inspection and notification within a few days, more recent cases have suggested one month as a presumptive deadline. The nature of the goods is also important. One U.S. case thus indicated that, for a complicated piece of machinery, notice "within a matter of weeks" was not practicable. As a special protection for remote or unsophisticated buyers, however, CISG Article 44 preserves the buyer's Article 50 remedy of a reduction in price "if he has a reasonable excuse for his failure to give the required notice." Note also that a seller may be deemed to have waived its right to timely notice, such as (as the German *Bundesgerichtshof* has held) when it agrees to take back the goods after the buyer raised potential concerns.

After it has declared a proper avoidance of the contract, the buyer is entitled to a return of any purchase price paid under the restitutionary provisions of Article 81. In return, however, that Article grants the seller a concurrent right to recover any goods delivered to the buyer. Indeed, the buyer loses the right to declare an avoidance of the contract if he cannot return the goods "substantially in the condition in which he received them." Article 82(1).

In addition, CISG Articles 85 through 88 impose certain obligations on the buyer to preserve the goods pending their return to the seller. A buyer who declares an avoidance after delivery of the goods must take "reasonable" steps to preserve them (Article 86(1)), which may include depositing the goods in a warehouse at the seller's expense (Article 87). If the seller has no agent in the buyer's location, but the goods have "placed at [the buyer's] disposal at their destination," the buyer must take possession of them "on behalf of the seller" if this can be done without payment of the price (*i.e.*, without paying for a negotiable bill of lading) and without "unreasonable inconvenience or unreasonable expense." Article 86(2). After such a taking of possession on behalf of the seller, the buyer must again take "reasonable" steps to preserve them. If the goods are perishable, an aggrieved buyer in possession may have to try to sell them and remit any proceeds to the seller, less the expenses of preserving and selling them. Article 88(2). The CISG does not, however, contain any provisions that would require an aggrieved buyer in possession to follow the seller's instructions, such as to resell on the seller's behalf, whether seemingly reasonable or not.

Action for Damages. CISG Articles 74-78 provide an aggrieved buyer (as well as an aggrieved seller, *see* below) with an action for damages, even when the buyer has avoided the contract and when the seller has successfully cured defects in its performance. There is no requirement that the buyer prove that the seller was at "fault" as a prerequisite to a recovery of damages. Nor is there a requirement that the buyer prove what caused the defect, only that the goods were nonconforming (as described above). Both direct and consequential damages are recoverable; and expectancy, reliance and restitutionary interests are all protected.

Article 74 defines the basic principle that an aggrieved party is entitled to "a sum equal to the loss, including loss of profit, suffered as a consequence of the breach." But that Article also limits consequential damages in the familiar manner that they may not exceed the loss that the party in breach "foresaw or ought to have foreseen at the time of the conclusion of the contract." However, this may not be the same as the common law *Hadley v. Baxendale*, 156 Eng. Rep. 145 (Ex. Ct. 1854) test, because recovery is available if the loss suffered is foreseeable as a "possible consequence" of the breach. The aggrieved buyer also must take "reasonable measures" to mitigate its damages under Article 77. Incidental damages relating to interest are allowed separately in Article 78 (although substantial dispute exists over how to calculate the interest rate).

Articles 75 and 76 then state alternative specific measures of recovery for an aggrieved party. Article

75 first allows the recovery, in addition to the general damages under Article 74, of the difference between the contract price and the "price in [a] substitute transaction," which in the case of an aggrieved buyer means the purchase of replacement goods (compare "cover" under UCC § 2-712). This measure is only allowed, however, if the replacement purchase occurs in a reasonable manner and within a reasonable time after avoidance. As an alternative, Article 76 permits recovery based on the difference between the contract price and the "current price" (*i.e.*, the market price) for the goods. Where this current price differential is used, the price in the market is to be measured at the time of "avoidance," unless the buyer had already "taken over" the goods. In the latter case, the market price is measured at the time of "taking over."

Although the Convention provides for recovery under either measure, if the buyer actually makes a replacement purchase, presumably it may use only the first. The general requirement of "reasonable measures" to mitigate damages under Article 77 would seem to require this result. The Convention gives no guidance, however, on how to determine whether any particular purchase by the buyer is a replacement purchase, or is instead an ordinary buildup of inventory.

In most civil law countries, the litigation loser also pays part of the winner's attorneys' fees, typically according to a statutory formula. This is regarded as part of the damages necessary to make the aggrieved party whole. United States courts generally have rejected such an award on the ground that rules relating to attorneys' fees are procedural, not substantive. The problem with such decisions is that they have engaged carefully neither with the interpretive rules in CISG Article 7 nor with the thoughtful analyses of foreign courts on the subject (which is also required by Article 7(1)).

BUYER'S PERFORMANCE OBLIGATIONS

CISG Article 53 defines two primary obligations of the buyer in a contract governed by the Convention: to pay the price (*see also* Articles 54 and 55), and to take delivery of the goods (*see also* Article 60). The former duty is the more important of the two. In addition, there are several derivative preliminary duties which might be referred to as "enabling steps."

Unless the sale contract expressly grants credit to the buyer, the sale is a cash sale, and the seller may make payment a condition for handing over the goods or the related documents. Article 58(1). Under the same provision, payment is due when the seller places the goods, or their documents of title, "at buyer's disposal" in accordance with the contract and the Convention. If the sales contract involves carriage of the goods, Article 58(2) gives the seller the right to ship the goods under negotiable documents of title and demand payment against those documents, even though the parties agreed on no particular method of payment. In general, the buyer has a right to examine the goods before payment. If, however, the buyer has expressly agreed to "pay against documents" (such as through the use of a CFR or CIF term, see "Commercial Terms" below), the buyer has thereby agreed to pay upon tender of the documents, regardless of whether the goods have yet arrived, and without inspection of the goods. Article 58(3).

If the buyer is to pay against "handing over" of the documents, or handing over the goods, the place of "handing over" is the place of payment. Otherwise, the seller's place of business is the place of payment, unless the contract provides otherwise. Article 57. Such a rule requires the buyer to "export" the funds to the seller, which is a critical issue when the buyer is from a country with a "soft" currency, or with other restrictions on the transfer of funds. In addition, the buyer has an obligation under Article 54 to cooperate and take all necessary steps to enable payment to be made, including the satisfaction of whatever formalities may be imposed by the buyer's country to obtain administrative authorization to make a payment abroad. Failure to take such steps may reflect a breach by the buyer even before payment is due.

The buyer's second obligation, to take delivery, also poses duties of cooperation. It includes a duty to make the expected preparations to permit the seller to make delivery and may include such acts as providing for containers, transportation, unloading, and import licenses. Article 60. This obligation may also have significance for the passing of the risk of loss when the contract contemplates shipment of the goods. Under Article 69(1), the risk of loss of or damage to the goods in such a case passes to the buyer when it fails to "take over" the goods in due time and the buyer thereby commits a breach by failing to take delivery.

SELLER'S REMEDIES UPON BUYER'S BREACH

The CISG provisions on the seller's remedies for a breach by the buyer parallel the structure for the buyer's remedies upon breach discussed above. Under CISG Articles 61 through 65, if the buyer breaches any of its obligations, the seller has three basic types of remedies: (a) an action for the price; (b) "avoidance" of the contract; and in any event (c) an action for damages.

Action for the Price. The preferred remedy for an aggrieved seller, if the buyer should breach, is a cause of action for the price, which is the seller's functional equivalent of an action for specific performance. A cause of action for damages, but not the price, is distinctly secondary. In addition, the seller may wish to reclaim the goods if they are delivered or obtain some protection for them if it "avoids" the contract after delivery to the buyer.

As to the seller's recovery of the price, CISG Article 62 gives the seller an unqualified right to require the buyer to pay the price, but no CISG Article expressly states that the seller has a cause of action for payment of the price. Of course, there are implicit conditions on this right: First, the seller must itself have performed as required by the contract (Article 30); second, the payment of the price must actually be due (Article 58); and, third, the seller must not have already resorted to an "inconsistent" remedy (such as reselling the goods with an eye to recovering corresponding damages). Such an action for the price, however, may constitute a claim "for specific performance," for which as noted above Article 28 imposes the important restriction that a court need only grant the remedy if it would do so under its domestic law. If it is an action for specific performance, therefore, then an aggrieved seller would have to meet the requirements of UCC § 2-709, as well as of CISG Article 62, before a United States court could order the buyer to pay the full price rather than damages. If, however, an action for the price does not require the entry of a "judgment for specific performance," then it would seem that CISG Article 28 would not apply, and the seller could seek this remedy directly under CISG Article 62. The courts and scholars continue to disagree on this question.

Avoidance. The CISG also provides two separate grounds for the seller to declare an "avoidance of the contract" upon a breach by the buyer. First, Article

64(1)(a) permits the seller to make such a declaration in the case of a "fundamental breach" by the buyer—again, as defined in Article 25 (*see* above). Second, if the buyer does not pay the price or accept delivery of the goods, Articles 63 and 64(1)(b) give the seller a right to set a *Nachfrist*—that is, to notify the buyer that performance is due by a stated new date after the contract date for performance; in such a case, the buyer's failure to perform by the new date is a fundamental breach. Like the corresponding limitation on aggrieved buyers, after the buyer has paid the price the seller loses the right to declare an avoidance if it does not do so within a reasonable time as defined in Article 64(2).

If an unpaid seller is unable (for any reason) to obtain the price, may it reclaim the goods from the defaulting buyer, *after* delivery, by "avoiding" the contract? Such a reclamation is difficult under the UCC (*see* UCC §§ 2-507 and 2-702). The Convention, however, seems to allow such reclamation, because Article 64, which gives the seller the power to declare the contract "avoided," does not distinguish between pre-and post-delivery situations, and Article 81 requires "restitution . . . of whatever the first party has supplied" after avoidance. This analysis, however, is available only so long as third parties (the buyer's creditors and trustees in bankruptcy) are not involved, for the CISG does not affect title to the goods and third party rights (Article 4), and again does not require a court to order "specific performance" which it would not order under its own law. Article 28.

Action for Damages. As to damages, CISG Articles 74-78 grant the aggrieved seller an action for damages and the general principles are the same as in the discussion of the buyer's remedies for a breach by the seller. The same two alternatives also exist for the measurement of the seller's specific damages: (a) the difference between the contract price and the price in a "substitute transaction," which in the case of an aggrieved seller is a resale of the goods (*see* Article 75); and (b) the difference between the contract price and the "current price" (*i.e.*, the market price) for the goods at the time of avoidance of the contract (*see* Article 76). The Convention provides for recovery according to either of these measures, but if the seller actually resells the goods, only the first measure should be available in light of the general mitigation requirement of Article 77.

The major practical problem concerning unpaid sellers is that the "lost volume" seller is not adequately protected by the above two measures of damages. Nonetheless, CISG Article 74 states as a general principle that an aggrieved party is entitled to all damages "including loss of profit" suffered "as a consequence of the breach." Thus, the courts have granted full protection to the lost volume seller by awarding "lost profits" damages, and by subtracting from those losses only the variable costs saved by the termination of the first sale contract. Such a recovery requires, however, that the seller actually had the intent and capacity to conclude the second sale in addition to the breached first sale contract.

RISK OF LOSS

The identification of the moment at which the risk of loss of or damage to the goods passes from the seller to the buyer is especially important for transactions governed by the CISG. This is because significant geographical distances often separate the parties, and as a result most contracts governed by the CISG will involve a transportation of the goods. The basic rule under the CISG is that the buyer bears the risk of loss to the goods during their transportation by a carrier, unless the contract provides otherwise. Such a contractual agreement to allocate the risk of loss typically comes through the inclusion of a "commercial term" (such as FOB or CIF, *see* "Commercial Terms" below), and such agreements supersede the CISG provisions under Article 6.

In absence of a contrary contractual agreement, CISG Articles 67 through 70 set forth specific risk of loss rules which depend on the nature of the seller's delivery obligation. A first set of rules relates to transactions that "involve[] carriage of the goods":

(a) If the contract does not obligate the seller to hand over the goods "at a particular place" (a "shipment contract"), the risk of loss will pass under Article 67(1) when the goods are delivered "to the first carrier" for shipment to the buyer. (b) If instead the contract obligates the seller to hand over the goods to the <u>carrier</u> "at a particular place," then the risk of loss passes under the same Article when the seller hands over goods to the carrier at that place. Under either, the goods need not be on board the means of transportation—any receipt by a carrier will do. Further, the seller need not "hand over" the goods to an ocean-going or international carrier—possession by the local trucker who will haul them to the port is sufficient. However, if the seller uses its own vehicle to transport the goods, the seller bears the risk until the goods are handed over to an independent carrier, or to the buyer.

(c) If, however, the contract requires the seller to deliver the goods to the <u>buyer</u> at the buyer's location or "at" some other distant location (a "destination contract"), the seller bears the risk of loss until it puts the goods at the buyer's disposal at that location at the delivery time and the buyer becomes aware of that fact. Article 69(2).

Thus, in a contract between a Buffalo, N.Y., seller and Beijing, China, buyer: (1) in a shipment contract under the CISG, the risk would pass to the buyer when the goods were delivered to the first carrier in Buffalo; (2) in a destination contract (where the seller is obligated to deliver at Beijing), the seller would bear the risk during transit, and the risk would not pass to the buyer until the goods were put at the buyer's disposal in Beijing. (Again, specific commercial terms—such as "FOB", FAS", and CIF"—have more detailed rules on risk of loss; *see* "Commercial Terms" below.)

A second set of risk of loss rules relates apply to transactions that do not involve carriage of the goods from the seller to the buyer. (d) If the goods are not to be transported by a carrier (*e.g.*, when the buyer or an agent are close to the seller and will pick up the goods), the risk passes to the buyer when he "takes over" the goods or, if he is late in doing so, when the goods are "placed at his disposal" and he commits a breach by not taking delivery. Article 69(1). The goods cannot, however, be "at his disposal" until they have first been identified to the contract. Article 67(2). (e) If the goods are already in transit when sold, the risk passes under Article 68 when the contract is "concluded" (unless the circumstances indicate otherwise or the seller knew or ought to have known of a loss or damage in transit and did not disclose this to the buyer). The challenge for the buyer under this latter rule is that it may be practically impossible to determine whether damage to goods in a ship's cargo hold occurred before or after the parties concluded the sales contract.

In most situations, title and risk are treated separately. Thus, manipulation of title through the use of documents of title, such as negotiable bills of lading, is irrelevant and has no effect on the point of transfer of risk of loss. *See* Article 67(1). Just as title and risk are treated separately, so also breach and risk generally are treated separately. The one exception to this approach (noted above) is where the buyer is obligated to pick up the goods and commits a breach by failing to do so in a timely manner. *See* Article 69(1). In all other cases, including any breach by the seller, the basic risk of loss rules are not changed by claims of breach (which is contrary to the position of UCC § 2-510). Thus, a breach by the seller, whether a "fundamental beach" under Article 25 or not, is irrelevant to determine risk allocation or the point at which the risk of loss passes to the buyer. In specific, if the seller has in fact already committed a fundamental breach, the risk of loss rules in Articles 67, 68, and 69 will not impair the remedies available to the buyer on account of that breach (and especially the right to avoid the contract). Article 70.

EXCUSE FOR NON-PERFORMANCE

The CISG has a general provision, Article 79, which recognizes an excuse for non-performance. Unlike UCC § 2-615, CISG Article 79 applies to a performance either by the seller or by the buyer, and extends to "any" obligations (not just the seller's delivery obligation). A party asserting an excuse under CISG Article 79 must prove three elements: (a) first, that the failure to perform was due to an external impediment beyond the party's control. Although Article 79 refers to an "impediment," the standard for exemption is not strict impossibility. Rather, the prevailing view is that an extreme hardship will suffice, that is, such extreme difficulty in performance as constitutes impossibility as a practical matter under the circumstances; (b) second, that the party could not reasonably be expected to have taken the impediment into account at the time of the conclusion of the contract; and (c) that the party could not reasonably have avoided or overcome the impediment or its consequences. The non-performing party also must give reasonable notice of the excuse to the other party.

Article 79(2) extends the excuse for a contract party to a failure to perform by "a third party whom [it] has engaged to perform the whole or a part of the contract." This provision is narrower, however, than appears at first glance. According to the consensus view, Article 79(2) extends only to persons employed to perform the specific contractual obligation in dispute and thus does not cover, for example, the failure of an upstream supplier to perform under a separate contract. In any event, Article 79(5) makes clear that any covered excuse only provides protection against a claim for damages by the other party; any other rights or remedies, such as avoidance of the contract for fundamental breach, are unaffected.

THE LIMITATIONS CONVENTION

Following its acceptance of the CISG, the United States in 1994 also ratified a parallel treaty that addresses the limitation period for international sales contracts (which U.S. lawyers would know as the "statute of limitations"). As noted above, over two dozen other countries have ratified this Limitations Convention (as amended by a 1980 Protocol).

The provisions on the scope of the Limitation Convention in large measure parallel those of the CISG. Under Article 1(1), the Limitation Convention applies to "claims based on contracts for the international sale of goods." Similar to the CISG, a contract of sale is "international" under the Limitation Convention if: (a) the parties have their "places of business" in different states (and if a party has more than one, the relevant place of business is the one with the "closest relationship" to the contract and its performance); and (b) either both of those states are Contracting States to the Convention *or* the relevant conflict of law rules lead to the application of the law of a Contracting State. *See* Article 2. Unlike the CISG, the United States has not declared a reservation on the latter option. In parallel with CISG Article 6, Article 3(2) of the Limitations Convention permits the parties to exclude its application to their transaction.

Under Article 8, the standard period of limitation is four years, and this period begins to run upon accrual of the cause of action. Article 10 then defines when a cause of action "accrues": A cause of action for a standard breach of contract accrues at the time of breach; one based on defects or other nonconformities, in contrast, accrues on delivery or refusal of a tender of delivery; and a cause of action for fraud accrues when the fraud "was or reasonably could have been discovered."

The Convention also contains an analog to the UCC's "warranty of future performance" exception (*see* § 2-725(2)). Under Article 11, if the seller has given an "express undertaking" relating to the goods "which is stated to have effect for a certain period of time," a cause of action will not accrue on tender of delivery, but rather on the date the buyer "notifies the seller of the fact on which the claim is based." Recall in this regard that CISG Article 39 requires that the buyer give the seller timely notice of any breach. Putting the two rules together, if the buyer satisfies its notice obligation, a cause of action for breach of an express undertaking that extends to the future will accrue within a reasonable time after the buyer "discovered or ought to have discovered" the breach.

The Limitation Convention nonetheless has certain rules that differ from U.S. concepts in important particulars. First, Article 22 precludes the parties from modifying the Convention's limitation period in advance, even by an express contractual agreement. The party in breach may extend the period, but only after it has begun to run. The Convention also sets an absolute ten year limitation period from when any particular period has "commenced to run." *See* Article 23. Finally, and unusually, the Limitations Convention includes a form of a procedural rule that precludes a party from relying on the expiration of a limitations period unless it has timely raised a corresponding defense in a relevant legal proceeding. *See* Article 24.

THE UNIDROIT PRINCIPLES OF INTERNATIONAL COMMERCIAL CONTRACTS

The UNIDROIT Principles of International Commercial Contracts represent a different approach to unification and harmonization of international commercial law. The CISG and its comparable conventions in other fields attempt to create positive law on specific international transactions, and their success depends on adopting rules that gain "consensus" approval of national governments. That approach thus is much like that of the National Conference of Commissioners on Uniform State Laws (the co-drafters of the UCC). With the Principles, in contrast, UNIDROIT (The International Institute for the Unification of Private Law in Rome) has proposed something quite different. Instead of positive law, the Principles are the equivalent of an international "Restatement of Commercial Contracts," and generally apply to all such contracts, whatever the specific type. And because they are not designed for ratification as a convention, the Principles do not need the approval of any national government.

In transactions to which the CISG is applicable, the courts should generally apply the rules of the CISG. However, where the CISG is silent or ambiguous or otherwise contains gaps, CISG Art. 7(2)'s instruction to consult the "general principles" of the Convention may permit reference to the UNIDROIT Principles. The latter will not act of their own force, but rather may serve as a source of guidance on the contemporary meaning of the general principles of the Convention.

As a more general statement of international contract principles, as of 2012 nearly three hundred decisions have referred to the Principles in some respect. These numerous references reflect the fact that arbitrators may use the Principles in the absence of any choice of law by the parties. The parties themselves also may expressly choose the Principles as the law to govern their contract. Finally, the drafters hoped that the Principles might serve as a model law, especially for LDCs. Note that, in all these uses, the effectiveness of UNIDROIT's Principles depends upon their persuasive value.

To promote maximization of their persuasive value, UNIDROIT assembled subject matter experts and requested that they draft the Principles to reflect current trade practices. These practices could be reflected either in conventions, such as the CISG, or in private contracts, such as general conditions or (international) standard form contracts in use by industry groups. Where no common trade practice existed, the drafters were instructed to formulate solutions best adapted to international commercial transactions, whether they were in fact part of any existing legal regime or not. Thus, they do not necessarily represent the national rule of a majority of states.

The principles initially were drafted over a period of 20 years, and were adopted by UNIDROIT's Governing Council in May, 1994. UNIDROIT intends to update the Principles on a regular basis (and in fact did so in 2004 and again in 2010). The Principles thus are more comprehensive (and perhaps more "modern") than the CISG. For example, they include modern provisions on how a contract may be formed, on confirmation of agreements, on contracts with open term clauses, on negotiations in bad faith, on the duty of confidentiality, on merger clauses, on use of standard forms, and on the battle of the forms. More innovative concepts also exist, such as on "gross disparity" as an element of the analysis of validity and on "hardship" as a basis for excuse of performance. There are provisions on payment, not only by "cheque," but also by funds transfers and other methods and on the currency to be paid in the absence of specification.

This Nutshell cannot provide a detailed, comprehensive description of the Principles, but it will provide three examples as illustrations of their approach to three known and difficult problems: the battle of the forms, the unilateral use of standard form contracts, and excuse of performance by changed circumstances.

Battle of the Forms. In the battle of the forms, Article 2.1.22 of the Principles eschews the traditional "mirror image" and "last shot" rules. Instead of the mirror image rule, it provides that if both sides propose "standard terms," a contract nonetheless is concluded if the parties have reached an agreement on all terms other than those in the "standard terms." The meaning of standard terms in the modern world of computer-generated contract clauses may prove difficult, but Article 2.1.19 broadly defines the concept to include all such terms prepared in advance and for repeat use and which are in fact used without negotiation. The approach of Article 2.1.22 should also refuse effect to clauses in standard terms that state that no agreement is formed unless the other party accepts all proposed standard terms ("my way or the highway" clauses). If such a clause is contained in the standard terms, it is ineffective, but its use in "non-standard terms"—*i.e.*, if raised expressly in negotiation—would prevent the formation of the contract. Thus, the rationale of this provision is that where the parties agree on those terms that they are willing to raise individually and negotiate, they should be bound to a contract (even if they both have submitted standard terms not included in their express negotiations).

What are the terms of that contract? Instead of adopting the traditional "last shot" doctrine, or even the modified "first shot" doctrine of UCC § 2-207, the Principles adopt the "knock-out" (or perhaps better, "overlap") rule. The terms of the contract include (1) the "agreed terms"; (2) those standard terms that are "common in substance," unless objected to; and (3) the default rules of the Principles. Thus, the rationale of the Principles is that, where the parties agree on terms which they are willing to raise individually and negotiate, those agreed terms are the terms of the contract. The typically unread standard terms prepared in advance by the parties' respective lawyers, in contrast, do not become part of the contract unless they agree in substance (a relatively rare occurrence).

Standard Terms. Where only one party proposes standard, preformulated terms without negotiation, there is no "battle" of forms, but such terms nonetheless may be one-sided. Article 2.1.21 states the obvious principle that an express agreement prevails over any such standard terms. But under Article 2.1.20 of the Principles, a standard term also is not "effective" if the "other party could not reasonably have expected it." Thus, the Principles relate such terms to the expectations of the non-drafting party, and adopt as a norm the real world assumption that standard terms are rarely read.

The Comments to the Principles indicate that the non-drafting, non-reading party is bound to many, but not all, terms that are standard in an industry. Such a party is not bound, however, by a "surprising" term. One example in the Comments of a "surprising" term relates to a travel agency tour package under which the agency assumes full responsibility for the tour, but the standard terms then state that the agency is merely an agent of the hotelkeeper and is not liable for hotel accommodations. Other examples include choice of forum clauses that choose courts or arbitral tribunals located outside the jurisdiction of the immediate parties to the contract. Thus, unexpected terms can be surprising *either* because of their content *or* because of their language or presentation. In some respects, this resembles the unconscionability doctrine, but there is less emphasis on finding both "harsh terms" and "unequal bargaining power" in the contracting process.

Excuse for Non-Performance. The Principles provide two different paths for asserting excuse from performance by changed circumstances. One is labeled *"Force Majeure"* and the other is labeled "Hardship." These two paths are not the equivalent of the common law doctrines of impossibility and impracticability. Instead, the concepts in the Principles have civil law foundations.

The *force majeure* provisions in Article 7.1.7 are similar to those in CISG Article 79, and include the concept of "impediment." The non-performance must be due to an impediment that the non-performing party could not control and "could not reasonably be expected to have taken . . . into account." The Article nonetheless leaves the precise parameters of the concept of an "impediment" beyond a party's "control" undefined. Some assert that it requires a complete impossibility and not a mere "impracticability"; others support a slightly more flexible view. But even those who read in more flexibility would

require an extreme burden, so the difference between the two views may not be substantial in actual cases. The non-performing party must give notice
of the impediment, and loses its right claim excuse if
it fails to do so, but the Principles do not specify
when the notice must be given.

The "hardship" provisions in Article 6.2, however,
are completely different from any concepts in the
CISG or in the common law—but principally as to
the remedy. Hardship occurs when "events fundamentally alter" the cost or value of a promised performance. Illustrations include a ten-fold increase in
prices of products to be supplied or a 99% decline in
the currency of payment. This would be in line with
many of the "price unconscionability" cases in the
United States. (An original comment to the Principles that a 50% change might be sufficient to trigger
the application of the doctrine, however, has since
been removed, presumably for substantive reasons.)

The novel aspect of "hardship" under the Principles is the remedy. Even if proven, hardship does
not by itself excuse performance. Instead, under Article 6.2.3, the effect of hardship is merely to entitle
the disadvantaged party to "request renegotiations."
This request, however, does not "in itself" entitle the
disadvantaged party to withhold performance. If the
attempt to renegotiate fails, either party may seek
intervention by a court with appropriate jurisdiction. Whether intervention by an arbitral tribunal is
available as an alternative is not expressly stated. A

court that finds the hardship criteria to be satisfied can "adapt" the contract so as to restore its "equilibrium," or may even terminate the contract.

COMMERCIAL TERMS AND THEIR ROLE IN INTERNATIONAL SALES TRANSACTIONS

Where the goods are to be carried from one location to another as part of the sale transaction, the parties will often adopt a commercial term to define the delivery obligations of the seller. Such terms include FOB (Free on Board), FAS (Free Alongside) and CIF (Cost, Insurance and Freight). These terms are defined in the domestic UCC (*see* §§ 2-319, 2-320), but the UCC definitions are seldom used intentionally in international trade. In fact, the UCC definitions are increasingly obsolescent because the statutory terms do not include the new terminology associated with air freight, containerization, or multi-modal transportation practices.

In international commerce the dominant source of definitions for commercial delivery terms is "Incoterms," a set of rules published by the International Chamber of Commerce (ICC). The Incoterms, an acronym for International Commercial Terms, provide rules for determining the obligations of both the seller and the buyer when defined commercial terms (such as FOB or CIF) are used. They state what acts the seller must do to deliver, what acts the buyer must do to accommodate delivery, what costs each party must bear, and at what point in the delivery process the risk of loss passes from the seller to the buyer. Each of these obligations may be different for different commercial terms. Thus, the obligations, costs, and risks of the seller and the buyer are different under FOB than they are under CIF.

Since the ICC is a non-governmental entity, Incoterms is neither a national legislation nor an international treaty. Thus, they cannot be "the governing law" of any contract. Instead, they are a written form of custom and usage in the trade, which the parties can, and often do, expressly incorporate in their international contracts for the sale of goods. Alternatively, if the Incoterms are not expressly incorporated in the contract, they nonetheless may have effect as an implicit term of the contract in the form of an international trade usage. Courts in the U.S., France, Germany, and elsewhere have so ruled, describing Incoterms as a widely-observed usage for commercial terms. This description has allowed Incoterms to qualify under CISG Article 9(2) as a "usage . . . which in international trade is widely known to, and regularly observed by, parties to" international sales contracts.

Although the UCC has definitions for some commercial terms (*e.g.*, F.O.B., F.A.S., C.I.F.), these definitions are expressly subject to "agreement otherwise." *See* § 2-319. Thus, an express reference to Incoterms will supersede the UCC provisions, and United States courts have so held. Such incorporation by express reference is often made in American international sales contracts, especially in Atlantic Ocean trade. Even if a contract does not make an express reference, and the UCC (rather than the CISG) otherwise might govern, Incoterms can still be applicable as a "usage of trade" under UCC Rev. § 1–303(c). The UCC criteria for such a usage is "a practice or method of dealing having such regularity of observance . . . as to justify an expectation that it will be observed with respect to the transaction in question." A usage need not be "universal" nor "ancient," just "currently observed by the great majority of decent dealers." *See* § 1-303, comment 4. Moreover, as revised in 2010, the Incoterms now expressly recognize that they may be used in "both domestic and international trade."

The 2010 revisions of the Incoterms, which formally entered into effect on January 1, 2011, were designed principally to respond to general developments in international trade and transport practices. The revisions had two principal purposes. First, they distilled and organized the eleven defined commercial terms into two general categories: those limited to sea and inland waterway transport, and those permitted for any mode of transport. The former category includes the most frequently used terms in large international transactions, CIF and FOB, as well as their more specific versions CFR (Cost and Freight) and FAS (Free Alongside Ship). The latter category includes the seven other terms that are also occasionally used in water transport, but are more common for air, land, and rail transportation.

The second principal purpose of Incoterms 2010 was to address specific legal and factual developments relating to the transportation of goods, and in particular electronic communication. Thus, the new rules endorse the substitution of paper communications with an "equivalent electronic record or procedure." Moreover, they broadly embrace such electronic communications where either the parties so agree or such is "customary" in the trade. This reference to trade custom should increasingly authorize buyers and sellers to fulfill communication and documentation requirements with electronic equivalents. Moreover, the new Incoterms adopt an open-ended definition of "electronic records" to permit adaptation to new technologies in the future.

Incoterms 2010 give the parties a menu of eleven (formerly, thirteen) different commercial terms to describe the delivery obligations of the seller and the reciprocal obligations of the buyer to accommodate delivery. Each defines ten specific obligations for the seller and for the buyer. One can also align the eleven terms along a spectrum according to the respective responsibilities of the seller and the buyer. At one end of the spectrum would be EXW (Ex Works), under which the seller must merely make the goods available at its own place of business (or other named place); at the other end would be DDP (Delivered Duty Paid), which obligates the seller to place the goods at the buyer's disposal at the destination location and to assume the responsibility and cost of both export and import customs clearance. The others fall along the spectrum and thus permit the parties to choose the term that best fits their specific commercial transaction. The eleven Incoterms rules—listed only alphabetically—are as follows:

1) CFR (Cost and Freight)

2) CIF (Cost, Insurance and Freight)

3) CIP (Carriage and Insurance Paid)

4) CPT (Carriage Paid To)

5) DAP (Delivered at Place)

6) DAT (Delivered at Terminal)

7) DDP (Delivered Duty Paid)

8) EXW (Ex Works)

9) FAS (Free Alongside Ship)

10) FCA (Free Carrier)

11) FOB (Free On Board)

One may organize these eleven different terms in a variety of ways. One is a division between the one term which does not assume that a carrier will be involved (EXW), and all the ten other terms. Another, noted above, is along a spectrum of responsibilities (from EXW to DDP). A third, also suggested above, is between those four terms which require water-borne transportation (FAS, FOB, CFR, CIF) and the seven other terms which are applicable to any mode of transportation, including multi-modal transportation (CIP, CPT, DAP, DAT, DDP, EXW, and FCA). The UCC has none of the latter seven terms, although the types of transactions they are designed for arise routinely, and although the parties may be able to achieve the same results with careful adjustments to the UCC designations "F.O.B. place of shipment," "C. & F.", "C.I.F.," and "F.O.B. named place of destination."

The ten terms requiring transportation can also be divided into "shipment contract" terms (FCA, FAS, FOB, CFR, CIF, CPT, and CIP)—although the precise agreements of the parties may affect this— and "destination contract" terms (DAP, DAT, and DDP). The UCC and the CISG each use a form of these concepts. *Compare* UCC §§ 2-503, 2-504, and CISG Art. 31. The underlying notion is that in shipment contracts the seller need merely put the goods in the hands of a carrier and arrange for their transportation, but transportation is at the buyer's risk and expense. *Compare* UCC § 2-504. In destination contracts, in contrast, the seller is responsible to put the goods in the hands of the carrier, arrange their transportation, and bear the cost and risk of transportation to the named location. Unfortunately, many aspects of transportation usages have changed since the UCC was drafted in 1952, and the UCC concepts do not always fit the practices that the newly updated Incoterms are able to address.

Incoterms—a copyrighted work of the ICC—are periodically revised, typically about once every ten years. As noted, the last revision was in 2010 and is set forth in ICC Publication No. 715. The following is a brief discussion of each of the Incoterms rules. They are addressed in the two principal groupings identified by the ICC: the rules for sea and inland waterway transport, and the rules for any mode or modes of transport:

Rules for Sea and Inland Waterway Transport

Under the Incoterms Free Alongside Ship (FAS) commercial term, the seller is obligated to deliver the goods alongside a ship arranged for and named by the buyer at a named port of shipment (or to "procure" rights to goods already in transit). The seller must bear the costs and risks of inland transportation to the named port of shipment. The risk of loss also will transfer to the buyer at the time the goods are delivered alongside the ship. The seller has no obligation to arrange transportation or insurance for the "main" (or water-borne) part of the carriage, but does have a duty to notify the buyer that the goods have been delivered alongside the ship. The seller must provide a commercial invoice and the "usual proof" that the goods have been so delivered (or an equivalent electronic record for either). The seller is obligated to obtain any licenses or other approvals for export clearance.

The Incoterms definition has no provisions on either payment or post-shipment inspection. Under the UCC "F.A.S. vessel" term (§ 2-319(2)), the buyer must pay against a tender of documents, such as a negotiable bill of lading, before the goods arrive at their destination and before the buyer has any post-shipment opportunity to inspect the goods. UCC § 2-319(4). Otherwise, the UCC "F.A.S." term is similar to the Incoterms "FAS" term, including obligating the seller only to deliver the goods alongside a named vessel and not obligating the seller to arrange transportation to a final destination. The Incoterms FAS term does not require that the seller obtain a negotiable bill of lading or that buyer pay against documents, but also does not restrict the buyer's right of inspection before payment.

Under the Incoterms Free on Board (FOB) commercial term, the seller is obligated to deliver the goods on board a ship arranged for and named by the buyer at a named port of shipment. Thus, this term is also appropriate only for water-borne transportation. The seller must bear the costs and risks of inland transportation to the named port of shipment, and until it has placed the goods "on board the vessel nominated by the buyer" (or has "procured" rights to goods already in transit). The seller has no obligation to arrange transportation or insurance, but does have a duty to notify the buyer that the goods have been delivered on board the ship. The seller "may" arrange carriage at the buyer's expense if requested by the buyer, or if it is "commercial practice" for the seller to do so and the buyer does not timely object. But even under such circumstances, the seller may refuse to make such arrangements as long as it so notifies the buyer. The risk of loss will transfer to the buyer at the time the goods are "on board the vessel." The seller must provide a commercial invoice and the "usual proof" that the goods have been so delivered (or an equivalent electronic record for either), as well as an export license for the goods.

Again, the Incoterms FOB definition has no provisions on either payment or post-shipment inspection. The UCC also defines "F.O.B.," but it is not a term requiring water-borne transportation. Thus, the UCC "F.O.B." is more closely aligned with the Incoterms FCA term (*see* below). But the UCC also has a term "F.O.B. vessel" (§ 2-319(1)(c)), which relates only to water-borne transportation, and therefore is most closely linked to the Incoterms FOB term. Under the UCC, however, the term "F.O.B. vessel" requires the buyer to pay against a tender of documents, such as a negotiable bill of lading, before the goods arrive at their destination and before the buyer has any post-shipment opportunity to inspect the goods. UCC § 2-319(4). Otherwise, the UCC "F.O.B. vessel" term is similar to the Incoterms FOB term, including obligating the seller only to deliver the goods on board the ship and not obligating the seller to arrange transportation to a final destination. The Incoterms FOB term is not intended to require payment against documents or to restrict inspection before payment, unless such a term is expressly added or there is a known custom in a particular trade. In addition, it is more likely that negotiable bills of lading are not intended to be used with Incoterms FOB shipments, unless the parties specify "payment against documents" in the sale contract.

Under the Incoterms Cost, Insurance and Freight (CIF) commercial term, the seller is obligated to arrange for both transportation and insurance to a named destination port and to deliver the goods on board the ship arranged by the seller (or to "procure" rights to the goods already in transit). Thus, the term also is appropriate only for water-borne transportation. The seller must arrange the transportation, and pay the freight costs to the *destination port*, but has completed its delivery obligations when the goods are placed "on board the vessel" at the *port of shipment*. Similarly, the seller must arrange and pay for insurance (with a "company of good repute" and for 110% of the contract price) during transportation to the *port of destination*, but the risk of loss transfers to the buyer at the time the goods are on board the vessel at the *port of shipment*. The seller must merely give the buyer any notice normally needed "to enable the buyer to take the goods." The seller must provide a commercial invoice and "the usual transport document" for the destination port (or an equivalent electronic record for either), any obtain any necessary export license.

The Incoterms CIF definition has no express provisions on either payment or post-shipment inspection. However, perhaps the most important aspect of the CIF term is a requirement that the seller provide a transport document that will enable the buyer "to claim the goods from the carrier" and, unless otherwise agreed, "to sell the goods in transit by the transfer of the document to a subsequent buyer or by notification to the carrier." As is explained below in the materials on bills of lading, the traditional manner of enabling the buyer to do this, in either the "payment against documents" transaction or a letter of credit transaction, is for the seller to obtain a negotiable bill of lading from the carrier and to tender that negotiable document to the buyer through a series of banks. The banks allow the buyer to obtain possession of the document (and control of the goods) only after the buyer pays for the goods. Thus, the buyer "pays against documents," while the goods are at sea, and before any post-shipment inspection of the goods is possible.

The UCC also has a definition of "C.I.F.," which requires the buyer to "make payment against tender of the required documents." UCC § 2-320(4). The UCC "C.I.F." term is otherwise similar to Incoterms CIF, in that it requires the seller to deliver the goods to the carrier at the port of shipment and bear the risk of loss only to that port, but to pay freight costs and insurance to the port of destination.

The Incoterms Cost and Freight (CFR) commercial term is similar to the CIF term, except that the seller has no obligations with respect to either arranging or paying for insurance coverage of the goods during transportation. Under the CFR term, the seller is obligated to arrange for transportation to a named destination point and then to deliver the goods on board the ship arranged for by the seller (or to "procure" rights to the goods already in transit). Thus, the term is appropriate only for waterborne transportation. The seller must arrange the transportation and pay the freight costs to the *destination port*, but has completed its delivery obligations when the goods are placed "on board the vessel" at the *port of shipment*. The seller has no express obligation to arrange or pay for insurance on the goods during transportation, and the risk of loss transfers to the buyer at the time the goods are on board the vessel at the *port of shipment*. The seller must give the buyer any notice needed to enable the buyer to take the goods. The seller must provide a commercial invoice and "the usual transport document" for the destination port (or an equivalent electronic record for either), any obtain any necessary export license. As with CIF, the Incoterms CFR definition has no provisions on either payment or post-shipment inspection. However, like CIF it requires a transport document that will enable the buyer "to sell the goods in transit by the transfer of the document to a subsequent buyer or by notification to the carrier." This again is commonly understood to mean a negotiable bill of lading and thus a payment against documents transaction. Both the UCC and prior versions of Incoterms regarded this term as requiring payment against documents while the goods were still at sea, thus restricting post-shipment inspection of the goods before payment. These provisions should still be regarded as the norm under Incoterms CFR.

Rules for Any Mode or Modes of Transport

Under the Incoterms Ex Works (EXW) commercial term, the seller must only tender the goods by placing them "at the disposal of the buyer" at an agreed point. But if there is no agreed point, the seller "may select the point that best suits its purpose," and this most often will be its own premises. Thus, the seller has no obligation to deliver the goods to a carrier or to load the goods on any vehicle. This term is best suited for those sellers who are new to international export transactions. The seller must also give the buyer any notice necessary for it to take delivery of the goods, but the seller has no obligation to arrange for transportation or insurance. The risk of loss transfers to the buyer at the time the goods are placed at buyer's disposal. The seller must provide a commercial invoice, or an equivalent electronic record, but has no obligation to obtain a document of title (or any other transport document) or an export license. The Incoterms definition has no effect upon either payment or inspection rights under the contract (although of course the buyer must assume any costs of pre-shipment inspection). The Incoterms risk of loss provision is contrary to the default rules of both the UCC (§ 2-509) and the CISG (Art. 69), which delay passing the risk in a non-delivery transaction until the buyer's actual receipt of the goods, both because the seller is more likely to have insurance and because the seller has a greater ability to protect the goods.

Under the Incoterms Free Carrier (FCA) commercial term, the seller is obligated to deliver the goods, cleared for export, into the custody of a carrier nominated by the buyer, usually the first carrier in a multi-modal transportation scheme. The seller has no obligation to pay for transportation costs or insurance. However, the seller "may" arrange transportation at the buyer's expense if requested by the buyer, or if it is "commercial practice" for the seller to do so and the buyer does not timely object. But even under such circumstances, the seller may refuse to make such arrangements as long as it so notifies the buyer. Even if the seller does arrange transportation, it has no obligation to arrange for insurance coverage during transportation, and need only notify the buyer that the goods "have been delivered" either by loading at the seller's premises or into the custody of the carrier or other person nominated by the buyer. The risk of loss transfers to the buyer upon such delivery, although the buyer may not receive notice until after that time. The seller must provide a commercial invoice or an equivalent electronic record, any necessary export license, and "the usual proof that the goods have been delivered"—or an equivalent electronic record. The Incoterms definition has no provisions on either payment or post-shipment inspection.

This FCA term is the Incoterms commercial term that is most comparable to the UCC's "F.O.B. place of shipment" term under § 2-319(1)(a). However, there are two levels of confusion. One is that Incoterms has its own "FOB" term, which is different; this creates a risk of a false comparison between the UCC "F.O.B." term and the Incoterms "FOB" term. The other is that the obligations under FCA and the UCC "F.O.B. place of shipment" term are, in fact, different. Under the UCC's "F.O.B. place of shipment" term, the seller must arrange transportation (UCC §§ 2-319, 2-504), while the seller need do so under Incoterms FCA only by special agreement. Further, under UCC § 2-504, the seller under an F.O.B. place of shipment term must also "obtain and promptly deliver ... any document necessary to enable the buyer to obtain possession of the goods." Under Incoterms FCA, the seller need merely provide, at buyer's request, "assistance" to the buyer in obtaining a transport document.

The Incoterms Carriage and Insurance To Paid (CIP) and Carriage Paid To (CPT) commercial terms are similar to its CIF and CFR terms, except that they may be used for any type of transportation, including multimodal transportation, and thus are not just for waterborne transportation. Under the CIP term, the seller is obligated to arrange and pay for both transportation and insurance to a named *destination* place. However, the seller completes its delivery obligations, and the risk of loss passes to the buyer, upon delivery to the first carrier at the place of *shipment.* Thus, the term is appropriate for multimodal transportation. The CPT commercial term is similar, except that the seller has no duty to arrange or pay for insurance coverage of the goods during transportation.

Under both CIP and CPT, the seller must notify the buyer that the goods have been delivered to the first carrier, and also give any other notice required to enable the buyer "to take the goods." Under both, the seller must also provide a commercial invoice, or an equivalent electronic record, any necessary export license, and "the usual transport document." But—unlike CIF and CFR—the seller is obligated to obtain a document that would "enable the buyer to sell the goods in transit" (such as a negotiable bill of lading) *only if* this is "agreed or customary." Thus, unless the parties expressly agree to a "payment against documents" term or a special trade usage exists, the CIP or CPT commercial term does not require payment against documents or restrict inspection rights before payment. These Incoterms definitions contain no other payment or post-shipment inspection provisions. As with all of the other seven Incoterms rules for any mode of transport, the UCC has no definition for a CIP or CPT term.

The Incoterms 2010 have two new terms, DAP (Delivered at Place) and DAT (Delivered at Terminal), which replace four former terms (DES, DEQ, DAF, and DDU). Both can again be used with any type of transportation, including multimodal transport. In both, the seller is required to arrange transportation, pay the freight costs, and bear the risk of loss to a named destination point. Although these definitions have no provisions on insurance during transportation, because the seller bears the risk of loss during transport, it is well-advised to arrange and pay for insurance or it otherwise will act as a self-insurer. There are also no provisions on payment or post-shipment inspection, but there is no requirement for use of a negotiable bill of lading, and delivery occurs only after arrival of the goods. Thus, there is no reason to imply a "payment against documents" requirement if none is expressly stated. On the other hand, the parties (as always) are free to agree expressly on both a destination commercial term and a payment against documents term.

Under the Incoterms DAP rule, the seller bears the responsibility, costs, and risks of delivering the goods at the destination specified in the contract. The seller completes its delivery obligations under DAP when the goods reach the named place and are placed at the disposal of the buyer on the arriving means of transport ready for unloading by the buyer. Thus, the seller is obligated to arrange and pay for transportation to the named destination port and (although not obligated) is well advised to arrange and pay for insurance on the goods during transportation. The risk of loss also will transfer to the buyer when the seller completes its delivery obligation. The seller (obviously) must clear the goods for export, but is not responsible for import duties or other import formalities.

The Incoterms DAT rule is similar to DAP, for seller again bears the responsibility, costs, and risks of delivering the goods to the terminal at the location specified in the contract. Terminal includes all forms of terminals (whether quay, container or rail yard, or road, rail, or air terminal). Unlike DAP, however, the seller also is responsible for unloading the goods from the arriving means of transport. The seller completes its delivery obligations, and the risk of loss passes to the buyer, when the goods are unloaded from the arriving means of transport and are placed at the disposal of the buyer at the named terminal at the place of destination. Like DAP, the seller is responsible for export clearance, but is not responsible for import clearance.

The final Incoterm rule, DDP (Delivered Duty Paid), places the highest level of responsibility on the seller (and thus the lowest responsibility on the buyer). Under the DDP commercial term, delivery occurs and the risk of loss passes when the goods are placed at the buyer's disposal at the named place in the country of destination, cleared for importation into that country. The buyer is responsible for unloading the goods from the arriving means of transport, but the seller must obtain the import license, pay all import duties and terminal charges, and complete all customs formalities at its risk and expense. The closest UCC commercial term is "F.O.B. destination," § 2-319(1)(b), but it lacks substantial detail as compared to the Incoterms DDP term.

In each of these latter three terms, DAT, DAP, and DDP, the seller must give the buyer any notice necessary to allow it "to take measures that are normally necessary to enable the buyer to take delivery of the goods." Under each, the seller also must provide a commercial invoice or an equivalent electronic record and must provide the buyer with a document "enabling the buyer to take delivery of the goods" at the point identified under each respective term.

THE "PAYMENT AGAINST DOCUMENTS" TRANSACTION

What is a "payment against documents" transaction and how does it work? Such a transaction arises if, upon the conclusion of the parties' contract for the sale of the goods, the seller insists that the buyer "pay against the documents," rather than after delivery and inspection of the goods. Such a payment term must be bargained for and expressed in the sales contract. As noted above, it may also arise from the use of specific commercial terms (such as CIF and CFR). But it otherwise will not normally be implied. Such an arrangement often is especially important to a seller in an international transaction. If the buyer rejects the goods after international shipment, the seller is left with goods at a foreign location and with no payment from the buyer. Its options are then limited to assuming the expense and hassle of a return shipment or a distress sale at the foreign port.

In a payment against documents transaction, the seller will pack the goods and prepare a commercial invoice. If the commercial term so requires (*e.g.*, under a "CIF" term), the seller will also procure an insurance certificate (another form of contract) covering the goods during transit. The seller then delivers the goods to the carrier, which issues a bill of lading as a combination receipt and contract. As a general matter, the bill of lading contract may require that the carrier, in return for payment of the freight charge, deliver the goods *either* (a) to the named "consignee" in a "straight," or non-negotiable, bill of lading, or (b) to the person in possession ("holder") of a properly indorsed "order," or negotiable, bill of lading (*i.e.*, "to seller or order"). But for a payment against documents transaction, only an order bill of lading is appropriate, because it will permit the buyer to obtain delivery of the goods *only if* the buyer has physical possession of the bill of lading properly indorsed over to it. Such an "order" (negotiable) bill of lading thus authorizes the carrier to deliver the goods only to the seller or a person the seller may designate through an appropriate indorsement (*i.e.*, through an "order") on the bill of lading itself. (For more on "order" bills of lading, *see* the "Bills of Lading" section below.)

From its nature, in short, a negotiable bill of lading controls the right to obtain the goods from carrier, but also provides valuable assurances to both the buyer and the seller. To the buyer, it provides assurance that the goods have been delivered to the carrier and are destined for the buyer and not some third party. To the seller, and any collecting banks acting on seller's behalf, it provides assurance that the carrier will deliver the goods to the buyer only if the buyer has obtained possession of the bill of lading. And of course, the seller and its collecting banks will deliver the negotiable bill of lading to the buyer only after it has paid the purchase price for the goods. Thus, when a bank undertakes to collect funds from the buyer for the seller, it receives from the seller a "document of title" (the bill of lading) issued by the carrier which gives the bank control of carrier's delivery of the goods—because the buyer cannot obtain possession of the goods from a carrier without possession of the negotiable bill of lading. And because the banks have received this document of title from the seller only on the condition of payment, they can obtain payment (or a legally binding assurance of payment) from the buyer before the buyer receives the ability to obtain the goods from carrier.

Once the seller has obtained a negotiable bill of lading made out to its "order," how does this payment arrangement actually work? First, it prepares and forwards along with the bill of lading a "draft," together with an invoice and any other documents required by the sales contract. Like a check drawn on a bank, the draft functions as a legal vehicle for "withdrawing" from the buyer the amount owed to the seller under the sales contract. The seller uses the banking system as a collection agent for the draft. The draft (sometimes also called a "bill of exchange") will usually be a "sight draft," which is payable on demand ("on sight") when presented to the buyer. The draft is drawn for the amount due under the sales contract, and it is payable to the seller's order.

The seller then indorses both the negotiable draft and the negotiable bill of lading and delivers them (along with any other required documents) to Seller's Bank. If no letter of credit is involved in the transaction, the bank will usually take these documents only "for collection," although it is also possible for the bank to "discount," or buy, the documents outright and become the owner. If Seller's Bank acts for collection only, the seller will also provide a collection form that describes the condition for release of the bill of lading to the buyer (typically, full payment).

Seller's Bank is then required to send the draft, the bill of lading, and the other accompanying documents for presentment to the buyer through "customary banking channels." Seller's Bank deals with "for collection" items individually, without assuming that they will be honored, and therefore without giving the seller a provisional credit in the seller's account until the buyer pays the draft. If no other intermediary banks are involved, Seller's Bank will deliver the document to Buyer's Bank (the "presenting bank"), which will notify the buyer of their arrival. Buyer's Bank will demand that the buyer "honor" the draft, which means paying the amount of a demand draft, or "accepting" (bindingly promising to pay later) a time draft. The buyer may require the bank to "exhibit" the draft and other documents (especially, the bill of lading) to it to allow the buyer to determine whether they conform to the contract. The buyer typically has three banking days after presentment to decide whether to honor the draft, if mere notice is sent. However, if the draft and documents are exhibited directly to the buyer, the buyer must decide whether or not to honor the draft by the close of business on that same day, unless there are extenuating circumstances.

The buyer must "pay against the documents" and not the goods themselves. This is why it is preferable to specify the terms of the documents in the original contract for the sale of goods. Once the buyer has paid, or arranged to pay, Buyer's Bank will give possession of the bill of lading to the buyer. Only then will the buyer be able to obtain the goods from carrier. The buyer never sees the goods, only the documents—so it inspects the documents rigorously to determine that they comply exactly with the requirements of the sale contract. Substantial performance by the seller in the tender of documents is not acceptable.

An international sale of goods transaction involving payment against documents is illustrated by the following diagram:

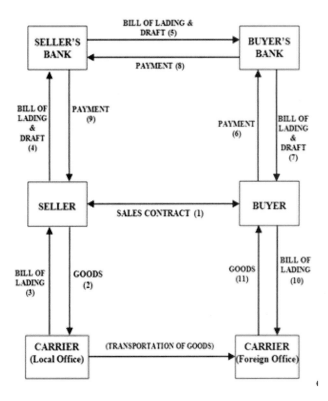

Note the risks to each party. If the seller ships conforming goods as stated on the bill of lading, it will be paid before the documents (and of course the goods) are released to the buyer. Thus, the seller will not lose control of the goods without being paid for them. If the buyer pays Buyer's Bank, the proceeds are remitted immediately and automatically

to the seller's bank account in the seller's home
country.

What can go wrong from the seller's point of view?
The seller has shipped the goods to a foreign buyer
without advance payment, and with no absolute
guarantee of payment from anyone other than the
buyer. The buyer may refuse to pay the sight draft
when it arrives. This would give the seller a cause of
action, but often it is usable only in the buyer's jurisdiction, which means bringing a suit abroad with
its extra expense, delay, and uncertainty. In particular, the seller could feel that it will be the target of
discrimination in the courts of another country.

The seller would still have control of the goods,
because after dishonor of the draft, the colleting
banks will return the bill of lading to the seller.
However, the goods would now be at a foreign destination—one at which the seller likely has no agents,
and no particular prospects for resale. In addition, if
the seller wishes to bring the goods back to its base
of operations (and normal sales territory), it would
have to arrange and pay a second transportation
charge, and this may be substantial in relation to
the value of the goods. The seller will be somewhat
better situated under a documentary transaction,
because the buyer may review only the documents
(especially, the bill of lading) in deciding whether it
will pay. But a dishonor of the draft by the buyer
also can create economic circumstances in which the
seller's only rational option is a distress sale at a

foreign location. This risk to the seller is inherent in the payment against documents transaction, unless the seller requires that the buyer also arrange for the issuance of a letter of credit. (*See* Chapter 3 for a complete description and discussion of the letter of credit transaction.)

On the other hand, for its payment of the price, the buyer has a document from the carrier entitling it to delivery of the goods, likely an insurance certificate protecting against casualty loss in transit, and—if it had the foresight to arrange this in advance (*see* below)—perhaps even a third-party inspection certificate confirming that the goods conform to the sale contract. In other words, the buyer should receive what it bargained for—delivery of conforming goods or insurance proceeds sufficient to cover any loss. However, without the ability to inspect the actual goods before payment, the buyer cannot be absolutely assured that they conform to the contract.

What can go wrong from the buyer's point of view? *At least* six distinct problems could arise:

(a) The goods could be lost or stolen.

(b) The carrier could stow the goods or operate so negligently that they are damaged in transit, which would require resort to the specialized body of law governing carrier liability.

(c) The seller could ship goods that do not conform to the sales contract. The nonconformity could range from the seller shipping scrap paper to the labeling on the packaging being incorrect (which can cause problems with customs officials in both countries).

(d) The bill of lading and attached draft could be stolen and presented to the buyer by a thief—with any necessary indorsements having been forged. If the carrier learns of the forged indorsement, it then will not deliver the goods to the buyer.

(e) The goods could fail to conform to the bill of lading, so that the documents state that goods of a particular description will be delivered but the goods actually delivered are of a different description.

(f) The bill of lading could be forged (i.e., without the carrier's knowledge or approval)—and no goods shipped.

Some of these problems are recognized and dealt with in the standard handling of the "payment against documents" transaction. For example, insuring the goods against loss or theft is required by a CIF transaction. Other problems, such as payment before inspection, make buyers feel unprotected, and they have searched for devices within the transaction that can afford them more protection. Such a device, in common use in modern transactions, is the Inspection Certificate. This involves the buyer arranging for an inspection of the goods by an independent third party before the seller delivers them to the carrier. The buyer then has the inspection certificate as a separate verification—beyond that of the seller and of the carrier in the bill of lading—of what goods the seller actually shipped.

Three problems nonetheless may remain that are uniquely related to any transaction using a bill of lading. These will be considered in the materials below:

(a) The loss or theft of the bill of lading, followed by the forgery of a necessary indorsement and carrier's misdelivery (delivery of the goods to the wrong person under a bill of lading).

(b) The misdescription of the goods by the seller/shipper and in the bill of lading, followed by carrier's delivery of goods that do not conform to the description in the bill of lading.

(c) The forgery of a complete bill of lading by a malevolent shipper without carrier's knowledge or approval.

THE ROLE OF BILLS OF LADING IN INTERNATIONAL SALES TRANSACTIONS

Bills of lading play a significant, indeed essential, role in international sales transactions. There are two different types of bills of lading—a "straight" (or non-negotiable) bill of lading, and an "order" (or negotiable) bill of lading. These are often known in the trade as "white" and "yellow" for the different colors of paper on which they traditionally have been printed. Each represents the shipper's contract with the carrier, and will set forth the terms of that contract expressly or incorporate the carrier's terms and tariffs by reference. As noted above, a bill of lading, whether negotiable or non-negotiable, represents a "document of title," in that the piece of paper defines who is legally entitled to possession of the goods (*i.e.*, to whom the carrier may and must deliver the goods). Nonetheless, for the reasons explored in more detail below, the typical large international sale of goods transaction of its nature will require a negotiable bill of lading.

State, federal, and international law all have rules governing bills of lading. Uniform Commercial Code Article 7 (as revised in 2003) broadly regulates "Documents of Title," including bills of lading. But the regulation of bills of lading, and in particular the relationship of the carrier to its customers, also is the subject of three international conventions and three United States federal statutes. The three conventions—the so-called Hague Rules, Hague/Visby Rules, and Hamburg Rules—all cover the same subject matter, but are progressively more customer-oriented. With this multiplicity of treaties governing the terms of the bill of lading and its use, conflicting concepts should be expected. Such concerns have led to the negotiation and conclusion of an entirely new treaty, the United Nations Convention on Contracts for the International Carriage of Goods Wholly or Partly by Sea (2009). These so-called "Rotterdam

Rules"—which the United States has signed but not yet ratified as of 2012—may well be acceptable to a noteworthy majority of maritime states, whether principally supportive of buyers, sellers, or carriers.

As of 2012, the United States has enacted the Hague Rules into its domestic law as the Carriage of Goods by Sea Act (COGSA)(now in a statutory note to 46 U.S.C. § 30701). It also has in force more limited pre-COGSA legislation, the Harter Act, 46 U.S.C. § 30701 *et seq.* COSGA defines the basic obligations of the carrier regarding the care for and transportation of the goods. It also establishes the fundamental rule that the bill of lading is "prima facie evidence of the receipt by the carrier of the goods as therein described." COGSA, § 3(4).

The most important federal law regulating bills of lading, however, is the Federal Bill of Lading Act (FBLA, also known by its earlier name, the Pomerene Act). 49 U.S.C. § 80101 *et seq.* The FBLA governs all interstate and all outbound international shipments that involve a bill of lading issued by a common carrier and to that extent it entirely preempts UCC Article 7. The word "carrier" is not defined, so it is not clear whether documents issued by freight forwarders are covered. Further, the term "bill of lading" is not defined, so it is not clear whether air waybills or inland waterway documents are included. Nonetheless, depending on the specific circumstances, strong arguments support application of the FBLA to both subjects.

As noted in the preceding section, the important role of bills of lading in international sale of goods transactions may be illustrated by an examination of three of the most common forms of bill of lading disputes: (a) misdelivery of the goods by the carrier; (b) misdescription of the goods in the bill of lading; and (c) forgery of the bill of lading in the first place. The following materials will analyze these three issues in turn.

Misdelivery. As noted in the introduction above, bills of lading come in two principal forms: non-negotiable and negotiable. A non-negotiable, or "straight," bill of lading is issued to a named person, the consignee. Under a non-negotiable bill of lading, the carrier obligates itself to deliver the goods at the destination point to the consignee named in the bill of lading. 49 U.S.C. § 80110. Possession of the actual straight bill of lading does not confer rights over the goods or against the carrier. Rather, the carrier is obligated to deliver the goods *only* to the named consignee. Further, indorsements on such a straight bill of lading are irrelevant to the rights of the "indorsee" and to the obligations of the carrier. In short, the carrier is liable to the consignee of a straight bill of lading for misdelivery if it delivers the goods to anyone other than the consignee (or a person whom that consignee delegates to receive them). Thus, straight bills of lading are not appropriate for a "payment against documents" transaction, and the case reporters are full of litigation where an attorney tried a shortcut using a straight bill of lading as the "easy" way to do this transaction—and sacrificed the client's interests in the process. Straight bills of lading are also called "air waybills," "sea waybills," and "freight receipts" (among other names) depending upon the principal method of transportation for the goods.

For a negotiable bill of lading, in contrast, physical possession is essential to determining the rights to the goods and the delivery obligations of the carrier. A negotiable bill of lading may be issued either to "bearer" or to the "order" of a named person. A bearer bill of lading is transferred by delivery alone, and anyone in possession may demand delivery of the goods from the carrier. Because of the inherent risks of such a practice, negotiable bills of lading issued to bearer are substantially less common in international transactions.

An "order" bill of lading allows the named person (the consignee) to indorse the bill of lading and thereby "order" delivery of the goods to others. If possession of the bill of lading is transferred to a third party, and the bill of lading is indorsed to that third party (either specially or in blank), then the third party becomes a "holder" of the bill of lading. Under a negotiable bill of lading, the carrier obligates itself to deliver the goods to the "holder" of the bill of lading at the destination point. 46 U.S.C. § 80110. Thus, possession of the negotiable bill of lading becomes crucial. The carrier must see the actual bill of lading to confirm that the person demanding the goods has possession of the bill and that the bill has the proper chain of indorsements over to that person.

The original consignee may indorse the negotiable bill of lading two ways: (1) "in blank," that is, with a bare signature ("*Ralph Folsom*"); or (2) by a "special indorsement," which identifies the next intended holder by name ("Deliver the goods to Michael Gordon, or order. *Ralph Folsom*"). 46 U.S.C. § 80104. Under a blank indorsement, any person in possession becomes a holder, and is thus entitled to demand delivery from the carrier. Under a special indorsement, in contrast, only the named indorsee can become a holder, and only that person can demand delivery from the carrier (or indorse the bill of lading to still another party so as to make it a holder). Thus, the special indorsement protects the interests of the parties from thieves and forgers much better than a blank indorsement.

By obtaining possession of the actual negotiable bill of lading, properly indorsed over to him, a person becomes a "holder" and acquires rights over the goods and against the carrier. In turn, the carrier is liable to the holder of a negotiable bill of lading for misdelivery if it delivers the goods to anyone but the holder. It is in this sense that the negotiable bill of lading is an especially secure "document of title," because possession of it, properly indorsed to the possessor, controls title to the document, title to the goods, and the direct obligation of the carrier to deliver the goods only to the holder. For this reason, the negotiable bill of lading is appropriate for a "payment against documents" transaction. The collecting banks can use their possession of such bills of lading to control title to both the goods and the document until they have collected the price from the buyer. Some other commercial countries, for regulatory reasons, recognize only "straight" bills of lading and not negotiable bills of lading; but as this brief review illustrates, the negotiable bill of lading provides important security to an international sale of goods transaction.

The holder of the bill of lading does not have absolute title to the goods in all cases, but nearly so. If the shipper was not the owner of the goods in the first place—for example if a thief steals the goods from the "true owner" at gunpoint—then no holder of the bill of lading will have title to the goods because the shipper's claim of title was "void" from the beginning. However, if the owner voluntarily parted with the goods but was defrauded by the shipper (*e.g.*, a "cash sale" in which the check bounces later), then the shipper obtains "voidable" title and can pass good title to a holder of the document who purchases it in good faith for value without notice. UCC § 7-503(a) (with reference to § 2-403). The rights of such a good faith holder for value are also superior to any seller's lien or right to stop delivery of the goods in transit.

Under the Federal Bill of Lading Act, as under the UCC, any forgery of a necessary indorsement is not effective to create or transfer rights, whether the forgery is perfect or inept. Further, any unauthorized signature by an agent is treated as a forgery, as long as it was made without actual, implied, or apparent authority. The protection is illustrated in the situation where a thief steals a negotiable bill of lading from the holder who was in possession of the document under a special indorsement. As described above, the holder's indorsement is necessary to transfer rights to the document and the goods to any other party. Without that indorsement, the thief is not a holder and has no rights to the document or goods. If the thief forges the holder's signature, that forgery is ineffective, and the thief is still not a holder and still has no rights. If the thief transfers the document to another party, that party also is not a holder and cannot obtain rights under the document without the original holder's signature. *See* the famous case of *Adel Precision Products Corp. v. Grand Trunk Western R. Co.*, 51 N.W.2d 922 (Mich. 1952). The carrier is still obligated to deliver the goods only to the holder, the victim of theft.

If the carrier nonetheless delivers to the forger, or to someone who received the document from the forger without the holder's indorsement, the carrier is liable for misdelivery under 49 U.S.C. § 80111. (The forger of course is also liable, if he can be found.) The concept is that each person who takes the bill of lading should "know its indorser." If the goods are misdelivered, the person who wrongfully received the goods is liable. Such a person, as well as all other transferees after the forger, all made warranties under 49 U.S.C. § 80107 that they had "a right to transfer the bill and title to the goods described in the bill"—but they had no such right or title. Each person has a warranty action against its transferor and each transferor, in turn, has a warranty action against its transferor—and so on back up the chain of transfers. This is not very efficient, but the purpose is to push liability back up the chain of transfers to the person who took from the forger (and, if he can be found, to the forger himself).

Collecting banks that transfer the document for value also can be subject to this warranty liability. If the buyer pays, and those funds are transmitted to the forger, then the collecting banks have received value. However, such banks have several potential escape valves. One is to disclaim such warranty liability when indorsing or transferring the bill of lading. The FBLA provides that its transfer warranties do not arise if "a contrary intention appears." 49 U.S.C. § 80107(a). Thus, an indorsement "XYZ Bank—no warranties, prior indorsements not guaranteed" would clearly disclaim liability for such a warranty. Banks may similarly argue that banking custom relieves them from any duty to examine documents, with the result that an implicit blanket statutory "contrary intention" exists as a matter of custom. A second avenue is to claim that the bank is only holding the document "as security for a debt," because the statute exempts such holders from warranty liability. The difficulty with this avenue is that a collecting bank does not pay the seller until after it receives payment, so it never becomes a creditor, secured or otherwise. Finally, if a bank incorporates by reference the ICC's Uniform Rules for Collections (1995) when it forwards the documents, it may effectively avoid liability for problems not apparent on the face of the documents. Each of these approaches has analytical difficulties, but they may indicate a blanket intention to disclaim the statutory warranties by implication. In any event, any bank found to have warranty liability can pass this liability back to its transferor, as long as it can identify and find that transferor.

The principal party subject to liability in the case of a misdelivery, however, will be the carrier. As noted, in the case of a non-negotiable bill of lading the carrier will be liable if it delivers the goods to anyone other than the named consignee (or its designee); and in the case of a negotiable bill of lading the carrier will be liable if it delivers the goods to anyone other than the holder. In the case of such a misdelivery, the FBLA provides that the carrier is liable to "a person having title to, or right to possession of," the goods. 49 U.S.C. § 80113. For a negotiable bill of lading, this of course will be the holder (if still in possession). But this will not be the case with a forged indorsement, because the carrier will have received possession of the bill from the forger and likely will have cancelled it as part of its standard practices. Thus, the proper plaintiff commonly will be the buyer in the underlying sales transaction because under the UCC, title to the goods generally will pass from the seller to the buyer at the time of shipment (unless seller was obligated to deliver at the buyer's location).. *See* § 2-401(2). But if the buyer has already wrongfully refused to pay (although obviously not in a "payment against documents" transaction), the seller may be able to obtain a right to possession of the goods and thus have the rights against the liable carrier.

Misdescription. The carrier responsible for transporting the goods is not a party to the contract between (*i.e.*, is not in "privity" with) the seller and the buyer in the sale of goods transaction. Therefore, the carrier has no obligation to deliver goods that conform to the sale contract. However, when the seller/shipper delivers the goods to the carrier, the bill of lading issued by the carrier will contain a description of the goods. COGSA in fact requires the carrier to issue a bill of lading with information on "[e]ither the number of packages or pieces, or the quantity, or weight, as the case may be, as furnished in writing by the shipper." COGSA § 3(3). The carrier in turn will have an obligation to deliver goods that conform to the description in the bill of lading. As noted above, COSGA declares that the bill of lading is "prima facie evidence of the receipt by the carrier of the goods as therein described." COGSA, § 3(4). And under the Federal Bill of Lading Act, a carrier is liable for any failure to deliver goods that correspond to the description in the bill of lading. 49 U.S.C. § 80113(a). This obligation is owed to the owner of the goods under a straight bill of lading and to the holder of a negotiable bill of lading, provided the owner or holder "gave value in good faith relying on the description."

The problem with this obligation is that the carrier usually does not know what it is carrying, because the goods are often in containers. Thus, the carrier knows that it received a *container* labeled "100 Apple iPads." But it will not, and is not expected to, open the container to check whether it contains iPads, or to count how many items actually are in it. Even if it opened the container, the carrier would not be expected to check whether each iPad is in working order. Even if it did so check, it is not likely to have the expertise to determine whether each can perform as expected or is otherwise fit for the ordinary uses of such a device. Thus, the carrier is not expected to warrant the description and capability of packaged goods given to it to transport.

To solve this problem, carriers are allowed, under the FBLA, to disclaim, through what are generally known as "Shipper's weight, load, and count" or "SLC" clauses, their obligations to deliver goods that conform to the description in the bill of lading. Appropriate disclaimer language is set forth in the statute, and includes the following phrases:

- "contents or condition of contents of packages unknown";

- "said to contain"; and

- "shipper's weight, load, and count."

Other language conveying the same meaning can be used; the statutory linguistic formulas are not required. The FBLA defines two further requirements for the effectiveness of such a clause. First, a disclaimer is effective only to the extent that the carrier "does not know whether any part of the goods were received or conform to the description." 49 U.S.C. § 80113(a). If the carrier has actual knowledge of a problem, it may not passively allow the shipper to provide a misdescription in the bill of lading.

Second, the goods must actually have been loaded on the vessel by the shipper. When goods are loaded by a carrier, the carrier is obligated to count the number of packages and is expected to note the condition of the packages. If it loads, the carrier is also obligated to "determine the kind and quantity" (although not the quality) of the goods. For bulk freight, even where it is loaded by the shipper, the carrier must still determine the kind and quantity of the freight if the shipper so requests and provides adequate facilities for the carrier to weigh the freight. In situations where the carrier must count packages or weigh the goods, disclaimers such as "shipper's weight, load, and count" will not be effective.

The requirement that the shipper actually load the goods seems appropriate for disclaimers of the "shipper's weight, load, and count" variety; but it seems inapposite for disclaimers of the "said to contain" or "contents or condition of contents of packages unknown" variety. Nonetheless, the carrier will be liable for a misdescription even with an otherwise clear "SLC" disclaimer if it issues a bill of lading and the shipper in fact never loaded anything on board the carrier's vessels.

More generally, the carrier must make at least a "reasonable inspection" of the goods under the circumstances. Thus, what is established is a system in which the carrier is responsible for checking readily observable facts—quantity, the number of cartons, obvious information about the weight of a shipment, and the like. These are items which the carrier is likely to check in any event, to be certain that cartons are not inadvertently left behind, and to determine the appropriate freight charge.

However, the carrier is not required to check most quality terms, such as what goods are in a container and whether or not they are in operating condition. Thus, it can truthfully say that it has received 100 cartons "said to contain" Apple iPads, without opening the cartons; but it does need to count the number of cartons. The intersection of these rules arises when the carrier accepts a sealed container supposed to contain 2000 tin ingots weighing 35 tons, and issues a bill of lading for a container "said to

contain 2000 tin ingots." If the container is empty
and weighs less than a ton, and this information is
readily apparent to the carrier, the carrier's disclaimer is not likely to provide protection. *Berisford
Metals Corp. v. S/S Salvador*, 779 F.2d 841 (2nd
Cir. 1985)(also addressing the separate limitation in
COGSA on the *amount* of carrier liability).

Forged Bill of Lading. If the carrier issues a
bill of lading for which there are no goods, the carrier is likely to be liable, as is described above. However, suppose the carrier never issued a bill of lading in the first place. Instead, a person unrelated to
the carrier created (forged) the bill of lading in the
name of the carrier, with no authority from the carrier. The buyer who pays upon receipt of such a bill
of lading (such as in a "payment against documents"
transaction) or otherwise purchases such a forged
bill of lading has paid funds, probably through a
series of banks, but finds that the carrier has no
goods to deliver. There is no misdelivery or
misdescription claim against the carrier, for no one
ever delivered goods to the carrier that it could
misdescribe or misdeliver. If the carrier did not issue the bill of lading and its "signature" is a forgery
or otherwise unauthorized, that signature is not "effective," and carrier will not be liable on the bill,
absent some sort of actionable negligence.

The forger of course is liable for the fraud, if he
can be found. But unlike the forged indorsement
situation, no one has received any goods, for there

were never any goods to deliver. Nonetheless, like the forged indorsement situation, each party that transferred the bill of lading for value makes warranties to later parties, and the first warranty is that "the bill is genuine." 49 U.S.C. § 80107(a)(1). If the bill of lading itself is forged, that warranty is breached. Thus, all parties who transferred the bill and received payment may be liable in a breach of warranty action by later transferees. The concept is that the last person to purchase the bill will "know its transferor," and be able to recover against that transferor. That transferor can, in turn, recover against *its* transferor, and so on up the chain of transfers, until the loss falls either on the forger or on the person who dealt with and took the bill from the forger.

Again, collecting banks that have transferred the document for value can be subject to this warranty liability. But again, such banks will have the same three potential escape valves discussed under forged indorsements above: (1) an express disclaimer of warranty that indicates "a contrary intention"; (2) a claim that the bank is holding the document only "as security for a debt"; and (3) the limitation in the ICC Collection Rules that banks need examine only the appearance of the documents. Again, each of these approaches has analytical difficulties, but they may reflect a blanket, implicit indication to disclaim the statutory warranties. In any event, any bank found to have warranty liability can pass this

liability back to its transferor, as long as it can identify and find that transferor.

ELECTRONIC BILLS OF LADING

The Federal Bills of Lading Act does not define
"bill of lading" and does not require that it be written on a piece of paper or have a physical signature
by anyone. Thus, use of electronic bills of lading
would seem to be a technical possibility. However,
all of the primary rules of this federal law are
founded on an implicit assumption that the bill of
lading is a paper document. The references to
indorsement (in blank or to a specified person),
transfer by delivery, and "person in possession"
make sense only for a paper document.

However, telecommunications technology can
provide electronic messages that perform the main
functions of the bill of lading: as a receipt, a
transport contract, and a document of title. Thus,
several types of bill of lading equivalents are currently in use; but most of them are used only as receipts for the goods generated by the carrier. Their
utility is enhanced where a "straight," or non-
negotiable, bill of lading (or waybill) does not need
to be presented to a carrier to obtain possession of
the goods. Unfortunately, the FBLA requires the
carrier to deliver the goods only to a person who
"has possession of the bill," even under a straight
bill of lading (49 U.S.C. § 80110(a)(2)), and makes
the carrier liable for damages if it does not take and
cancel the bill when delivering the goods. These re-

quirements are often ignored by carriers in practice, and the parties merely exchange printed forms, but the statutory requirements nonetheless inhibit the acceptance of electronic bills of lading in the United States.

Despite these requirements, the Interstate Commerce Commission now authorizes the use of uniform electronic bills of lading, both negotiable and non-negotiable, for both motor carrier and rail carrier use. *See* 49 CFR Part 1035. More generally, at least two federal courts also have recognized the effectiveness of electronic bills of lading, at least in certain respects. These developments, however, relate to the role of bills of lading merely in evidencing a carriage contract and in communicating information about the goods, the shipper, and the consignee. The recognition by the Interstate Commerce Commission and the court cases do not address issues relating to defining the rights and obligations of the parties to the electronic bill. Thus, the bills do not allow for further sale or rerouting of the goods in transit, or for using the bills of lading to finance the transaction. Under the I.C.C. regulations, for example, negotiable uniform electronic bills of lading must "provide for indorsement on the back portion" (49 CFR § 1035.1), but there is no explanation of how an electronic message has a "back portion," or how "indorsement" is to be effected.

Carriers also have attempted to create programs that utilize electronic carrier-issued international receipts for goods. Most of these efforts relate to non-negotiable electronic waybills under which shippers provide relevant information through the carrier's website and the shipper or consignee then prints out a waybill document at either the origin or destination. Atlantic Container Lines, for example, has used dedicated lines between terminals at its offices in different ports to send messages between those offices. It generated a Data Freight Receipt which was given to the consignee or notify party. Such a receipt was not negotiable, however, and gave buyers and banks little protection from further sale or rerouting of the goods by the shipper in transit. A program was similar, but also an advance over the prior approach, because it included a "no disposal" term in the shipper-carrier contract. Thus, this electronic message protected the buyer from further sale or rerouting by the seller in transit. It still could not be used to finance the transfer, however, because the electronic receipt, even if it named a bank as consignee, was not formally a negotiable document of title. The receipt was believed to give the bank only the right to prevent delivery to the buyer, not a positive right to take control of the goods for itself.

The Chase Manhattan Bank also attempted to create the Seaborne Trade Documentation System (SEADOCS), which involved a Registry for negotiable electronic bill of lading for oil shipments. The Registry acted as custodian for an actual paper negotiable bill of lading issued by a carrier, and maintained a registry of transfers of that bill from the original shipper to the ultimate "holder." The transfers were made by a series of electronic messages, each of which could be authenticated by "test keys", or identification numbers, generated by SEADOCS. SEADOCS would then, as agent, indorse the paper bill of lading in its custody. At the end, SEADOCS would electronically deliver a paper copy of the negotiable bill of lading to the last indorsee to enable it to obtain the goods from the carrier. While SEADOCS was a legal success, showing that such a program was technically feasible, it was not a commercial success, lasting less than a year.

The Comite Maritime International (CMI) has adopted Rules for Electronic Bills of Lading (1990). Under those rules, any carrier can issue an electronic bill of lading as long as it will act as a clearinghouse for subsequent transfers. Upon receiving goods, the carrier sends an electronic message to the shipper describing the goods, the contract terms and a "private key" which can be used to transfer shipper's rights to a third party. Under the CMI Rules, the shipper has the "right of control and transfer" over the goods, and is called a "holder." Under Rules 4 and 7, an electronic message from shipper which includes the private key can be used to transfer the shipper's rights to a third party, who then becomes a new holder. The carrier then cancels the shipper's "private key" and issues a different private key to the new holder. Upon arrival, the carrier will deliver the goods to then-current holder or a consignee designated by the holder. The original parties to the transaction must agree that the CMI Rules will govern, but this is done merely through adoption in the carriage contract. All parties also must agree that electronic messages satisfy any national law requirements that a bill of lading be in writing. This is an attempt to create an "electronic" writing which is a negotiable document of title by contract and estoppel. Some commentators have observed that this is an attempt by private parties to create a negotiable document, a power usually reserved to legislatures.

The Commission of the European Committees has sponsored the BOLERO electronic bill of lading initiative, which is based on the CMI Rules. However, under the BOLERO system neither a bank nor a carrier is the repository of the sensitive information of who has bought and sold the cargo covered by the electronic bills of lading. Instead, BOLERO establishes as the operator of the central registry a third party who is independent of the shipper, the carrier, the ultimate buyer and all intermediate parties.

Most bankers have been skeptical of the device created by the CMI Rules. The registries maintained by each carrier do not have the same level of security associated with SWIFT procedures. (*See* "Electronic Letters of Credit" in Chapter 3.) In addition to fraudulent transactions, there is a risk of misdirected messages. Thus, a bank could find itself relying on non-existent rights from a fraudulent actor impersonating the carrier. The banks are concerned as to whether carriers will accept liability in their new role as electronic registrars for losses due to such fraudulent practices. The banks are also concerned that the full terms and conditions of the contract of carriage are not available to subsequent "holders." Thus, use of the CMI Rules does not yet seem to be widely adopted, at least in the United States, and bills of lading are still primarily paper-based in both the "payment against documents" and letter of credit transactions.

Two recent legal developments nonetheless may facilitate and promote the future development of commercially viable electronic bills of lading. First, recent revisions to the Uniform Commercial Code expressly contemplate "electronic documents of title," including electronic bills of lading. Revised UCC Article 1 defines an electronic document of title as one "evidenced by a record consisting of information stored in an electronic medium" (§ 1-201(b)(16)) and then broadly defines a "record" to include information that is "stored in an electronic medium and is retrievable in perceivable form" (§ 1-201(b)(31)). The 2003 revisions to UCC Article 7 then address issues concerning the security of electronic bills of lading through the concept of "control." At the core of this concept is a requirement that "a single authoritative copy of the document exists which is unique, identifiable, and [with certain defined exceptions] unalterable." Rev. § 7-106(b). Article 7 then has specifically tailored rules for the "negotiation" of an electronic document of title.

Second, a recently concluded international treaty, the 2009 United Nations Convention on Contracts for the International Carriage of Goods Wholly or Partly by Sea (the so-called "Rotterdam Rules"), creates an explicit legal framework for the creation, transfer, and enforcement of "negotiable electronic transport records." Deliberately medium and technology neutral, these rules should both accommodate and foster future technological innovations. Although only one country has ratified the Rotterdam Rules as of 2012, there are positive indications that many countries will do so (including the United States).

INTERNATIONAL ELECTRONIC COMMERCE

The rapid and phenomenal growth of E-Commerce in the modern economy caught the legal regimes of the world unprepared. None was ready for the legal problems caused by the new forms of contract-making, payment, performance, and information exchange. They have done their best to adapt traditional rules to new transaction patterns, but each legal regime has adapted in a different manner. Thus, although some fundamental principles are the same, there is little consistency in the rules applicable to E-Commerce transactions which cross national borders.

Such a lack of consistency is not new, but the problems are magnified by another aspect of E-Commerce: The parties often do not know when an E-Commerce transaction is in fact across jurisdictional boundaries. A website with a ".com" address may literally be located anywhere in the world. Thus, the website address of each party, which may be the only information each about of the other, may not reveal the transborder nature of the transaction.

E-Commerce also raises a number of important challenges for the traditional rules of contract law. These include how to satisfy writing and signature requirements, authentication and attribution without personal contact, security and integrity of electronic messages, and express and implied terms for both commercial and consumer contracts. It also raises jurisdiction issues, ranging from choice of law to sufficient contacts for the exercise of personal jurisdiction, to "presence" in a jurisdiction for purposes of regulation by public authorities. The public authorities not only wish to prevent fraud and deception by E-Merchants, but also to regulate privacy, intellectual property, and taxation issues, among others. In all these areas, there are very few statutory rules or decided cases; and, where there are, the existing rules and approaches to E-Commerce differ from one legal regime to another.

Thus, there is a growing need not only for statutory rules to facilitate E-Commerce, but also for uniform rules across jurisdictional borders (because, again, it is not usually clear where the parties are located). Promoting similar rules could be accomplished by either an international multilateral treaty or proposed model legislation. A first international effort in the latter direction was a Model Law on Electronic Commerce adopted in 1996 by UNCITRAL (the organization which developed the CISG). The Model Law is a minimalist approach to legislation, seeking to facilitate E-Commerce transactions and not to regulate them. This Model Law is now available to all legal regimes for enactment to provide guidance for E-Merchants and their customers.

In its general provisions, the UNCITRAL Model Law provides equality of treatment for paper documents and electronic messages. It provides that "data messages" are not to be denied legal effect because they are electronic, and that any "writing" requirement is satisfied by a data message which is accessible for subsequent reference. Legal requirements for a "signature" are met by a data message if there is a method that is "reasonable for the circumstances" both to identify the person sending the message and to indicate that person's approval of the message. (A separate UNCITRAL Model Law on Electronic Signatures (2001) provides more detail on this point.) An electronic data message will also satisfy any evidentiary requirements, including for "an original document" if "there exists a reliable assurance as to the integrity of the information" and "that information is capable of being displayed to the person to whom it is to be presented." Finally, record retention requirements may be satisfied by retaining data messages if the information therein is "accessible so as to be usable for subsequent reference," retained in its original format and "can be demonstrated" to be accurate, and permits "identification of the origin and destination of a data message and the date and time when it was sent or received."

The UNCITRAL Model Law also contains more specialized rules that may be varied by agreement between the parties. These rules concern contract formation, attribution of messages, and acknowledgment and time of receipt of data messages. As to attribution, a message is deemed to be sent by a designated originator if it is sent either by an authorized person or by a machine that is programmed by the originator to operate automatically. The addressee of the data message is authorized to rely on it as being from the originator if either an agreed-upon security procedure has been used or the originator enabled the actual sender to gain access to a message identification method.

A major problem with electronic data messages is that they get lost—or are caught in spam or similar computer filters—much more often than messages sent in paper form. Thus, acknowledgment of receipt of electronic messages is much more important to the parties than is acknowledgment of paper-based messages, and the parties often stipulate in their agreements that data messages must be acknowledged. If they so agree, under the UNCITRAL Model Law, such an acknowledgment can be accomplished either by the method agreed upon or, in absence of such an agreement, any sufficiently clear communication or conduct. Even where the parties have not agreed to require acknowledgment, the originator of a data message may unilaterally require it by stating in the body of the message that it is conditional on acknowledgment. In such a case, the data message "is treated as though it has never been sent, until the acknowledgement is received." Receipt of a message generally requires that the message enter an information system outside the control of the originator or its agents.

Other provisions in the UNCITRAL Model Law are specific to the contracts for the carriage of goods and to transportation documents. These provisions generally permit electronic data messages to replace bills of lading and waybills, even where local statutes require a paper document. They also provide that legal rules that require the use of paper documents in carriage contracts are satisfied by such data messages.

The UNCITRAL Model Law on Electronic Commerce has had a significant influence on domestic legislation. As of 2012, more than forty national laws, various EU Directives, as well as uniform acts in nearly every state of the U.S. and nearly every province of Canada have incorporated some or all of its provisions and concepts. Further enactments are expected.

More recently, UNCITRAL also has proposed a formal treaty, the United Nations Convention on the Use of Electronic Communications in International Contracts (2005). This treaty also is designed to ensure that a communication or contract is not "denied validity or enforceability on the sole ground that it is in the form of an electronic communication." Similar to the CISG, the Convention would apply to electronic communications exchanged between parties whose "places of business" are in different states, provided at least one party has its place of business in a Contracting State. The parties may also "opt into" the Convention, but may also "opt out" or otherwise vary the effect of the Convention when it would apply. Again like the CISG, this Convention would not apply to communications involving consumers, negotiable instruments, or documents of title, but also not to those involving estate law or certain types of financial transactions.

The core principles of the Convention parallel those of the Model Law. First, a communication may not be denied legal effect solely because it is in electronic form. Second, this basic principle applies with specific force for the enforceability of contracts concluded by electronic means, including, interestingly, without individual actions by natural persons. The Convention nonetheless defines specific remedies for input errors by natural persons relating to automated message systems. Finally, and as a more general proposition, the Convention declares a principle of functional equivalence between electronic communications and paper documents, including with reference to electronic methods of authentication and signature requirements. With only two ratifications as of 2012, however, the future influence of this treaty remains quite unclear.

In the United States, a federal statute from 2000, the Electronic Signatures in Global and National Commerce Act (E–Sign), also has served as a significant impetus to the legal enforceability of E-Commerce transactions. E-Sign was not adopted to displace the substantive rules of contract law, but rather to facilitate the use of electronic records and signatures in interstate and foreign commerce. At its core is the familiar principle that electronic signatures, records, and contracts may not be denied validity or effect solely because they are in an electronic form. E–Sign generally preempts state laws and regulations, but it also contains an express exception that permits states to adopt their own legislation in its place as long as the legislation does not conflict with the rules and basic philosophy of E-Sign.

Even before E-Sign, however, the National Conference of Commissioners on Uniform State Laws—one of two institutions principally responsible for the UCC—adopted two different proposed uniform acts to facilitate electronic commerce. One is the

Uniform Electronic Transactions Act (UETA), which is similar in scope and substance to the UNCITRAL Model Law. UETA applies to all types of electronic messages and contracts, and seeks to validate and facilitate their use at a very basic level. Like E-Sign, UETA provides that "a record or signature may not be denied legal effect or enforceability solely because it is in electronic form" and that "a contract may not be denied legal effect or enforceability solely because an electronic record was used in its formation." Because of E-Sign's express exception for such state statutes, UETA has had a much more significant practical impact in promoting and facilitating electronic commerce.

The second legal product of the Uniform Commissioners on the subject of E-Commerce is the Uniform Computer Information Transactions Act (UCITA). UCITA applies to transactions involving the transfer of computer information, but primarily governs software licensing transactions (such as downloads over the internet). It then broadly addresses, in quite detailed provisions, nearly every significant aspect of transactions effected solely through computers. Its format is similar to UCC Article 2 on sales of goods, and at one time was intended to be UCC Article 2B, until it was rejected by the American Law Institute as not sufficiently balanced. The Uniform Commissioners then proposed UCITA as their own, separate uniform act. But it has not received broad acceptance, with only two state adoptions (Maryland and Virginia). Although it too embraces the core principle of the validity of electronic contracts and communications, UCITA has much more detailed (and controversial) provisions on a variety of issues and departs in important particulars from the concepts in both the UNCITRAL Model Law and UETA.

In short, the many efforts to create a foundation for electronic commercial transactions have many similarities in their goals and basic principles. But many differences remain. Moreover, many countries have not at all adapted their local legal rules to address the subject, and thus have left the matter to traditional principles of uncertain relevance. These differences in state, national, and international legal rules on E-Commerce are likely to continue to cause difficulties for the participants in international transactions, especially where the location of the parties is unknown even to them. And the challenges and potential conflicts are likely to grow as more non-U.S. parties participate in E-Commerce, and a greater proportion of such transactions are across national boundaries.

CHAPTER 3

FINANCING THE INTERNATIONAL SALE OF GOODS

THE INTERNATIONAL DOCUMENTARY SALE AND DOCUMENTARY LETTER OF CREDIT

THE PROBLEM

Unlike most domestic sales transactions, in a sale of goods across national borders the exporter-seller and importer-buyer may not have previously dealt with one another; or each may know nothing about the other; or each may be unfamiliar with the other's national legal system. The seller does not know: (1) whether buyer is creditworthy or trustworthy; (2) whether information received on these subjects from buyer's associates is reliable; (3) whether exchange controls will hinder payment by the buyer (especially if buyer's country has a "soft" currency, but payment is in a "hard currency"); (4) how great the exchange risk is if payment in buyer's currency is permitted; and (5) what delays may be involved in receiving unencumbered funds from buyer.

On the other hand, buyer does not know: (1) whether seller can be trusted to ship the goods if buyer prepays; (2) whether the goods shipped will be of the quantity and quality contracted for; (3) whether the goods will be shipped by a reliable carrier and properly insured; (4) whether the goods might be damaged in transit; (5) whether the seller will furnish to buyer sufficient ownership documentation covering the goods to allow buyer to claim them from customs officials; (6) whether seller will provide the documentation necessary to satisfy export control regulations and import customs and valuation regulations (*e.g.*, country of origin certificates, health and other inspection certificates, etc.); and (7) what delays may be involved in receiving unencumbered possession and use of the goods at buyer's location.

Where the parties are strangers, these risks are significant, possibly overwhelming. Because they operate at a distance from each other, seller and buyer cannot concurrently exchange the goods for the payment funds *without the help of third parties*. An international letter of credit can work to bridge this and similar problems. In specific, the documentary sale involving the use of a letter of credit illustrates how the potentially large risks reviewed above can be distributed to third parties who have special knowledge, can properly evaluate each risk assumed, and thereby can reduce the transaction risks to insignificance.

THE DOCUMENTARY SALE TRANSACTION WITH A CONFIRMED LETTER OF CREDIT

The third party intermediaries enlisted are banks (at least one in buyer's home country and usually a second one in seller's home country) and at least one carrier. Thus, the parties involved are: (1) a buyer;

(2) the bank at which buyer does its banking (hereafter, Buyer's Bank); (3) a seller; (4) a bank with an office in seller's country (hereafter "Seller's Bank"); and (5) at least one carrier. These parties are able to take a large risk not subject to firm evaluation by any one of them, and divide it into several small, calculable risks, and then allocate these smaller risks to the parties best able to evaluate them. Thus, the documentary sale with a letter of credit is an example that not all risk allocation is a "zero sum game," but may in fact create a "win-win" situation.

These parties will be related by a series of contracts—but not all of the parties to the transaction will be parties to each contract. The contracts include (a) the sale of goods contract between buyer and seller; (b) the bill of lading, a contract with and a receipt issued by the carrier; and (c) the letter of credit, which represents a promise by Buyer's Bank (and, if confirmed, also by Seller's Bank) to pay seller under certain conditions concerning proof that seller has shipped the goods.

(a) The contract underlying the entire series of transactions is the contract for the sale of goods from seller to buyer. Buyer and seller are parties to this contract, but not the banks or the carrier. Seller is responsible to deliver the contracted quantity and quality of goods, and buyer is responsible for taking the goods and paying the stated price. As described in Chapter 2, the law governing international sale of goods contracts in modern commerce is commonly, and increasingly so, the United Nations Convention on Contracts for the International Sale of Goods (CISG). (For a detailed examination of the scope and content of this international treaty, *see* Chapter 2.)

(b) In documentary sales, buyers and sellers are usually distant from each other, and the goods must be moved. Thus, an international carrier of the goods is usually employed, and either seller or buyer will make a contract with the carrier to transport the goods. (For our illustration, seller will make that contract.) Seller (or, in the language of a contract of carriage, "shipper") makes a contract with carrier that obligates carrier to transport the goods to buyer's location or some other distant place.

This second contract in our transaction will be expressed in a "bill of lading," which is "issued" by carrier. Under the terms of the bill of lading contract, in return for payment of the freight charge, carrier promises to deliver the goods to either (1) the named "consignee" in a "straight" (or nonnegotiable) bill of lading, or (2) the person in possession ("holder") of an "order" (or negotiable) bill of lading. The order (negotiable) bill of lading should be used in the documentary sale (especially one involving a letter of credit), so that the buyer is able to obtain delivery of the goods *only if* buyer has physical possession of the bill of lading properly indorsed over to it. Such a bill of lading controls access to and delivery of the goods, so that the bill of lading is also a "document of title." Chapter 2 above has a more detailed examination of the role of bills of lading in such a documentary transaction.

(c) Before it delivers the goods to the carrier, seller ("shipper") wants assurance that payment will be forthcoming. A simple promise from a foreign buyer may not be sufficient. Even a promise from a bank in buyer's country may not be sufficient, because seller likely does not know foreign banks or even about them. Instead, seller wants a firm, legally binding promise from a bank known to it, preferably one in seller's jurisdiction and locality.

What seller wants is the third contract in our transaction—a confirmed, irrevocable letter of credit. A letter of credit is a specialized contract involving a promise by a bank (Buyer's Bank) that it will pay to seller the amount of the contract price subject to defined conditions. In the distinctive language of letter of credit law, the promise will be that the bank "will honor drafts drawn on the bank by seller." But again, seller also will want a payment promise from a bank in its own country and region. Thus, if required by the sales contract, buyer must arrange for a "confirmed" letter of credit. This occurs through Buyer's Bank requesting a bank in seller's location to obligate itself, through a separate "confirmation" letter sent to seller, to honor the drafts presented by seller. Often, seller will learn of both actions in the one confirmation letter from its local bank.

The banks' promises will be conditioned upon seller presenting documentary evidence that the goods have been shipped via a carrier to arrive at buyer's location, along with any other documents required by the contract for the sale of goods. What would furnish such evidence? The key document is the bill of lading issued by carrier—the second contract in our transaction—, which furnishes the evidence that seller has shipped the goods as described therein.

Further, a negotiable (or "order") bill of lading will be required, one that thus also controls the right to obtain the goods from carrier. Thus, and as described in more detail in Chapter 2 above, a negotiable bill of lading delivered by seller to Seller's Bank will serve three distinct functions: (1) it will provide evidence that the goods have been delivered to carrier; (2) it will show that the goods are destined for buyer and not some third party; and (3) it will assure the banks that they can control carrier's delivery of the goods to buyer by simply retaining possession of the order bill of lading. In other words, when a bank pays seller under the letter of credit, it receives from seller a "document of title" issued by carrier which gives the bank control over carrier's delivery of the goods. Buyer cannot obtain possession of the goods from carrier without physical possession of the bill of lading, so after the banks have paid seller for that piece of paper, they can obtain payment (or a binding commitment of payment) before buyer receives the ability to obtain the goods from carrier.

How does the international documentary sales transaction involving a letter of credit work? Consult the following diagram:

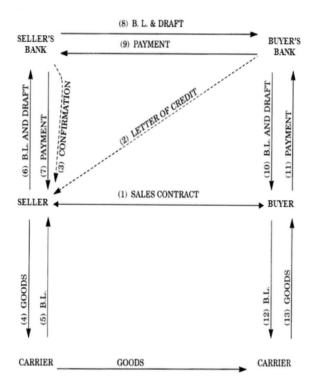

The process begins with the sale of goods contract. When buyer and seller are forming their contract, seller will insist that it include both a "price term" and a "payment term." For maximum protection, seller will seek payment by "Confirmed, Irrevocable Letter of Credit," and should also specify what documents are required with great detail. The reason for specifying this payment term in the sales contract is that generally the buyer will have a right to inspect the goods before payment. This is not true with a "payment against documents" transaction, but even here buyer will have a right to inspect the documents before payment, and this inspection will come after the seller has shipped the goods through the carrier. To avoid the risk of nonpayment by the buyer, seller must bargain for and include in the sales contract a term that requires payment by a confirmed and irrevocable letter of credit. Such an agreement will not normally be implied.

What documents will the banks require as a condition to payment under the letter of credit? In addition to the draft (see below), they usually include the following:

(1) A negotiable bill of lading showing carrier's receipt of the described goods and an obligation to deliver them only to the holder of the document;

(2) a commercial invoice, which is a form of an itemized bill that sets out the terms of the sale, grade and quantity of goods, amount owed, etc.;

(3) a packing list, which is a separate confirmation from seller's shipping department of

any goods packed in sealed cartons or containers;

(4) a policy of marine insurance (if goods are to be transported by sea);

(5) a certificate of inspection, which is issued by a commercial inspecting firm and independently confirms that the required number and type of goods are being shipped (although buyer must separately contract for such an inspection);

(6) an export license and/or health inspection certificate showing that the goods are cleared for export; and

(7) a certificate of origin, which documents the source of the goods sold and—depending on the trade agreements between the exporting and importing country—may be used by customs personnel in the importing country to determine tariff assessments.

If buyer agrees to a letter of credit payment term, buyer (the "account party," or, in the language of letter of credit law, the "applicant") will contract with Buyer's Bank ("issuer" or "issuing bank") to issue a letter of credit ("credit") in favor of seller ("beneficiary"). The letter of credit is a direct promise by the issuing bank that it will pay the contract price to the seller/beneficiary, if seller presents to it the documents specified in the letter of credit. Buyer's Bank will be aware of buyer's creditworthiness, and will make appropriate arrangements to receive the funds from buyer (through either immediate payment or future repayment of a loan secured by appropriate collateral). These arrangements will be made before the letter of credit is issued, for with an irrevocable letter of credit Buyer's Bank is independently bound after issuance to pay according to the credit's terms.

If the sales contract requires a "confirmed" letter of credit, buyer must also arrange for a payment promise by a local bank in seller's area ("confirmer" or "confirming bank"). Buyer's Bank will forward its letter of credit to seller through another bank, Seller's Bank, and request that Seller's Bank add its confirmation. By merely indicating "We confirm this credit," Seller's Bank makes a direct and independent promise to seller that it will pay the contract price to seller, if seller presents the required documents. (Why do the banks provide these services? For an appropriate fee, of course. But these fees are quite small, typically 1-2% of the amount of the letter of credit.) If the sales contract does not require a confirmation of the credit, Buyer's Bank can forward the letter of credit through an "advising bank" (also known as a "notifying bank") located near seller. Such a bank will not be obligated to seller, but will merely inform seller of the issuance and may then later take the presented documents from seller and forward them to Buyer's Bank for collection purposes only. (Another role a bank may play is as a "nominated bank," one the issuer authorizes (typically later) to honor a presentation, but which does not add its independent confirmation in advance.)

Once the letter of credit is issued and confirmed, seller will pack the goods, prepare a commercial invoice, and procure an insurance certificate (another form of contract) covering the goods during transit. If an inspection certificate is required by the sales contract, the goods will be made available to the designated inspection firm (which is engaged according another contract), and it will issue a certificate stating that the goods conform to the description in the sales contract. If so required by the terms of the sales contract, seller also will prepare the necessary documents for the customs officials in its home country (e.g., an export license) and in buyer's country (e.g., a certificate of origin). Seller then sends the goods to the carrier, which issues the negotiable bill of lading as a combination receipt and contract. As described above, in a letter of credit transaction this bill of lading must be negotiable, and will commonly require carrier to deliver the goods only "to seller or order"—i.e., only to seller or a person seller designates by an appropriate indorsement, provided in either case that the person is also in possession.

Seller now has the complete set of the required documents, and takes these documents to Seller's Bank, which (as a confirming bank) is obligated to pay seller the contract price upon presentation of the documents. Because the letter of credit is merely a promise to pay, seller also must use a legal vehicle to "draw on" the credit. To do this, seller prepares a "draft" and then presents it to the bank along with the other required documents. The draft (sometimes known by an earlier term, "bill of exchange") resembles a check written by seller and typically drawn on Buyer's Bank (the original issuer) for the amount of the contract price. A draft can be payable on demand ("at sight"), or at a defined later time (e.g., "30 days after sight"). If a "demand draft" is used, the bank—in our case, Seller's Bank (the confirming bank)—will pay the amount immediately, usually by crediting seller's bank account; if a time draft is used, the bank will "accept" it (i.e., stamp its name on it) and thereby bindingly obligate itself to pay at the defined later time. In the latter case, seller can still raise funds immediately by selling the paper on the strength of the bank's credit.

Seller's Bank never sees the goods, only the documents. Because of this, it inspects the documents rigorously to determine that they comply exactly with the requirements of the letter of credit—for the documents are its only protection. Substantial performance by seller is not acceptable. Thus, where a credit called for "100% acrylic yarn" and the invoice stated "imported acrylic yarn," the presentation did not satisfy the terms of the credit, even though the packing list stated "100% acrylic yarn."

In return for the bank's payment, seller will indorse both the draft and the negotiable bill of lading over to Seller's Bank and transfer the other required documents to it. Seller's Bank, in turn, will indorse the draft and the bill of lading and forward both with their accompanying documents to Buyer's Bank. As the issuer of the letter of credit, Buyer's Bank also is obligated to "honor" the draft and thus to reimburse Seller's Bank if the draft and the other documents from seller conform to the requirements in the letter of credit. Buyer's Bank then contacts buyer, presents the documents to buyer, and requests reimbursement. Buyer, like the banks, must pay "against the documents" and not the goods themselves, which is why it is necessary to specify the terms of the documents in the original contract for the sale of goods, and then repeat those specifications precisely in the letter of credit. Once buyer has paid, or arranged to pay, Buyer's Bank, buyer will obtain possession of the bill of lading and only then will it have the power to obtain the goods from carrier.

Note the limited risks to each party. If seller ships conforming goods, it has independent promises of payment from both buyer and two banks. The banks' promises are enforceable despite assertions of non-conformity of the goods, so long as the documents conform. Thus, as a practical matter, seller is exposed only if Seller's Bank fails, Buyer's Bank fails, and buyer is either unable or unwilling to pay, a constellation of events so unlikely that seller should have no noteworthy concern. If Seller's Bank unjustifiably refuses to perform its obligation, seller has a cause of action in a local court—which will use a familiar language and a familiar legal system—against a "deep pocket defendant."

Even though Seller's Bank is obligated to pay seller against the documents, its position also is generally secure. It is entitled to reimbursement from Buyer's Bank and from buyer, and practically is at risk only if both Buyer's Bank and buyer fail or refuse to perform their obligations—risks which Seller's Bank should be able to evaluate accurately. Finally, Buyer's Bank is at risk only if buyer fails or refuses to perform; but these again are risks which Buyer's Bank had an opportunity to evaluate before issuing the letter of credit, and for which it could adjust its price (the fee and the interest rate on any loan). Moreover, each bank has the security of the negotiable bill of lading, which will enable it to control the goods until it obtains reimbursement.

On the other hand, for its payment of the price to Buyer's Bank, buyer has a document from carrier entitling it to delivery of the goods, an insurance certificate protecting buyer against casualty loss in transit, and perhaps an inspection certificate warranting that the goods conform to the sales contract. In other words, buyer should receive what it bargained for—delivery of conforming goods or insurance proceeds sufficient to cover any loss.

THE GOVERNING LEGAL RULES

The law governing letters of credit developed before World War I principally in England, and thereafter in courts in the United States. As the U.S. national economy matured in the 20th century, the need for uniform national rules also led the drafters of the Uniform Commercial Code to include a separate article (Article 5) on letter of credit law. Nonetheless, as is true with the rest of the UCC, most of Article 5 is not mandatory law; as a result, nearly all of Article 5's provisions defer to the agreement of the parties as expressed in the terms of their contract.

For international letters of credit, the practically more significant rules are found in the Uniform Customs and Practices for Documentary Credits (UCP), which (like the Incoterms) are a set of contract terms prepared and published by the International Chamber of Commerce (ICC). The overwhelming majority of international letters of credit incorporate the UCP by express reference. The UCP constitutes a rather detailed set of rules that define the rights and obligations of the banks involved in letters of credit; but its legal status is as a statement of contract terms and banking trade usage, and not as generally applicable positive law. The unusual aspect of the UCP is that it takes effect by a unilateral declaration of a bank in the letter of credit, and not by formal agreement with the beneficiary. Nonetheless, the UCC expressly validates such an incorporation of the UCP in a letter of credit. *See* UCC § 5-116(c).

Both UCC Article 5 and the UCP exist in revised versions. The Uniform Commissioners and the American Law Institute revised Article 5 in 1995, and all 51 U.S. jurisdictions have since enacted this revised version into law. The most recent version of the UCP is the 2007 Revision (ICC Publ. No. 600). The rules set forth in the two generally are the same in substance, but some differences exist. Moreover, the UCP does not purport to define a comprehensive regulatory system for letters of credit, and UCC § 5-116(c) makes clear that, even if incorporated in a specific letter of credit, the UCP controls only to the extent of a conflict with the UCC.

The most prominent example of this is that the UCP has no rules that address fraud. As a result, UCC Article 5, and not the UCP, will provide the legal rules to resolve issues related to allegations of fraud in letter of credit transactions. Based on this relationship between the UCP and the UCC, this chapter will describe the UCP rules for all non-fraud issues, and the UCC provisions for issues of fraud.

The UCP describes four different roles of banks in letter of credit transactions: (1) issuing bank; (2) advising bank; (3) confirming bank; and (4) nominated bank. An issuing bank means the bank that issues a letter of credit at the request of an applicant, and thus promises to honor a presentation, if the presented documents conform to the terms of the letter of credit. An advising bank advises the beneficiary (usually the seller) of the documentary credit, but makes no promise to pay against documents. It is obligated to take "reasonable care" to check the authenticity of the credit before advising, but is not otherwise obligated. A confirming bank is one that confirms the letter of credit at the issuing bank's authorization or request, and thus adds its own promise to honor a conforming presentation. "Nominated bank" is a broader term under the UCP that includes any bank "with which the credit is available," which means a bank (typically in seller's locality) that is designated or authorized by the issuing bank to pay or negotiate the draft presented by the beneficiary. It may, or may not, also be a confirming bank.

The letter of credit rules in the UCP (and also in UCC Article 5) are founded on two fundamental principles. One is that the banks' obligations under the letter of credit are independent of the buyer's and seller's obligations under the contract for the sale of goods. In the words of UCP Article 4, banks "are in no way concerned with or bound by such contract," even if the letter of credit refers to it. The second, closely related, is that banks deal only with documents, and not with performance of the underlying sales contract (or any other contract). UCP Article 5. Thus, the promises of an issuing bank or a confirming bank are not subject to claims or defenses by the applicant (buyer) that the beneficiary (seller) has not performed its obligations under the sales contract. UCP Article 4(a). (However, the applicant may seek an injunction from a court against payment by the bank if it can prove fraud by the beneficiary, as is discussed in more detail below.)

When the beneficiary (seller) presents the required documents, an issuing or a confirming bank has two duties. One is to examine the documents to determine whether they conform to the terms of the letter of credit. The second is to respond if it finds any discrepancies. As to the first, because the banks pay the beneficiary against the documents, and never see the goods, they insist on "strict compliance" with all documentary conditions. Under UCP Article 14(a), banks "must examine a presentation to determine, on the basis of the documents alone, whether or not the documents appear, on their face, to constitute a complying presentation." Compliance is not explicitly defined in the UCP. But Article 14(d) provides that, as measured against "the context of the credit" and "international standard banking practice," data in a presented document "need not be identical to, but must not conflict with," the terms of the credit. This language has generated substantial judicial and scholarly debate, but the prevailing view is that the "strict compliance" standard remains. To provide at least some guidance, the ICC publishes and periodically updates an "International Standard Banking Practice" (ISBP) manual. *See* ICC Publ. No. 681E (2007).

The primary document for describing the goods in a documentary sale transaction is the commercial invoice. The description in the commercial invoice must be specific and must "correspond with that appearing in the credit." UCP Article 18(c). Descriptions of the goods in all other documents "may be in general terms not conflicting with" the description in the credit. UCP Article 14(e). English courts have gained renown in applying the "strict compliance" standard, including in a famous case holding that the phrase "machine shelled groundnut kernels" did not comply with the required term "Coromandel groundnuts," even though it was "universally acknowledged" in the trade that both labels applied to the goods. *J.H. Rayner & Co. Ltd. v. Hambro's Bank, Ltd*, 1 K.B. 36 (1943). But this holding also reflects a further important principle—that banks are not responsible for, and are not expected to investigate, the customs or usages that may apply in a particular trade (other than in the banking trade).

The more difficult litigated issues concerning the strict conformity of documents seem to arise in transportation terms. Express conditions in the credit that loading, presentment, or other acts must be performed by a certain time will be strictly enforced. A credit calling for "full set clean on board ocean bills of lading," for example, is not satisfied by a tender of "a trucker's bill of lading," even though evidence was presented that such bills were in customary Mexican form and that Mexican truckers customarily do not specify on the bill of lading that the goods are "on board." *Marine Midland Grace Trust Co. of N.Y. v. Banco Del Pais, S.A.*, 261 F. Supp. 884 (S.D.N.Y. 1966).

Unfortunately, discrepancies in tendered documents are an everyday occurrence. Indeed, some estimates are that as many as two-thirds of all presentations contain at least one discrepancy, and that one-half of presentations are rejected on this basis. That rate of error should not be surprising if one understands that the presentation, as in some reported cases, may consist of many hundreds of pages of documents. However, it is clear that the "strict compliance" standard itself may cause difficult problems in application.

In any event, a clear typographical error seems to represent the edge of the strict compliance standard. The 2007 version of the ICC's ISBP manual states as an example of such an obvious "misspelling or typographical error" a description of the goods as "fountan pen" instead of "fountain pen." ICC Publ. 681E, at 22 (2007). This does not apply, however, where a misspelling is not an obvious linguistic error. Thus, one court held that an issuer was justified in dishonoring where the letter of credit mistakenly identified the beneficiary as Sung Jin Electronics, while the documents were correctly addressed to Sung Jun Electronics. *Hanil Bank v. Pt. Bank Negara Indonesia*, 148 F.3d 127 (2nd Cir. 1998). More generally, modern opinions as well as revised Article 5 reject a nascent line in some Amer-

ican cases that seemed to permit payment upon
substantial performance by the beneficiary. *See* § 5–
108 and Comment 1. What is left, as one court has
sensibly explained, is "a common sense, case-by-case
approach [that] permit[s] minor deviations of a typographical nature because such a letter-for-letter
correspondence between the letter of credit and the
presentation documents is virtually impossible."
Voest-Alpine Trading USA Corp. v. Bank of China,
167 F. Supp. 2d 940 (S.D. Tex. 2000).

If the bank discovers discrepancies, its second obligation is to notify the beneficiary of the "dishonor,"
state the grounds, and return the documents (or
follow any previous instructions). Article 16(c). The
bank may reject the documents without consulting
its customer, the applicant (buyer). However, in
many situations, the discrepancies may be trivial,
and the customer may want the payment made, and
the goods delivered, despite the discrepancy. Thus,
UCP Article 16(b) allows, but does not require, the
bank to consult the applicant for a waiver of the discrepancies it has discovered. Evidence suggests
that, if consulted, applicants in fact will waive discrepancies discovered by the bank about 90% of the
time. Thus, the system seems to work because the
non-bank parties (buyer and seller) want the transaction to be completed despite the technical difficulties imposed by letter of credit law.

A bank must not only be thorough in its examination, but also quick in its response. UCP Article

14(b) states that a bank has a "maximum of five banking days following the day of presentation to determine if a presentation is complying." (Under the UCC, the time limit is "a reasonable time ... but not beyond the end of the seventh business day," but this should be an example of where the UCC defers to the UCP.) If the bank discovers no discrepancies, there is no particular difficulty in meeting this deadline, and "the maximum" may be shorter than five days. In a famous case from the past, an issuing bank examined 967 pages of documents twice in two and a half days. *Banco Espanol de Credito v. State Street Bank and Trust Co.*, 385 F.2d 230 (1st Cir. 1967).

If the bank discovers discrepancies, however, it may be subject to time pressures. The "five banking days" deadline includes not only time to examine the documents presented, but also time to consult the bank's customer (buyer) about waiving the discrepancies *and* notifying the party from whom the documents were received. The latter two requirements, in particular, can create timing difficulties for the bank.

UCP Article 16(c) requires any bank that rejects a presentation of documents to state, "in a single notice" to the presenter, "each discrepancy in respect of which [it] refuses to honour." Under UCP Article 16(f), failure to state all the discrepancies, or to meet the time deadline, "precludes" the bank from claiming non-compliance due to any unstated discrepancy, without the necessity of proving waiver or estoppel. Thus, banks that reject documents have only one chance to identify all the discrepancies on which they can ever rely. The rationale for this rule is to inform the beneficiary (seller) of all the discrepancies at once, so that it can determine whether they are curable and whether such cure is cost-effective. But the rule can also lead the issuing bank to delay notification for additional re-examinations to ensure that all defects are discovered (as long as it does not breach the five day deadline).

As noted, under the UCP banks deal only in documents. UCP Article 5. The parties may provide conditions upon the credit, as long as compliance with those conditions can be satisfied through documentary evidence. Thus, letters of credit must state precisely the documents, and the terms of the documents, against which payment is to be made. It is the responsibility of the issuing bank and its customer, the applicant (buyer), to ensure that, for each condition, the letter of credit stipulates a document to indicate compliance. Otherwise, "banks will deem such condition as not stated and will disregard it." UCP Article 14(h).

Although, for the description of the goods, the commercial invoice is the document that must "strictly conform" to the letter of credit, the most important of the documents required by a letter of credit is the transportation document. Under prior versions of the UCP, this had referred to ocean bills of lading, evidencing an assumption that the goods would be carried by sea. New developments in the transport industry, however, have created new technological applications. Thus, the recent revisions of the UCP provide separate articles for negotiable ocean bills of lading; non-negotiable sea waybills; charter party bills of lading; multi-modal transport documents; air transport documents; road, rail or inland waterway transport documents; and courier receipts, post receipts, and certificates of posting.

Under UCP Article 20, an ocean bill of lading must name the port of loading, the port of discharge, and the carrier, and also specify the parties that will be acceptable signatories. Banks have no duty, however, to check the signature or initials accompanying an "on board" notation, absent a special arrangement with the bank. The bill of lading may indicate an "intended vessel." In such cases, any "on board" notation must specify the vessel on which the goods have been loaded. The medieval custom of issuing "a set" of bills of lading, and hoping one of them would arrive and be honored, is now disapproved; and the UCP seeks to have only a single original bill of lading issued as the norm.

A charter party bill of lading does not identify the carrier, and is now a permissible transport document for use with a letter of credit. UCP Article 22(b) relieves the banks from any duty to examine the terms of the charter party, under the assumption that only sophisticated parties with considerable knowledge of the trade will use them.

In multimodal transportation arrangements, the bill of lading is likely to be issued by a freight forwarder and not by a carrier. Thus, it does not name a carrier and it does not contain a receipt by the bailee (the carrier), which is the norm for documents of title. However, if the letter of credit authorizes the use of a signature of a named agent of the carrier, such a bill of lading may be used under UCP Article 19, if the freight forwarder issues it as a multimodal transport document as an agent for a carrier. Otherwise, such "house bills" of freight forwarders are not acceptable transport documents for letters of credit under the UCP.

The liability of the confirming bank is separate from and independent of, but parallels, the liability of the issuing bank. To establish the confirming bank's liability, UCP Article 8 permits the beneficiary to present the documents to the confirming bank or to any other nominated bank. The letter of credit must also specify, however, both a place for presentation of the documents and an expiration date for the presentation. A careful confirming bank should insist that its office is designated as the place for presentation of the documents. Once the presentation is made, the confirming bank has all of the examination, time, and notice obligations that apply to an issuing bank as described above. In turn, when a confirming bank accepts the documents from the beneficiary and presents them to the issuing bank, the latter has all of these examination, time, and notice obligations as against the confirming bank (which is now the "presenter").

ELECTRONIC LETTERS OF CREDIT

Electronic communications have taken over some aspects of letter of credit practice, but not others. They dominate the issuance process in bank-to-bank communications, and are sometimes used by applicants to initiate the issuance process. However, banks and other interested parties have not yet been able to create an entirely paperless transaction pattern for many reasons. First, the beneficiary still wants a piece of paper committing the banks to pay upon specified conditions. Second, even with an electronic letter of credit, most industries have not accepted electronic forms in the place of the significant documents typically required by a letter of credit. The principal example is an electronic negotiable bill of lading, which, for the reasons discussed in the preceding chapter, has not yet found broad or stable acceptance. Thus, in the presentation phase for letters of credit, physical documents will be used, while funds settlement (payment) likely will be electronic.

Over three quarters of letter of credit communication between banks, including the issuance, advice, and confirmation of letters of credit, is paperless; and nearly all informal communication is electronic. While bank-to-bank communication is electronic, bank-to-beneficiary (seller) communication is still paper-based. Letter of credit issuers can now communicate directly with beneficiaries' computers, however, and use of this practice both is widespread and should be expected to increase. The UCP rules also now expressly contemplate "teletransmission," which will continue to facilitate the use of electronic practices.

Most bank-to-bank communications concerning letters of credit are routed through the dedicated lines of SWIFT (the Society for Worldwide Interbank Financial Telecommunication). SWIFT is a Belgian not-for-profit organization owned by banks as a cooperative venture for the transmission of financial transaction messages. It requires all such messages to be structured in a uniform format, and uses standardized elements for allocating message space and for message text. Thus, messages can be communicated on a computer-to-computer basis without being re-keyed.

A bank issuing a letter of credit communicates that message to the nearest SWIFT access point. The message is then routed on a dedicated data transmission line to a regional processor, where it is validated (see below). From the regional processor, it is routed over a dedicated line to one of three main data centers, one each in the United States, the Netherlands, and Switzerland. From there it is routed through a regional processor to a SWIFT access point and to the receiving bank. The message switching, and sometimes necessary storage, can be performed by computers, if the standardization of the format of the financial messages is sufficiently developed and comprehensive. SWIFT seems to have achieved this level of uniformity.

The bank that receives a SWIFT electronic letter of credit message need not send a reply stating that it accepts the request to advise or confirm or the authorization to negotiate or pay the letter of credit. It needs only to perform by advising, confirming, negotiating, or paying, and it is entitled to reimbursement by the issuing bank. However, the SWIFT messages only transmit the letter of credit and their authorizations and requests. SWIFT messages do not effect the settlements of letters of credit or other transfers of funds between issuing banks and other banks. SWIFT is not a clearing house for bank settlements like, for example, CHIPS (Clearing House for Interbank Payment Systems). Under the SWIFT letter of credit system, participating banks must use other arrangements (such as CHIPS) to settle their accounts and accomplish a transfer of funds.

SWIFT relies upon both encryption of messages and authentication to provide security to its users. The authentication of SWIFT messages is accomplished by the use of algorithms, which are mathematical formulas that calculate the contents of a message from header to trailer. If a SWIFT message requires authentication, and all letter of credit messages do, the issuing bank computes the contents and compiles a result based on the number of characters and data fields. At the regional processor, SWIFT checks the authentication trailer for the number of characters in the authentication. However, a more rigorous authentication will be performed by the receiving bank, using an algorithm contained in an authentication key provided by the issuing bank. The computations involving these authentication procedures will indicate a mismatch if the message is fraudulent or has been altered. There are also "log in" procedures, application-selection procedures, message numbering and error checking capabilities, and control of access to the system hardware. SWIFT also retains records of each transaction. In all, the security devices are numerous and complex.

Most SWIFT messages are delivered within minutes of their issuance by a bank, although delays of up to two hours are possible. Thus, delays in the system are slight, but present. When is the issuer of an electronic letter of credit bound? The UCP provides no set rules on the issue, but UCC Article 5 establishes that such messages are effective and enforceable upon transmission by the issuer, not delivery to the receiving bank. UCC § 5-106(a) and SWIFT rules require no reply. This UCC rule conforms to the understanding of bankers involved in the trade.

Under SWIFT rules, Belgian law governs all relations between SWIFT and its users. SWIFT is liable for negligence or fraud of its own employees and agents and for those parts of the communication system that it controls, such as regional processors, main switches and the dedicated lines that connect them. But SWIFT disclaims liability for those parts of the communication system that it does not control, such as the bank computers that issue and receive messages and the dedicated lines from bank to a regional processor. Even where SWIFT is liable, its liability is limited to "direct" damages (loss of interest); the contracts with SWIFT thus expressly disclaim liability for indirect, special or consequential damages. Whether Belgian law also governs relations between SWIFT and the non-bank parties to the transaction (applicants and beneficiaries), or between banks and their customers, does not seem yet to have been tested in court.

It is now possible for an applicant (buyer, in the documentary credit transaction) to draft a proposed electronic letter of credit. The electronic proposed credit can then be transmitted to the issuing bank for issuance through the SWIFT system. This procedure is usually used where the applicant seeks multiple credits and there is a master agreement between the issuing bank and the applicant. The issuing bank will first check to see whether the proposed credit is authorized and contains the required security codes. Then it will determine whether it is within the previously authorized credit limits and is stated in the standardized elements and uniform format for electronic messages. Both SWIFT and UCP requirements must be analyzed, and changes in the proposed message may be necessary. Thus, the procedures are not yet fully automatic.

On the other end of the electronic communications, the beneficiary (seller, in the documentary sale), which must be induced to part with value (*i.e.*, ship the goods) on the basis of the bank's promises, wants a "hard copy," a written letter of credit in the traditional form. The receiving bank (such as a confirming bank) therefore will convert the SWIFT electronic message into such a written, paper credit. However, the SWIFT message has been designed for bank-to-bank use, and not necessarily for use by beneficiaries, which creates some problems. First, it does not bear a signature in the traditional sense, even though it has been thoroughly authenticated within the computer-based transmission mechanisms. Thus, the beneficiary is entitled to doubt whether the sending bank is bound to the beneficiary to perform by the written credit derived from the SWIFT electronic message.

The issue is usually framed as: "Is the SWIFT message to be considered to be *the* operative credit instrument as far as the beneficiary is concerned?" The issue is of importance to beneficiaries not only in the original issuance of the credit, but also in the myriad of amendments to the credit that may follow. Under SWIFT rules, SWIFT users treat the electronic message as a binding obligation, and treat the authentication as the functional equivalent of a signature. However, the beneficiary is not a SWIFT user, and banking practice has been that a beneficiary can rely on an electronic message only after it has been issued in a paper-based format, properly signed or otherwise authenticated. UCC § 5–104 states that a letter of credit "may be issued in any form," including an electronic format, but that provision does not necessarily answer the question as to whether the unsigned, paper-based transcription of a SWIFT message, generated by the recipient of that message, is the operative credit instrument and binds the issuing bank.

Under the UCP, whether an electronic message is the operative credit instrument or not depends upon the terminology in the message itself. UCP Article 11(a) states a basic rule that an authenticated electronic message "will be deemed to be the operative credit," and that "any subsequent mail confirmation shall be disregarded." It also states, however, that if the electronic message states "full details to follow (or words of similar effect)," then the electronic message will not be the operative credit, and the issuing bank "must then issue the operative credit without delay" in terms not inconsistent with the electronic message.

However, there is some doubt as to whether SWIFT-generated transcriptions are subject to the UCP. SWIFT internal rules provide that credits issued through its system are subject to the UCP, but the transcription into a hard copy may bear no reference to the UCP. UCP Article 1 states that the UCP provisions govern "where the text of the credit expressly indicates that it is subject to these rules."

Chapter 2 discussed the attempts to create an electronic bill of lading. If successful, an electronic bill of lading could help facilitate the electronic letter of credit transaction. However, to date, while an electronic bill of lading has been used successfully to replace the straight (non-negotiable) bill of lading, its use to replace the negotiable bill of lading has been met with skepticism. Although SEADOCS showed that an electronic approach was technically feasible, it was not a commercial success. American bankers have been skeptical of their rights to any actual goods under electronic bills of lading issued under CMI (Comité Maritime International) Rules. The BOLERO program of the Commission of the European Communities likewise has not received broad acceptance. Nonetheless, as described in Chapter 2, the new provisions of UCC Articles 1 and 7 on "electronic documents of title" as well as the new "Rotterdam Rules" of 2009 may provide a stable legal foundation for a broader acceptance of electronic bills of lading in the future. Moreover, in early 2012 the ICC and SWIFT agreed to collaborate toward creation of a new "Bank Payment Obligation (BPO)" system designed to create a stable foundation for electronic letters of credit. This collaboration between the two leading international institution in the field of letter of credit law is likely to bring about important advancements in electronic letters of credit.

STANDBY LETTERS OF CREDIT

Foreign governments, or other developers with sufficient bargaining power, often require a financial assurance (by way of a financial guarantee) that foreign firms that undertake to supply goods or to perform a construction project will do so competently and in accordance with the terms of the governing contract. Performance bonds can serve as an adequate assurance, but it is generally understood that United States banks are barred from issuing insurance contracts, including performance bonds. They have, however, developed an alternative—the "standby" letter of credit. This alternative form of a letter of credit transaction involves a credit that is issued by the seller's (or other performer's) bank and runs in favor of the buyer—truly a backwards arrangement as compared to the commercial letters of credit described above. A standby credit is payable against a writing that certifies that the seller has not performed its promises. Such a credit is not for the purpose of ensuring payment to the seller for goods shipped. Instead, it is used as a form of guarantee or insurance for the seller's performance. Thus, although not allowed to issue guarantees, performance bonds, or insurance policies, banks can achieve essentially the same end through standby letters of credit. The result is the creation of a new commercial device, which is now commercially accepted for its own value, and which has supplanted the performance bond in many fields of endeavor.

Consult the following diagram to illustrate the stages of the issuance and resort to a standby letter of credit:

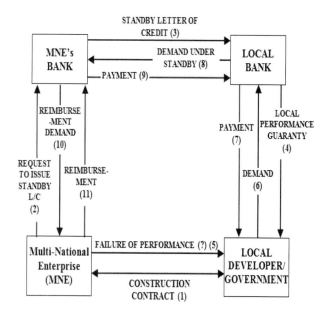

Below is also an example of a standby letter of credit issued by seller's bank in favor of the country of India. It is taken from *Dynamics Corp. of America v. Citizens & Southern Nat. Bank*, 356 F. Supp. 991 (N.D. Ga. 1973):

"... *TO: THE PRESIDENT OF INDIA*

INDIA

BY ORDER OF: ELECTRONICS SYSTEMS DIVISION OF DYNAMICS CORPORATION OF AMERICA

For account

of same

GENTLEMEN:

WE HEREBY ESTABLISH OUR IRREVOCABLE CREDIT IN YOUR FAVOR, FOR THE ACCOUNT INDICATED ABOVE, FOR A SUM OR SUMS NOT EXCEEDING IN ALL FOUR HUNDRED TEN THOUSAND FOUR HUNDRED SEVENTY TWO AND 60/100 US DOLLARS (US$410,472.60)—AVAILABLE BY YOUR DRAFT(S) AT sight,

DRAWN ON: us

Which must be accompanied by:

1. Your signed certification as follows: "The President of India being one of the parties to the Agreement dated March 14, 1971 signed and exchanged between the President of India and the Dynamics Corporation of America for the license to manufacture, purchase and supply of radio equipment as per Schedule I thereof for the total contract value of $1,368,242.00, does hereby certify in the exercise of reasonable discretion and in good faith that the Dynamics Corporation of America has failed to carry *out certain obligations of theirs under the said Order/Agreement. . ."*

In it, the seller (account party) has contracted to have the seller's bank (issuing bank) issue an irrevocable letter of credit in favor of the foreign government (beneficiary) that payment will be made upon presentation of a simple documentary statement by the beneficiary. This is merely a unilateral declaration by the beneficiary, "in the exercise of reasonable discretion and in good faith," that the account party has failed to carry out its obligations under a contract. Some standbys require no documentary presentation, but provide for payment to be made upon the beneficiary's demand (called a "suicide credit").

This transaction is almost a reverse mirror image of the letter of credit in the documentary sale. In the standby credit, the account party (applicant) is the seller or contractor, the beneficiary is the purchaser (not the seller), and the documents do not control the goods and have no independent value of their own. As noted, often the required documentation is a mere certification by the beneficiary that the contractor has failed to perform under the contract or, perhaps, has failed to return an advance payment.

A standby letter of credit may incorporate the UCP, and is then governed by the same rules as those applicable to documentary credits "to the extent to which they may be applicable." UCP Art. 1. Standby letters of credit may also have confirming banks; but it is also quite common for a standby to serve as support for a local performance guaranty by foreign banks (which are not subject to U.S. banking laws). If the documents presented conform precisely to the terms of the letter of credit, the confirming bank (if any) and the issuing bank are obligated to pay the beneficiary or otherwise to honor its draft. The beneficiary is not subject to defenses arising out of the underlying sales or project transaction, so the conformity of the goods or actual performance in the project is, with exceptions noted below, irrelevant to the bank's decision. The decision is to be based upon the documents alone. Further, the documents need not conform to the underlying contract either, so long as they comply with the letter of credit. This is the "independence principle" which underlies the legal setting for letters of credit generally.

Some legal commentators question whether the traditional "independence principle" of letter of credit rules should be applied to standby credits, in light of the fact that such letters do not assure an exporter about payment for goods to be shipped, but serve principally a non-payment function to protect an importer (beneficiary) if an exporter (the applicant/account party) does not deliver on its contract (to supply goods, services, or raw materials, or to construct a project). However, the text of both the UCP and UCC Article 5 make it clear that the drafters intended them to cover standby letters of credit, and to apply the "independence principle" to such bank obligations.

NEW INTERNATIONAL RULES FOR
STANDBY LETTERS OF CREDIT

Even though both the UCP and Revised UCC Article 5 expressly include standby letters of credit within their coverage, it is clear that they were designed principally to cover the documentary letter of credit transaction and not the standby transaction. Thus, they impose many unnecessary document-related conditions on the use of standbys. The UCP, in particular, contains many provisions on the proper presentation of transportation documents, all of which are irrelevant to the usual standby letter of credit transaction. The UCP also does not address several issues, such as fraud and choice of law, which are significant to standby transactions.

In response to these difficulties, the United Nations Commission on International Trade Law (UNCITRAL) has developed the United Nations Convention on Independent Guarantees and Standby Letters of Credit (1995), which entered into force on January 1, 2000. The Convention currently has eight Contracting States (Belarus, Ecuador, El Salvador, Gabon, Kuwait, Liberia, Panama and Tunisia). For the same reason, the International Chamber of Commerce (ICC) has developed the Rules on International Standby Practices (ISP 98), which became effective on January 1, 1999. The ISP 98 was designed to replace the UCP and be its equivalent in international practice regarding standby letters of credit. (A separate set of ICC rules, The Uniform Rules for Demand Guarantees (URDG 758, 2010), addresses the subject of demand guarantees, a civil law instrument more commonly used in foreign countries.)

The U.N. Convention on standbys applies to an "international undertaking." Article 1(1). Under Article 4(1), a letter of credit is "international" if the place of business of any two of the following typical actors are in different countries: the issuer, the beneficiary, the applicant, an "instructing party" (an entity that applies for the letter of credit on behalf of the applicant), or a confirmer. The Convention also provides choice of law rules, and allows the parties to choose the applicable law. If the parties do not agree on a choice of law, the Convention provides a default rule that the law of the issuer's place of business shall govern the transaction. Articles 21, 22.

Article 14 of the Convention states the basic principle that an issuer must "act in good faith and exercise reasonable care" and must adhere to "generally accepted standards of international practice" for stand-by letters of credit. The core provision of the Convention, however, is found in Article 16 on "examination of [the] demand and accompanying documents." Under that provision, the issuer must examine any demand for payment in accordance with the Article 14 standard, and determine "whether documents are in facial conformity with the terms and conditions of the undertaking, and are consistent with one another." The bank also has a "reasonable time, but not more than seven business days" following the demand to examine the documents and, if it decides not to honor, to give the beneficiary notice by "expeditious means ... indicat[ing] the reason for the decision not to pay."

The Convention also provides rules for allegations of fraud and the grounds for injunctive relief. Articles 19 and 20. Under these rules, an otherwise obligated bank, acting in good faith, may refuse payment if it is "manifest and clear" that (a) a document is not genuine or has been falsified, (b) no payment is due, or (c) "judging by the type and purpose of the undertaking, the demand has no conceivable basis." (For more on this, *see* immediately below.) A court may issue an order blocking payment or freezing proceeds of a standby credit if it finds "strong evidence" of such a circumstance.

ISP 98 deletes all the provisions concerning transportation documents, but does require that any official documents be certified. It also places a floor on the amount of information a beneficiary must provide, and requires "magic words" in regard to the presentation of certificates of default under a standby. The ISP also provides rules to govern electronic demands for payment under standby letters of credit. However, since the ISP is not a statute, but merely trade terms incorporated into the contract by reference, it does not attempt to include provisions on fraud and injunctive relief. Perhaps surprisingly, it also does not include any choice of law provisions.

THE FRAUD DEFENSE

One important tension that arises from a strict application of the "independence principle" in letter of credit law is the effect of fraud. The "independence principle" promotes the utility of the letter of credit transaction by offering certainty of payment to the beneficiary who complies with a credit's requirements. But where a required document is forged or fraudulent, or the beneficiary has engaged in material fraud beyond a "mere" breach of the underlying sales contract, a counter principle comes into play. As one court long ago observed, "There is as much public interest in discouraging fraud as in encouraging the use of letters of credit." *Dynamics Corp. of America v. Citizens & Southern Nat. Bank*, 356 F. Supp. 991 (N.D. Ga. 1973). The famous case in this regard is *Sztejn v. J. Henry Schroder Banking Corp.*, 31 N.Y.S.2d 631 (N.Y. Sup. 1941), in which the court observed that the principle of "the independence of the bank's obligation under the letter of credit" should not be extended to protect an unscrupulous beneficiary where its fraudulent actions become apparent before it presents the drafts and other documents for payment.

Thus, there are two competing principles, and the courts have created compromises to limit the impact of the independence principle when a transaction is tainted by beneficiary fraud or by forged or fraudulent documents. Vexing problems arise when an applicant makes a claim of fraud and, more particularly, of "fraud in the transaction"; but the doctrine that the "independence principle" is subject to a "fraud exception" is expressly stated in the UCC and otherwise seems to be generally recognized. The principle underlying this approach is that the courts will not allow their process to be used by a dishonest person to carry out a fraud. However, there is still a significant debate about how broad and extensive the fraud exception should be.

This "fraud exception" is available where the credit is expressly subject to the UCP, even though the UCP has no specific provisions on the subject. Because the UCP is silent, the courts have held that UCC Article 5 governs as a "gap-filler." *See, e.g., Mid-America Tire, Inc. v. PTZ Trading Ltd.*, 768 N.E.2d 619 (Ohio 2002). The courts generally have been skeptical regarding enjoining payment due to fraud in the documentary letter of credit transaction. This is less true, however, for the standby letter of credit transaction. A principal reason for the difference is that some of the limiting concepts in the documentary letter of credit transaction, such as the extensive documentary requirements and the "strict compliance" standard, become largely meaningless when the "document" involves a mere allegation by one party that the other party failed to perform properly under the contract. When the limitations that give structure to a transaction become meaningless, the transaction can become a breeding ground for fraud.

UCC § 5–109 imposes, however, a series of important limitations on the availability of the fraud exception. The first is an absolute requirement that an issuer honor a presentation by certain intermediary banks that have already paid in good faith. Thus, § 5-109(a)(1) provides that "the issuer shall honor" a conforming presentation made by either (i) "a nominated person who has given value in good faith without notice of forgery or material fraud," or (ii) "a confirmer who has honored its confirmation in good faith" (as well as in certain other similar, but very rare, situations). Thus, a confirming bank that has paid against the documents in good faith is entitled to reimbursement even if strong evidence of fraud or forgery later surfaces. The same applies when an advising bank later becomes a nominated bank through an authorization to pay against the documents (rather than merely to accept the documents for collection) if it has paid in good faith and without notice. Under the UCC, therefore, if such a good faith intermediary bank has already paid the beneficiary, and the documents appear on their face to comply with the credit, the issuing bank *must* provide reimbursement, even if the documents are forged or fraudulent or there is material fraud in the transaction.

A second limitation on the fraud exception is that, even if the documents are presented by anyone else (*e.g.*, the beneficiary or any other intermediary bank), the issuing bank *may* still pay, even though it has been notified that the documents are forged or fraudulent, or that there is fraud in the transaction. The only requirement is that the issuer act "in good faith," and Article 5 defines this term with the very limited notion of "honesty in fact." § 5-102(a)(7). The issuing bank *may* also refuse to pay, but for a variety of reasons that is not very likely. First, banks have a limited ability to evaluate the available evidence of fraud, especially on an *ex parte* basis, and have little desire to become involved in the buyer-seller dispute in any event. Second, banks are paid to handle documents, not to become judge and jury. Third, banks likely will be reluctant to develop a reputation as an unreliable source of funds in letter of credit transactions. Fourth, a decision to dishonor almost certainly will cause a lawsuit by the beneficiary for wrongful dishonor, with all of the attendant litigation and attorneys' fees for the bank. Finally, if the issuing bank honors a conforming presentation in good faith, even with no investigation whatsoever, Article 5 makes clear that it has an absolute right of reimbursement from the applicant. § 5-108(i). Thus, all of the incentives point in the direction of the issuer honoring and allowing the applicant and the beneficiary to fight it out among themselves.

The applicant (buyer) may, however, seek an injunction on its own. UCC § 5-109(b) grants an applicant the right to seek a court order against payment if it can prove forgery or fraud in a required document under the letter of credit or fraud by the beneficiary in the underlying transaction. Thus, under the UCC, if the applicant obtains an injunction against payment from a court having proper jurisdiction, the issuing bank will be compelled to refuse to pay. But UCC Article 5 leaves only a very narrow avenue for this option. To beneficiaries, the concept creates great uncertainty about prompt payment, because they may know nothing about a foreign judicial system and may fear the worst. To applicants in international sales transactions, the concept has created a theoretical argument, but very few reported cases have actually resulted in an injunction against payment.

UCC § 5-109(b) also limits the right to an injunction based on the fraud exception in several important ways:

First, the fraud must be "material," and this is a severe standard. The meaning of "material" of course will be decided on a case by case basis. Nonetheless, courts have generally imposed a very high burden, and have required proof of fraud that has "so vitiated the entire transaction that the legitimate purposes of the independence of the issuer's obligation would no longer be served." *See, e.g.,* *Ground Air Transfer, Inc. v. Westates Airlines*, Inc., 899 F.2d 1269 (1st Cir.1990). *See also* § 5-109, Comment 1 (endorsing this standard).

Second, the applicant must present sufficient evidence of fraud or forgery, not merely allegations of it.

Third, the applicant must satisfy all of the traditional equitable requirements for injunctive and similar relief. Thus, the applicant must demonstrate that it would suffer irreparable harm without an injunction and that a later money judgment would not be an adequate remedy (that there is "no adequate remedy at law"), and in most jurisdictions must also show that the balance of harm does not weigh too heavily against the beneficiary and that an injunction would not be contrary to the public interest.

Fourth, a court must require as a condition of an injunction that the beneficiary, the issuer, and any affected confirming or nominated banks are "adequately protected." This typically means that the applicant must post a bond against any losses by affected third parties. The Comments to § 5-109 expand this concept to include even protection against incidental damages, such as legal fees.

UCC § 5–109 also adds a final, significant limitation. A forgery or a fraud in a document required by the letter of credit may permit an injunction if perpetrated by anyone. But as to conduct in the underlying transaction, an injunction is permissible only if payment would facilitate a material fraud "by the beneficiary," and not by some third party, such as a carrier. The difference between the two concepts is illustrated by the approach of English and Canadian courts to allegations of fraud.

English and some Canadian courts also have recognized the "fraud exception," based upon fundamental contract principles and the persuasive precedent of the American cases. These courts, however, place great stress on the *scienter* requirements of common law fraud. Of equal importance, the courts require the applicant to establish that the beneficiary itself made, or was responsible for, the misrepresentation that is the foundation for the fraud claim. Fraudulent actions by any other party to the transaction would not permit an injunction against payment to the beneficiary. Thus, the House of Lords in the famous case of *The American Accord*, while recognizing the basic fraud concept, refused to extend it to protect the buyer when the fraud was committed by a third party (a loading broker) without seller's knowledge. *United City Merchants (Investments) Ltd. v. Royal Bank of Canada (The American Accord)*, [1983] 1.A.C.168. Under this approach, (1) where the credit requires loading by May 15 and the bill of lading shows loading on the 16th, the bank must dishonor under the basic "strict compliance" standard; (2) where the credit requires loading on May 15, and applicant can prove that the beneficiary altered a May 16 loading document to say May 15, a court may issue an injunction against honor; but (3) where the credit requires loading by May 15, but a freight forwarded altered the May 16 loading document to say May 15, a court may not issue an injunction against honor. Indeed, the English Court of Appeals in *Montrod Ltd. v. Grundkötter Fleischvertriebs GmbH*, [2002] 1 W.L.R. 1975, refused to allow any flexibility in the requirement of beneficiary involvement, even if a document presented under the letter of credit is so fraudulent as to be a "nullity."

Under § 5-109, in contrast, a court may issue an injunction if a document required by the letter of credit is forged or materially fraudulent, even if the beneficiary was not involved. In such a case, the identity of the perpetrator would be irrelevant.

The traditional difference between fraud doctrines and breach of contract concepts was that the former considered the state of mind of the seller, while breach of contract concerns only whether the goods lived up to particular objective standard set by their description. Fraud concepts have expanded enormously since the middle of the last century, however, and conduct that would not have been actionable then is now routinely within current case law concepts. The modern fraud doctrines often do not require any evil intent, but only that seller know that a particular fact is not true (or that he states a fact with indifference about its truthfulness) or that he believes that a fact is true when it is not, and a court decides that he should have made a more thorough investigation before speaking. In spite of all of this, in letter of credit law the courts have continued to place a high burden on applicants to demonstrate "material fraud" by the beneficiary.

Given the high standard for an injunction against payment, applicants have sought other means for protection. One option is a "notice injunction." Under this vehicle, an applicant with only limited evidence of fraud may nonetheless be able to convince a court to require that an issuer give some prior notice to the applicant (usually a matter of days) before honoring a presentation by the beneficiary. This would permit the applicant to accelerate its efforts to obtain sufficient evidence to justify a preliminary or permanent injunction against any payment by the issuer under the letter of credit.

As suggested above, injunctions against honor are rare in traditional commercial letters of credit, but are more common in standby letters of credit. The principal reason for this is the extremely limited documentary presentations typically required with standbys. Often, the beneficiary need merely make a documentary demand that states an entitlement to payment. Substantial political and economic upheavals thus often trigger "aggressive" demands under standby letters of credit. One prominent example is the political changes brought about by the revolution in Iran in the 1970s. After an initial period of strict adherence to the independence principle, U.S. courts became increasingly skeptical of demands made by governmental institutions and began issuing injunctions against honor under standby letters of credit that supported pre-revolution projects. *See, e.g., Harris Corp. v. Nat'l Iranian Radio and Television*, 691 F.2d 1344 (2nd Cir. 1982). At least one court has found similarly convincing evidence of fraud to justify such an injunction from the chaos surrounding the recent events in Iraq. *See, e.g., Archer Daniels Midland Co. v. JP Morgan Chase Bank, N.A.*, 2011 WL 855936 (S.D.N.Y. 2011).

As noted above, UNCITRAL also has attempted to bring about international uniformity on fraud allegations under the 1995 Convention on Independent Guarantees and Stand-by Letters of Credit. Article 19 of the Convention permits a bank to refuse payment and Article 20 permits a court to issue a "provisional order" against payment if the applicant can show that (1) a document is not genuine, (2) no payment is due, or (3) "the demand has no conceivable basis." The Convention also describes five expansions on the latter option. These include that (a) a covered risk "has undoubtedly not materialized"; (b) a court or arbitral tribunal has already declared the underlying obligation as "invalid"; (c) the underlying obligation "has undoubtedly been fulfilled to the satisfaction of the beneficiary"; (d) fulfillment of that obligation "has clearly been prevented by wilful misconduct of the beneficiary"; and (e) a confirming or similar bank seeking reimbursement has made payment "in bad faith." The Convention then expressly prohibits a court from enjoining payment on any other basis.

OTHER LETTER OF CREDIT TERMS; BACK TO BACK AND REVOLVING CREDITS

A complete understanding of international letters of credit also requires familiarity with a range of specialized terminology. Although documentary letters of credit in international commercial transactions most often are irrevocable (and the UCP establishes such a presumption), the parties may instead expressly agree that a letter of credit is "revocable." This gives the beneficiary a right to payment, but only until it is "cancelled" by the issuer or applicant. In absence of such an agreement, UCP Article 7(b) makes a letter of credit irrevocable from the time it is issued.

Letters of credit may be payable by "sight" draft (on demand) or "time" draft (*e.g.*, six months after presentation of documents). A letter of credit that contemplates a time draft will grant credit to the applicant and, upon a conforming presentation and acceptance by the issuer, give the beneficiary an instrument (an accepted draft) that it can negotiate (sell) to another financial institution to raise cash immediately. The confirming or issuing bank will "accept" the draft that accompanies the documents, thus making the bank primarily liable to pay the draft. A "general" letter of credit does not restrict the beneficiary's right to transfer its rights thereunder, while a "special" letter of credit limits permissible transferees, usually to one or more banks. A letter of credit is "fixed" if it can become "exhausted" either when drafts for payment have been drawn by beneficiary for the full amount of the letter. A letter of credit "expires" when the time period stated therein for the presentation of drafts and other documents has passed.

Brokers of goods have a problem because they often have two transactions in the same goods. They will sell the goods to a buyer in one transaction and then buy them from a supplier in a separate transaction. If both sales transactions involve payment by letters of credit, the broker will be the beneficiary (seller) of the letter of credit in the "downstream" transaction and the applicant (buyer) in the "upstream" transaction. This arrangement is known as a "back to back credit" and allows the broker to finance its purchase of the goods from supplier with the credit of its buyer. If the documents required by the two letters of credit are *identical,* the broker can use the downstream letter of credit as collateral for the issuance of the upstream letter of credit. It does this by assigning its rights under the downstream credit to the issuing bank of the upstream credit. Such arrangements are facilitated if the credits specify the use of time drafts (*e.g.,* "pay 30 days after sight"). They also work more easily using general letters of credit, although special credits can be used by giving an issuing bank a security interest in the proceeds of the downstream credit.

However, back to back credits can also become unworkable if one of the credits is amended, and no similar amendment is made to the other credit.

Thus, most banks prefer not to use the back to back letter of credit transaction. Instead, they recommend that sellers and brokers obtain financing through a "transferable letter of credit" or an "assignment of proceeds" from a letter of credit.

A transferable letter of credit is one that expressly states that it can be transferred by the original beneficiary to third parties, who become new and substitute beneficiaries. UCP Article 38. Thus, a broker who is the beneficiary of a transferable letter of credit can use its rights under that credit to finance the purchase of the goods from suppliers by transferring all or part of the broker's rights under the credit to the suppliers. Partial transfers are allowed, so the broker can use this device to finance purchases from several suppliers. However, although substitute commercial invoices and drafts may be used, all other necessary documents ultimately will be presented—through the issuing bank—to the original account party (applicant), which will reveal the identity of the substitute beneficiary. That may compromise commercially sensitive information, and so brokers tend to avoid use of such credits.

The beneficiary of a letter of credit may instead irrevocably assign a portion of the credit's proceeds to a third party. If the proceeds are assigned, an advising bank notifies the assignee of the assignment. Thus, a broker who is the beneficiary of a letter of credit that permits assignment of proceeds can use its rights under that credit to finance the purchase of the goods from a supplier by assigning a part of the broker's rights under the credit to the supplier. The assignment of proceeds does not change the parties to the letter of credit. Nonetheless, the original account party (applicant under the letter of credit) is obligated to pay only if it receives—through the issuer—documents that conform to the credit, so the assignee will not be paid unless it ships the goods using conforming documents. The assignee is not a party to the letter of credit and may not know what the terms of the credit are, so it must trust the broker (the beneficiary) to both accurately convey the content of and then later fulfill those terms. The assignment is not governed by the UCP, but by the applicable law of contract. UCP Article 39.

Rapid expansion of turn-key construction contracts (*e.g.*, for building a complete steel mill or cement plant such that a buyer need only to "turn a key" to begin plant operation) has expanded the use of "revolving" letters of credit. This form of a credit serves as a vehicle to enable contractors to receive progress payments promptly as sequential construction phases are completed, and in turn to support further construction phases. Revolving letters of credit are usually clean (no documents required) sight letters that work in the same way and are subject to the same legal rules as fixed amount letters of credit. The principal difference relates to the amount of the credit and how much the beneficiary may draw at any given time. They commonly are used when an importer (often a third world host government) pays, by way of a letter of credit, to import services (building skills) and raw materials rather than finished goods. The letter of credit is, however, funded in stages. Each time the construction company (the beneficiary) performs a defined set of services and then draws on the letter of credit for payment, the importer (the applicant under the letter of credit) engages to restore the amount of the letter (by arrangement with the issuer) to an agreed credit level in favor of the beneficiary. Revolving letters sometimes require presentation of specific documents such as certificates of construction phase completion (often prepared by a supervising architect). But "red tape" in obtaining such interim certifications prompts many contractors to seek less formal arrangements, requiring the applicant to trust the contractor not to draw upon the letter before such action is appropriate. In such a case, the payment ceiling (amount of credit) under the revolving letter may be a substantially smaller amount than the total value of the construction contract.

CHAPTER 4
TECHNOLOGY TRANSFERS

Issues surrounding the transfer of knowledge across national borders have provoked intense discussions during the last decade. The discussions promise to continue unabated. At the core is the desire of third world countries (often advanced developing countries like China, Brazil, and India) to obtain protected information quickly and affordably irrespective of the proprietary rights and profit motives of current holders (usually persons from the most developed countries). Developing countries want production processes which maximize inexpensive labor but which result in products that are competitive in the international marketplace. Capital intensive production processes (e.g., robot production of automobiles) may be of less interest. MNEs may be willing to share (by way of license or sale) a good deal of proprietary information, but are reluctant to part with their "core technology."

Among the industrialized countries, efforts often occur to acquire (even by way of stealing) "leading edge" technology. One example involved attempted theft of IBM computer technology by Japanese companies ultimately caught by the F.B.I. In the United States, the Office of Export Administration uses the export license procedure to control strategic technological "diversions." But falsification of licensing documents by prominent Norwegian and Japanese companies allowed the Soviets to obtain the technology for making vastly quieter submarine propellers. In the ensuing scandal, "anti-Toshiba" legislation was adopted in the U.S. Congress. See Section 2443 of the 1988 Omnibus Trade and Competitiveness Act. Leading Japanese executives resigned their positions, which is considered the highest form of apology in Japanese business circles.

The predominant vehicle for controlling technology transfers across national borders is the "license" or "franchise" contract. Some $180 billion in licensing royalties flow annually across borders. The holder of information in one country first acquires the legally protected right to own the information in another country. With few exceptions, IP rights are national in origin, products of territorial domestic regimes. This makes the acquisition of IP rights around the globe remarkably expensive. Once acquired, the holder then licenses the right, usually for a fee, to a person in that other country. The very sharing of information raises a risk that proprietary control of the technology may be lost or, at a minimum, that a competitor will be created. Absent authorized transfers, piracy of intellectual property is increasingly commonplace. Indeed, in some countries such theft has risen to the height of development strategy.

The developing nations (as a "Group of 77"), the industrialized nations and the nonmarket economy nations tried to agree in UNCTAD upon an international "Code of Conduct" for the transfer of technology. Wide disparities in attitudes toward such a Code were reflected by the developing nations' insistence that it be an "internationally legally binding Code", and the industrialized nations' position that it consist of "guidelines for the international transfer of technology". Some economics of the debate are illustrated by the fact that persons in the United States pay about one-tenth in royalties for use of imported technology than they receive in royalty payments from technology sent abroad. Many considered development of an international technology transfer Code the most important feature of the North-South dialogue. But it was not to be. Instead, to some degree, the TRIPs Agreement of the World Trade Organization functions as such a code.

THE TRIPS AGREEMENT

The World Trade Organization agreements effective January 1995 include an agreement on trade-related intellectual property rights (TRIPs). This agreement is binding upon the over 150 nations that are members of the World Trade Organization. In the United States, the TRIPs agreement was ratified and implemented by Congress in December of 1994 under the Uruguay Round Agreements Act. There is a general requirement of national and most-favored-nation treatment among the parties.

The TRIPs Code covers the gamut of intellectual property. On copyrights, there is protection for computer programs and databases, rental authorization controls for owners of computer software and sound recordings, a 50-year motion picture and sound recording copyright term, and a general obligation to comply with the Berne Convention (except for its provisions on moral rights).

On patents, the Paris Convention (1967) prevails, product and process patents are to be available for pharmaceuticals and agricultural chemicals, limits are placed on compulsory licensing, and a general 20-year patent term from the date of application is created. Patents on certain medical procedures, as well as plants and animals, maybe denied protection. United States law, which previously granted 17 year patents from the date of issuance, has been amended to conform. For trademarks, internationally prominent marks receive enhanced protection, the linking of local marks with foreign trademarks is prohibited, service marks become registrable, and compulsory licensing is banned. Geographical indicators of origin (Feta cheese, Bordeaux wines, Tennessee whiskey) are protected. In addition, trade secret protection is assisted by TRIPs rules enabling owners to prevent unauthorized use or disclosure. Integrated circuits are covered by rules intended to improve upon the Washington Treaty. Lastly, industrial designs are also part of the TRIPs regime.

Infringement and anticounterfeiting remedies are included in the TRIPs, for both domestic and international trade protection. There are specific provisions governing injunctions, damages, customs seizures, and discovery of evidence.

Pharmaceuticals

Late in 2001, the Doha Round of WTO negotiations were launched. These negotiations have reconsidered the TRIPs agreement, particularly as it applies to developing nations. In addition, a Declaration on the TRIPs Agreement and Public Health was issued at the Qatar Ministerial Conference. This Declaration includes the following statement:

> We agree that the TRIPs Agreement does not prevent Members from taking measures to protect public health. Accordingly, while reiterating our commitment to the TRIPs Agreement, we affirm that the Agreement can and should be interpreted and implemented in a manner supportive of WTO Members' right to protect public health and, in particular, to promote access to medicines for all.

By mid-2003, a "Medicines Agreement" was finally reached on how to implement this Declaration. Compulsory licensing and/or importation of generic copies of patented medicines needed to address developing nation public health problems are authorized. Such activities may not pursue industrial or commercial policy objectives, and different packaging and labeling must be used in an effort at minimizing the risk of diversion of the generics to developed country markets. Under pressure from the United States, a number of more advanced developing nations (such as Mexico, Singapore and Qatar) agreed not to employ compulsory licensing except in situations of national emergency or extreme urgency. Canada, on the other hand, has licensed production of drugs for Rwanda and other nations incapable of pharmaceutical production.

TRIPS Disputes

TRIPs disputes decided by WTO Panels or the Appellate Body have required India to reform its "mailbox rule" for pharmaceutical and agricultural chemical patent applications (patentable since 2005), Canada to give 20 year terms to pre-TRIPs patents and limit its generic pharmaceutical regulatory review and stockpiling patent rights' exceptions, the European Union to remove information technology tariffs and amend discriminatory regulations regarding geographical indicators, the United States to pay for small "business use" of copyrighted music and to remove a prohibition against registration of Cuban confiscated trademarks without the original owner's consent (HAVANA CLUB rum), and China's copyright coverage and entertainment product restraints.

PATENT PROTECTION

For the most part, patents are granted to inventors according to national law. Thus, patents represent *territorial* grants of exclusive rights. The inventor receives Canadian patents, U.S. patents, Mexican patents, and so on. Since over one hundred countries have laws regulating patents, there are relatively few jurisdictions without some form of patent protection. Approximately 2 million patents are issued around the world each year. However, legally protected intellectual property in one country may not be protected similarly in another country. For example, some third world nations refuse to grant patents on pharmaceuticals. These countries often assert that their public health needs require such a policy. Thailand was traditionally one such country and unlicensed or compulsory licensed "generics" have been a growth industry there, and also in Brazil and India.

Nominal patent protection in some developing nations may lack effective forms of relief-giving the appearance but not the reality of legal rights. Since international patent protection is expensive to obtain, some holders take a chance and limit their applications to those markets where they foresee demand or competition for their product. Nevertheless, U.S. nationals continue to receive tens of thousands of patents in other countries. But the reverse is also increasingly true. Residents of foreign countries now receive over 50 percent of the patents issued under U.S. law. In many countries, persons who deal with the issuance and protection of patents are called patent agents. In the United States, patent practice is a specialized branch of the legal profession. Obtaining international patent protection often involves retaining the services of specialists in each country.

What constitutes a "patent" and how it is protected in any country depends upon domestic law. In the United States, a patent issued by the U.S. Patent Office grants the right for 20 years to exclude everyone from making, using or selling the patented invention without the permission of the patentee. The United States traditionally granted patents to the "first to invent," not (as in many other countries) the "first to file." In 2011, the United States switched to first to file rules. Patent infringement, including the supply of "components" for patented inventions, can result in injunctive and damages relief in the U.S. courts. "Exclusion orders" against foreign-made patent infringing goods are also available. Such orders are frequently issued by the International Trade Commission under Section 337 of the Tariff Act of 1930, and are enforced by the U.S. Customs Service.

A U.S. patent thus provides a short-term legal, but not necessarily economic, monopoly. For example, the exclusive legal rights conveyed by the patents held by Xerox on its photocopying machines have not given it a monopoly in the marketplace. There are many other producers of non-infringing photocopy machines with whom Xerox competes.

There are basically two types of patent systems in the world community, registration and examination. Some countries (e.g., France) grant a patent upon "registration" accompanied by appropriate documents and fees, without making an inquiry about the patentability of the invention. The validity of such a patent grant is most difficult to gauge until a time comes to defend the patent against alleged infringement in an appropriate tribunal. In other countries, the patent grant is made following a careful "examination" of the prior art and statutory criteria on patentability or a "deferred examination" is made following public notice given to permit an "opposition." The odds are increased that the validity of such a patent will be sustained in the face of an alleged infringement. The United States and Germany have examination systems.

To obtain U.S. patents, applicants must demonstrate to the satisfaction of the U.S. Patent Office that their inventions are novel, useful and nonobvious. Nevertheless, a significant number of U.S. patents have been subsequently held invalid in the courts and the Patent Office has frequently been criticized for a lax approach to issuance of patents. Much of this growth is centered in high-tech industries, including computer software and business methods patents. The United States also been criticized for sometimes allowing patents on "traditional knowledge" (e.g., Mexican Enola Beans) found primarily in the developing world.

The terms of a patent grant vary from country to country. For example, local law may provide for "confirmation," "importation," "introduction" or "revalidation" patents (which serve to extend limited protection to patents already existing in another country). "Inventor's certificates" and rewards are granted in some socialist countries where private ownership of the means of production is discouraged. The state owns the invention. This was the case in China, for example, but inventors now may obtain patents and exclusive private rights under the 1984 Patent Law. Some countries, such as Britain, require that a patent be "worked" (commercially applied) within a designated period of time. This requirement is so important that the British mandate a "compulsory license" to local persons if a patent is deemed unworked. Many developing nations have similar provisions in their patent laws . . . the owner must use it or lose it.

INTERNATIONAL RECOGNITION OF PATENTS

The principal treaties regarding patents are the 1970 Patent Cooperation Treaty and the 1883 Convention of the Union of Paris, frequently revised and amended. To some extent, the Paris Convention also deals with trademarks, servicemarks, trade names, industrial designs, and unfair competition. Other treaties dealing with patents are the European Patent Convention (designed to permit a single office at Munich and The Hague to issue patents of 35 countries party to the treaty), and the proposed European Union Patent Convention (intended to create a single patent valid throughout the EU).

Paris Convention

The Paris Convention, to which over 170 countries including the United States are parties, remains the basic international agreement dealing with treatment of foreigners under national patent laws. It is administered by the International Bureau of the

World Intellectual Property Organization (WIPO) at Geneva. The "right of national treatment" prohibits discrimination against foreign holders of local patents and trademarks. Thus, for example, a foreigner granted a Canadian patent must receive the same legal rights and remedies accorded Canadian nationals. Furthermore, important "rights of priority" are granted to patent holders provided they file in foreign jurisdictions within twelve months of their home country patent applications. But such rights may not overcome prior filings by others in "first to file" jurisdictions.

Patent applications in foreign jurisdictions are not dependent upon success in the home country. Patentability criteria vary from country to country. Nevertheless, the Paris Convention obviates the need to file simultaneously in every country where intellectual property protection is sought. If an inventor elects not to obtain patent protection in other countries, anyone may make, use or sell the invention in that territory. The Paris Convention does not attempt to reduce the need for individual patent applications in all jurisdictions where patent protection is sought. Nor does it alter the various domestic criteria on patentability.

Patent Cooperation Treaty

The Patent Cooperation Treaty (PCT), to which about 140 countries including the United States are parties, is designed to achieve greater uniformity and less cost in the international patent filing process, and in the examination of prior art. Instead of filing patent applications individually in each nation, filings under the PCT are done in selected countries. The national patent offices of Japan, Sweden, Russia and the United States have been designated International Searching Authorities (ISA), as has the European Patent Office at Munich and The Hague. The international application, together with the international search report, is communicated by an ISA to each national patent office where protection is sought. Nothing in this Treaty limits the freedom of each nation to require expensive translations, establish substantive conditions of patentability and determine infringement remedies.

However, the Patent Cooperation Treaty also provides that the applicant may arrange for an international preliminary examination in order to formulate a non-binding opinion on whether the claimed invention is novel, involves an inventive step (non-obvious) and is industrially applicable. In a country without sophisticated search facilities, the report of the international preliminary examination may largely determine whether a patent will be granted. For this reason alone, the Patent Cooperation Treaty may generate considerable uniformity in world patent law. In 1986 the United States ratified the PCT provisions on preliminary examination reports, thereby supporting such uniformity.

KNOWHOW

Knowhow is commercially valuable knowledge. It may or may not be a trade secret, and may or may not be patentable. Though often technical or scientific, e.g. engineering services, knowhow can also be more general in character. Marketing and management skills as well as simply business advice can constitute knowhow. If someone is willing to pay for the information, it can be sold or licensed internationally.

Legal protection for knowhow varies from country to country and is, at best, limited. Unlike patents, copyrights and trademarks, you cannot by registration obtain exclusive legal rights to knowhow. Knowledge, like the air we breathe, is a public good. Once released in the community, knowhow can generally be used by anyone and is almost impossible to retrieve. In the absence of exclusive legal rights, preserving the confidentiality of knowhow becomes an important business strategy. If everyone knows it, who will pay for it? If your competitors have access to the knowledge, your market position is at risk. It is for these reasons that only a few people on earth ever know the Coca Cola formula, which is perhaps the world's best kept knowhow.

Protecting knowhow is mostly a function of contract, tort and trade secrets law. Employers will surround their critical knowhow with employees bound by contract to confidentiality. But some valuable knowledge leaks from or moves with these employees, e.g. when a disgruntled retired or ex-employee sells or goes public with the knowhow. The remedies at law or in equity for breach of contract are unlikely to render the employer whole. Neither is torts relief likely to be sufficient since most employees are essentially judgment proof, though they may be of more use if a competitor induced the breach of contract. Likewise, even though genuine trade secrets are protected by criminal statutes in a few jurisdictions, persuading the prosecutor to take up your business problem is not easy and criminal penalties will not recoup the trade secrets (though they may make the revelation of others less likely in the future).

The Economic Espionage Act of 1996 creates *criminal* penalties for misappropriation of trade secrets for the benefit of foreign governments or anyone. For these purposes, a "trade secret" is defined as "financial, business, scientific, technical, economic or engineering information" that the owner has taken reasonable measures to keep secret and whose "independent economic value derives from being closely held." In addition to criminal fines, forfeitures and jail terms, the Act authorizes seizure of all proceeds from the theft of trade secrets as well as property used or intended for use in the misappropriation (e.g., buildings and capital equipment).

Despite all of these legal hazards, even when certain knowhow is patentable, a desire to prolong the commercial exploitation of that knowledge may result in no patent registrations. The international chemicals industry, for example, is said to prefer trade secrets to public disclosure and patent rights with time limitations. Licensing or selling such knowhow around the globe is risky, but lucrative.

TRADEMARK PROTECTION

Virtually all countries offer some legal protection to trademarks, even when they do not have trademark registration systems. Trademark rights derived from the use of marks on goods in commerce have long been recognized at common law and remain so today in countries as diverse as the United States and the United Arab Emirates. The latter nation, for example, had no trademark registration law in 1986, but this did not prevent McDonald's from obtaining an injunction against a local business using its famous name and golden arches without authorization. However, obtaining international trademark protection requires separate registration under the law of each nation.

Over three million trademarks are registered around the globe each year. In the United States, trademarks are protected at common law and by state and federal registrations. Federal registration is permitted by the U.S. Trademark Office for all marks capable of distinguishing the goods on which they appear from other goods. U.S. law notably allows trademarks on distinct smells, colors, sounds and tastes. Unless the mark falls within a category of forbidden registrations (e.g. those that offend socialist morality in the People's Republic of China), a mark becomes valid for a term of years following registration.

In some countries (like the United States prior to 1989), marks must be used on goods before registration. In others, like France, use is not required and speculative registration of marks can occur. It is said that ESSO was obliged to purchase French trademark rights from such a speculator when it switched to EXXON in its search for the perfect global trademark. Since 1989, U.S. law has allowed applications when there is a bona fide intent to use a trademark within 12 months and, if there is good cause for the delay in actual usage, up to 24 additional months. Such filings in effect reserve the mark for the applicant. The emphasis on bona fide intent and good cause represent an attempt to control any speculative use of U.S. trademark law.

The scope of trademark protection may differ substantially from country to country. Under U.S. federal trademark law, injunctions, damages and seizures of goods by customs officials may follow infringement. Other jurisdictions may provide similar remedies on their law books, but offer little practical enforcement. Thus, trademark registration is no guarantee against trademark piracy. A pair of blue jeans labeled "Levi Strauss made in San Francisco" may have been counterfeited in Israel or Paraguay without the knowledge or consent of Levi Strauss and in spite of its trademark registrations in those countries. Trademark counterfeiting is not just a third world problem, as any visitor to a U.S. "flea market" can tell. Congress created criminal offenses and private treble damages remedies for the first time in the Trademark Counterfeiting Act of 1984.

In many countries trademarks (appearing on goods) may be distinguished from "service marks" used by providers of services (e.g., The Law Store), "trade names" (business names), "collective marks" (marks used by a group or organization), and "certification marks" (marks which certify a certain quality, origin, or other fact). Although national trademark schemes differ, it can be said generally that a valid trademark (e.g., a mark not "canceled," "renounced," "abandoned," "waived" or "generic") will be protected against infringing use. A trademark can be valid in one country (ASPIRIN brand tablets in Canada), but invalid because generic in another (BAYER brand aspirin in the United States).

Unlike patents and copyrights, trademarks may be renewed continuously. A valid mark may be licensed, perhaps to a "registered user" or it may be assigned, in some cases only with the sale of the goodwill of a business. A growing example of international licensing of trademarks can be found in franchise agreements taken abroad. And national trademark law sometimes accompanies international licensing. The principal U.S. trademark law, the Lanham Act of 1946, has been construed to apply extraterritorially (much like the Sherman Antitrust Act) to foreign licensees engaging in deceptive practices.

Foreigners who seek a registration may be required to prove a prior and valid "home registration," and a new registration in another country may not have an existence "independent" of the continuing validity of the home country registration. Foreigners are often assisted in their registration efforts by international and regional trademark treaties.

INTERNATIONAL RECOGNITION OF TRADEMARKS

The premium placed on priority of use of a trademark is reflected in several international trademark treaties. These include the Paris Convention, the 1957 Arrangement of Nice Concerning the International Classification of Goods and Services, and the 1973 Trademark Registration Treaty done at Vienna. The treaties of widest international application are the Paris Convention and the Arrangement of Nice, as revised to 1967, to which the United States is signatory. The International Bureau of WIPO plays a central role in the administration of arrangements contemplated by these agreements.

The Paris Convention reflects an effort to internationalize some trademark rules. In addition to extending the principle of national treatment in Article 2 and providing for a right of priority of six months for trademarks (see patent discussion ante), the Convention mitigates the frequent national requirement that foreigners seeking trademark registration prove a pre-existing, valid and continuing home registration. This makes it easier to obtain foreign trademark registrations, avoids the possibility that a lapse in registration at home will cause all foreign registrations to become invalid, and allows registration abroad of entirely different (and perhaps culturally adapted) marks. Article 6 bis of the Paris Convention gives owners of "well known" trademarks the right to block or cancel the unauthorized registration of their marks. One issue that frequently arises under this provision is whether the mark needs to be well known locally or just internationally to obtain protection.

The Nice Agreement addresses the question of registration by "class" or "classification" of goods. In order to simplify internal administrative procedures relating to marks, many countries classify and thereby identify goods (and sometimes services) which have the same or similar attributes. An applicant seeking registration of a mark often is required to specify the class or classes to which the product mark belongs. However, not all countries have the same classification system and some lack any such system. Article 1 of the Nice Agreement adopts, for the purposes of the registration of marks, a single classification system for goods and services. This has brought order out of chaos in the field.

The 1973 Vienna Trademark Registration Treaty (to which the United States is a signatory) contemplates an international filing and examination scheme like that in force for patents under the Patent Cooperation Treaty. This treaty has not yet been fully implemented, but holds out the promise of reduced costs and greater uniformity when obtaining international trademark protection. Numerous European and Mediterranean countries are parties to the Madrid Agreement for International Registration of Marks (1891, as amended). Since 2002, the United States has joined in the Madrid Protocol of 1989. This Protocol permits international filings to obtain about 60 national trademark rights and is administered by WIPO. A Common Market trademark has been developed by the European Union, an alternative to national trademark registrations and the "principle of territoriality" underlying IP laws.

COPYRIGHT PROTECTION

Nearly one hundred nations recognize some form of copyright protection for "authors' works." The scope of this coverage and available remedies varies from country to country, with some uniformity established in the roughly 80 nations participating in the Berne and Universal Copyright Conventions (below). In the United States, for example, the Copyright Act of 1976 protects all original expressions fixed in a tangible medium (now known or later developed), including literary works, musical works, dramatic works, choreographic works, graphic works, audiovisual works, sound recordings, computer programs and selected databases. It is not necessary to publish a work to obtain a U.S. copyright. It is sufficient that the work is original and fixed in a tangible medium of expression. Prior to 1989, to retain a U.S. copyright, the author had to give formal notice of a reservation of rights when publishing the work. Publication of the work without such notice no longer dedicates it to free public usage.

U.S. copyright protection now extends from creation of the work to 70 years after the death of the author. The author also controls "derivative works," such as movies made from books. Only the author (or her assignees or employer in appropriate cases) may make copies, display, perform, and first sell the work. Registration with the U.S. Copyright Office is not required to obtain copyright rights, but is important to federal copyright infringement remedies. Infringers are subject to criminal penalties, injunctive relief and civil damages. Infringing works are impounded pending trial and ultimately destroyed. But educators, critics and news reporters are allowed "fair use" of the work, a traditional common law doctrine now codified in the 1976 Copyright Act.

The marketing of copyrights is sometimes accomplished through agency "clearinghouses." This is especially true of musical compositions because the many authors and potential users are dispersed. In the United States, the American Society of Composers, Authors and Publishers (ASCAP) and Broadcast Music, Inc. (BMI) are the principal clearinghouses for such rights. Thousands of these rights are sold under "blanket licenses" for fees established by the clearinghouses and later distributed to their members. Similar organizations exist in most European states. Their activities have repeatedly been scrutinized under U.S. and EU antitrust law. A Joint International Copyright Information Service run since 1981 by WIPO and UNESCO is designed to promote licensing of copyrights in the third world. This Service does not act as an agency clearinghouse for authors' rights, a deficiency sometimes said to promote copyright piracy.

Copyright protection in other countries may be more or less comprehensive or capable of adaptation to modern technologies. The copyrightability of computer programs, for example, is less certain in many jurisdictions. In some developing countries, "fair use" is a theme which is expansively construed to undermine copyright protection. But these differences seem less significant when contrasted with the worldwide problem of copyright piracy, ranging from satellite signal poaching to unlicensed music and books.

In the United States, the Copyright Felony Act of 1992 criminalized all copyright infringements. The No Electronic Theft Act of 1997 (NET) removed the need to prove financial gain as element of copyright infringement law, thus ensuring coverage of copying done with intent to harm copyright owners or copying simply for personal use. The Digital Millennium Copyright Act of 1998 (DMCA) brought the United States into compliance with WIPO treaties and created two new copyright offenses; one for circumventing technological measures used by copyright owners to protect their works ("hacking") and a second for tampering with copyright management information (encryption). The DMCA also made it clear that "webmasters" digitally broadcasting music on the internet must pay performance royalties.

INTERNATIONAL RECOGNITION OF COPYRIGHTS

Absent an appropriate convention, copyright registrations must be tediously acquired in each country recognizing such rights. However, copyright holders receive national treatment, translation rights and other benefits under the Universal Copyright Convention (UCC) of 1952 (U.S. adheres). Most importantly, the UCC *excuses* foreigners from registration requirements provided notice of a claim of copyright is adequately given (e.g., © Folsom, Gordon, Spanogle, and Van Alstine, 2012). Some countries like the United States took advantage of an option *not* to excuse registration requirements. The exercise of this option had the effect at that time of reinforcing the U.S. "manufacturing clause" requiring local printing of U.S. copyrighted books and prohibiting importation of foreign copies. This protectionist clause finally expired under U.S. copyright law in 1986. The UCC establishes a minimum term for copyright protection: 25 years after publication, prior registration or death of the author. It also authorizes compulsory license schemes for translation rights in all states and compulsory reprint rights and instructional usage in developing countries.

National treatment and a release from registration formalities (subject to copyright notice requirements) can be obtained in Pan-American countries under the Mexico City Convention of 1902 and the Buenos Aires Convention of 1911, the United States adhering to both. Various benefits can be had in many other countries through the Berne Convention of 1886 (as revised). Like the UCC, the Berne Convention suspends registration requirements for copyright holders from participating states. Unlike the UCC, it allows for local copyright protection independent of protection granted in the country of origin and does not require copyright notice. The Berne Convention establishes a minimum copyright term of the life of the author plus 50 years, a more generous minimum copyright than that of the UCC. It also recognizes the exclusive translation rights of authors. The Berne Convention does not contemplate compulsory licensing of translation rights. Most U.S. copyright holders previously acquired Berne Convention benefits by simultaneously publishing their works in Canada, a member country.

In 1989, the United States ratified the Berne Convention. U.S. ratification of the Berne Convention creates copyright relations with an additional 25 nations. Ratification has eliminated U.S. registration requirements (reserved under the UCC) for foreign copyright holders and required protection of the "moral rights" of authors, i.e. the rights of integrity and paternity. The right of paternity insures acknowledgment of authorship. The right of integrity conveys the ability to object to distortion, alteration or other derogation of the work. It is generally thought that unfair competition law at the federal and state levels will provide the legal basis in U.S. law for these moral rights. A limited class of visual artists explicitly receive these rights under the Visual Artists Rights Act of 1990.

FRANCHISING IN THE UNITED STATES

Franchising is an important sector in the U.S. economy. Thousands of franchisors have created and administer franchise systems throughout the nation. U.S. franchisees number in the hundreds of thousands. These franchisees are typically independent business persons, and their local franchise outlets employ millions of people. It has been estimated that approximately one-third of all retail sales in the United States take place through franchised outlets. Just as U.S. franchisors have found franchising particularly effective for market penetration abroad, Canadian, European and Japanese companies are increasingly penetrating the U.S. market through franchising.

Franchising is a business technique that permits rapid and flexible penetration of markets, growth and capital development. In the United States, there are traditional distinctions between product franchises and business format franchises. Product franchises involve manufacturers who actually produce the goods that are distributed through franchise agreements. For example, ice cream stores, soft drink bottling companies and gasoline retailers are often the subject of product franchises. Business format franchises are more common. These do not involve the manufacture by the franchisor of the product being sold by the franchisee. More typically, the franchisor licenses intellectual property rights in conjunction with a particular "formula for success" of the business. Fast food establishments, hotels, and a variety of service franchises are examples of business format franchising.

U.S. regulation of franchise relationships occurs at both the federal and state levels of government. Such regulation can be as specific as the Federal Trade Commission Franchising Rule and state franchise disclosure duties or as amorphous as the ever present dangers of state and federal antitrust law.

INTERNATIONAL FRANCHISING

International franchising raises a host of legal issues under intellectual property, antitrust, tax, licensing and other laws. The significance of these issues is magnified by the rapid growth of international franchising. Many U.S. franchisors start in Canada, with Japan and Britain following. Some U.S. investors have found franchising the least risky and most popular way to enter Central and Eastern Europe. U.S. franchising in China is expanding rapidly. Franchising is not just a U.S. export. Many foreign franchisors have entered the U.S. market.

Most franchisors have standard contracts which are used in their home markets and receive counsel on the myriad of laws relevant to their business operations. Such contracts need to be revised and adapted to international franchising without significantly altering the franchisor's successful business formula. Franchise fees and royalties must be specified, the provision of services, training, and control by the franchisor detailed, the term and area of the franchise negotiated ("master franchises" conveying rights in an entire country or region are common in international franchise agreements), accounting procedures agreed upon, business standards and advertising selected, insurance obtained, taxes and other liabilities allocated, and default and dispute settlement procedures decided. At the heart of all franchise agreements lies a trademark licensing clause conveying local trademark rights of the franchisor to the franchisee in return for royalty payments.

Were franchising unaffected by regulation, the attorney's role would be limited to negotiation and drafting of the agreement. But international franchising is increasingly regulated by home and host jurisdictions, including regional groups like the EU. In third world countries, especially Latin America, technology transfer laws, aimed principally at international patent and knowhow licensing, also regulate franchise agreements. These laws benefit franchisees and further development policies, e.g., conservation of hard currencies by control of royalty levels. In 1986, the European Court of Justice issued its first major opinion on the legality of franchise agreements under competition law. The *Pronuptia* decision indicates that European law can depart significantly from leading American antitrust law on market division arrangements for distributors. The Europeans subsequently implemented a comprehensive regulation on franchise agreements, which in turn was replaced by the EU "vertical restraints" Regulation No. 330/10.

There is often a perception of being invaded culturally that follows franchising. Local laws sometimes respond to the cultural impact of foreign franchises, as when McDonald's wishes to introduce its large golden arch into the traditional architecture of Europe. But this did not stop McDonald's from opening in Moscow with great success. In India and Mexico, nationalist feelings hostile to the appearance of foreign trademarks on franchised products have produced laws intended to remove such usage. For example, the Mexican Law of Inventions and Tradenames (1976, repealed 1987) anticipated requiring use of culturally Mexican marks in addition to marks of foreign origin. Other nations require local materials (olive oil in the Mediterranean) to be substituted. This could, for example, alter the formula for success (and value) of fast food franchises. Still others (e.g., Alberta, Canada) mandate extensive disclosures by franchisors in a registered prospectus before agreements may be completed. Disclosure violations can trigger a range of franchisee remedies: rescission, injunction, and damages. Such laws are also found in many of the American states.

Franchise advertising must conform to local law. For example, regulations in the People's Republic of China prohibit ads which "have reactionary . . . content." Antitrust and tax law are important in international franchising. Double taxation treaties, for example, will affect the level of taxation of royalties. Antitrust law will temper purchasing requirements of the franchisor, lest unlawful "tying arrangements" be undertaken. Tying arrangements involve coercion of franchisees to take supplies from the franchisor or designated sources in return for the franchise. Such arrangements must, by definition, involve two products: the tying and tied products. They are subject to a complex, not entirely consistent, body of case law under the U.S. Sherman Antitrust Act, Articles 101 and 102 of the Treaty on the Functioning of the European Union (TFEU) and other laws.

For example, U.S. antitrust case law on franchise tying arrangements is quite diverse. One decision treats the trademark license as a separate tying product and the requirement of the purchase by fast food franchisees of non-essential cooking equipment and paper products unlawful. Another case permits franchisors to require franchisees to purchase "core products" (e.g., chicken) subject to detailed specifications, or from a designated list of approved sources. Sometimes, the "core product" (e.g., ice cream) and the trademark license (e.g., Baskin-Robbins) are treated as a single product incapable of being tied in violation of the law. Still another leading case involving McDonald's suggests that anything comprising the franchisor's "formula for success" may possibly be tied in the franchise contract. This may be especially lawful if there was full pre-contract disclosure by the franchisor.

INTERNATIONAL PATENT AND KNOWHOW LICENSING

This section concerns the most common form of lawful international technology transfer-patent and knowhow licensing. Before any patent licensing can take place, patents must be acquired in all countries in which the owner hopes there will be persons interested in purchasing the technology. Even in countries where the owner has no such hope, patent rights may still be obtained so as to foreclose future unlicensed competitors. Licensing is a middle ground alternative to exporting from the owner's home country and direct investment in host markets. It can often produce, with relatively little cost, immediate positive cash flows.

International patent and knowhow licensing is the most critical form of technology transfer to third world development. From the owner's standpoint, it presents an alternative to and sometimes a first step towards foreign investment. Such licensing involves a transfer of patent rights or knowhow (commercially valuable knowledge, often falling short of a patentable invention) in return for payments, usually termed royalties. Unlike foreign investment, licensing does not have to involve a capital investment in a host jurisdiction. However, licensing of patents and knowhow is not without legal risks.

From the licensee's standpoint, and the perspective of its government, there is the risk that the licensed technology may be old or obsolete, not "state of the art." Goods produced under old technology will be hard to export and convey a certain "second class" status. On the other hand, older more labor intensive technologies may actually be sought (as sometimes done by the PRC) in the early stages of development. Excessive royalties may threaten the economic viability of the licensee and drain hard currencies from the country. The licensee typically is not in a sufficiently powerful position to bargain away restrictive features of standard international licenses. For all these reasons, and more, third world countries frequently regulate patent and knowhow licensing agreements. Such law is found in the Brazilian Normative Act No. 17 (1976) and the Mexican Technology Transfer Law (1982, repealed 1991), among others. Royalty levels will be limited, certain clauses prohibited (e.g., export restraints, resale price maintenance, mandatory grantbacks to the licensor of improvements), and the desirability of the technology evaluated.

Regulation of patent and knowhow licensing agreements is hardly limited to the third world. The Common Market, for example, after several test cases before the European Court of Justice, issued a "block exemption" controlling patent licensing agreements. Many of the licensing agreement clauses controlled by this 1984 Regulation were the same as those covered by third world technology transfer legislation. Its successors, Regulations 240 of 1996 and 772 of 2004, broadly cover technology transfer agreements (including, since 2004, software copyright licensing). EU regulation prohibits production restraints, forbids the fixing of retail prices for the licensed product by the licensor, limits the licensor's power to select to whom the licensee may sell, controls the "grant back" of product improvements and determines the licensee's right to challenge the validity of intellectual property. It also affects exclusive licensing arrangements, the allocation of geographic territories among licensees, trademark usage, tying arrangements, fields of use, the duration of the license, quality controls, and discrimination between licensees by the licensor. Regulation of patent, knowhow and software copyright licensing in the United States is less direct and predominantly the concern of patent and antitrust law (e.g., tying practices).

The licensor also faces legal risks. The flow of royalty payments may be stopped, suspended or reduced by currency exchange regulations. The taxation of the royalties, if not governed by double taxation treaties, may be confiscatory. The licensee may produce "gray market" goods (*infra*) which eventually compete for sales in markets exclusively intended for the licensor. In the end, patents expire and become part of the world domain. At that point, the licensee has effectively purchased the technology and becomes an independent competitor (though not necessarily an effective competitor if the licensor has made new technological advances).

Licensing is a kind of partnership. If the licensee succeeds, the licensor's royalties (often based on sales volumes) will increase and a continuing partnership through succeeding generations of technology may evolve. If not, the dispute settlement provisions of the agreement may be called upon as either party withdraws from the partnership. Licensing of patents and knowhow often is combined with, indeed essential to, foreign investments. A foreign subsidiary or joint venture will need technical assistance and knowhow to commence operations. When this occurs, the licensing terms are usually a part of the basic joint venture or investment agreement. Licensing may also be combined with a trade agreement, as where the licensor ships necessary supplies to the licensee, joint venturer, or subsidiary. Such supply agreements have sometimes been used to overcome royalty limitations through a form of "transfer pricing," the practice of marking up or down the price of goods so as to allocate revenues to preferred parties and jurisdictions (e.g., tax havens).

PROTECTION FROM PIRACY

Theft of intellectual property and use of counterfeit goods are rapidly increasing in developing and developed countries. Such theft is not limited to consumer goods (Pierre Cardin clothing, Rolex watches). Industrial products and parts (e.g., automotive brake pads) are now being counterfeited. Some developing countries see illegal technology transfers as part of their economic development. They encourage piracy or choose not to oppose it. Since unlicensed producers pay no royalties, they often have lower production costs than the original source. This practice fuels the fires of intellectual property piracy. Unlicensed low cost reproduction of entire copyrighted books (may it not happen to this book) is said to be rampant in such diverse areas as Nigeria, Saudi Arabia, and China. Apple computers have been inexpensively counterfeited in Hong Kong. General Motors estimates that about 40 percent of its auto parts are counterfeited in the Middle East. Recordings and tapes are duplicated almost everywhere without license or fee. And the list goes on.

Section 337 Proceedings

Legal protection against intellectual property theft and counterfeit goods is not very effective. In the United States, trademark and copyright holders may register with the Customs Service and seek the blockade of pirated items made abroad. Such exclusions are authorized in the Lanham Trademark Act of 1946 and the Copyright Act of 1976. Patent piracy is most often challenged in proceedings against unfair import practices under Section 337 of the Tariff Act of 1930. Section 337 proceedings traditionally involve some rather complicated provisions in Section 1337 of the Tariff Act of 1930. Prior to 1988, the basic prohibition was against: (1) unfair methods of competition and unfair acts in the importation of goods, (2) the effect or tendency of which is to destroy or substantially injure (3) an industry efficiently and economically operated in the United States Such importation was also prohibited when it prevented the establishment of an industry, or restrained or monopolized trade and commerce in the United States.

The Omnibus Trade and Competitiveness Act of 1988 revised Section 337. The requirement that the U.S. industry be efficiently and economically operated was dropped. The importation of articles infringing U.S. patents, copyrights, trademarks or semiconductor chip mask works is specifically prohibited provided a U.S. industry relating to such articles exists or is in the process of being established. Proof of injury to a domestic industry is not required in intellectual property infringement cases. Such an industry exists if there is significant plant and equipment investment, significant employment of labor or capital, or substantial investment in exploitation (including research and development or licensing).

Determination of violations and the recommendation of remedies to the President under Section 337 is the exclusive province of the International Trade Commission (ITC). Most of the case law under Section 337 concerns the infringement of patents. While not quite a per se rule, it is nearly axiomatic that any infringement of U.S. patent rights amounts to an unfair import practice for purposes of Section 337. Section 337 proceedings result in general exclusion orders permitting seizure of patent counterfeits at any U.S. point of entry. However, the Customs Service finds it extremely difficult when inspecting invoices and occasionally opening boxes to ascertain which goods are counterfeit or infringing. Many counterfeits do look like "the real thing."

For most seizure remedies to work, the holder must notify the customs service of an incoming shipment of offending goods. Use of private detectives can help and is increasing, but such advance notice is hard to obtain. Nevertheless, the Customs Service seizes millions of counterfeit goods each year. In 2009, U.S. officials seized about $260 million in counterfeit goods. Chinese gangs accounted for the bulk of these goods, which were most often footwear, consumer electronics, luxury goods and pharmaceuticals. U.S. military and civilian procurement agencies have begun actively targeting counterfeit suppliers. An Anti-Counterfeiting Trade Agreement (ACTA) is in the works, though China is not expected to participate.

Patent-based Section 337 proceedings are multiplying. ITC decisions take about 12 to 15 months, versus three to five years for federal court lawsuits. General exclusion orders are typically sought. Hearings are held before one of four administrative law judges specializing in patent law, with final decisions taken by the ITC. Infringing products are excluded from importation during the appeals process. About one-fourth of all 337 proceedings find infringements.

An increasing number of foreign owners of U.S. patents are invoking 337 procedures. About half of all such complaints are settled, often using cross-licensing among the parties.

In 2007, in a major decision, the ITC excluded the importation of cell phones containing Qualcomm microchips found to infringe Broadcom patents. In 2011, Apple obtained an exclusion order against patent-infringing Android phones. Invocation of Section 337 in patent disputes will be influenced by the U.S. Supreme Court's ruling in *KSR International Co. v. Teleflex, Inc.* (April 30, 2007) where it unanimously held that a patent combining pre-existing elements is invalid if the combination is no "more than the predictable use of prior art elements according to their established functions" (obvious). *Likewise, the Supreme Court's cautious consideration of business method process in Bilski v. Kappos (June 28, 2010) will influence section 337 disputes.*

National and International Remedies

Infringement and treble damages actions may be commenced in U.S. courts against importers and distributors of counterfeit goods, but service of process and jurisdictional barriers often preclude effective relief against foreign pirates. Even if such relief is obtained, counterfeiters and the sellers of counterfeit goods have proven adept at the "shell game," moving across the road or to another country to resume operations. Moreover, the mobility and economic incentives of counterfeiters have rendered the criminal sanctions of the Trademark Counterfeiting Act of 1984 largely a Pyrrhic victory. Ex parte seizure orders are also available under the 1984 Act and the Lanham Trademark Act when counterfeit goods can be located in the United States. Goods so seized can be destroyed upon court order.

International solutions have been no less elusive. The WTO agreement on TRIPs addresses these problems by mandating certain national remedies, but their effectiveness remains to be tested. Various U.S. statutes authorize the President to withhold trade benefits from or apply trade sanctions to nations inadequately protecting the intellectual property rights of U.S. citizens. This is true of the Caribbean Basin Economic Recovery Act of 1983, the Generalized System of Preferences Renewal Act of 1984, the Trade and Tariff Act of 1984 (amending Section 301 of the 1974 Trade Act), and Title IV of the 1974 Trade Act as it applies to most favored nation tariffs. Slowly this carrot and stick approach has borne fruit. Under these pressures for example, Singapore drafted a new copyright law, Korea new patent and copyright laws, and Taiwan a new copyright, patent, fair trade and an amended trademark law. Brazil introduced legislation intended to allow copyrights on computer programs. Though these changes have been made, there is some doubt as to the rigor with which the new laws will be enforced when local jobs and national revenues are lost.

France and Italy have made it illegal to knowingly purchase counterfeit goods. For example, if a student buys a "Louis Vuitton" bag for $15 in a Paris or Florence flea market, he or she may be arrested, fined and imprisoned. France has gone a step further. A new agency monitors Internet piracy. French offenders are subject to a "three strikes" rule: Two warnings are issued before Net accesses can be terminated and fines imposed by court order. South Korea and Taiwan also employ warnings and penalties against illegal downloading.

GRAY MARKET GOODS

One of the most controversial areas of customs law concerns "gray market goods," goods produced abroad *with authorization* and payment but which are imported into *unauthorized* markets. Trade in gray market goods has dramatically increased in recent years, in part because fluctuating currency exchange rates create opportunities to import and sell such goods at a discount from local price levels. Licensors and their distributors suddenly find themselves competing in their home or other "reserved" markets with products made abroad by their own licensees. Or, in the reverse, startled licensees find their licensor's products intruding on their local market shares. In either case, third party importers and exporters are often the immediate source of the gray market goods, and they have little respect for who agreed to what in the licensing agreement. When pressed, such third parties will undoubtedly argue that any attempt through licensing at allocating markets or customers is an antitrust or competition law violation.

In the early part of the century, gray market litigation provoked a Supreme Court decision in *A. Bourjois & Co. v. Katzel*, 260 U.S. 689 (1923) blocking French cosmetics from entering the United States. A U.S. firm was assigned the U.S. trademark rights for French cosmetics as part of the sale of the American business interests of the French producer. The assignee successfully obtained infringement relief against Katzel, an importer of the French product benefitting from exchange rate fluctuations. The Supreme Court reversed a Second Circuit holding which followed a line of cases allowing "genuine goods" to enter the American market in competition with established sources. The Supreme Court emphasized the trademark ownership (not license) and independent public good will of the assignee as reasons for its reversal.

Genuine Goods Exclusion Act

Congress, before the Supreme Court reversal, passed the Genuine Goods Exclusion Act, now appearing as Section 526 of the Tariff Act of 1930. This Act bars *unauthorized importation* of goods bearing trademarks of U.S. citizens. Registration of such marks with the Customs Service can result in the seizure of unauthorized imports. Persons dealing in such imports may be enjoined, required to export the goods, destroy them or obliterate the offending mark, as well as pay damages. The Act has had a checkered history in the courts and Customs Service. The Customs Service view (influenced by antitrust policy) was that genuine (gray market) goods may be excluded only when the foreign and U.S. trademark rights are not under common ownership, or those rights have been used without authorization. The practical effect of this position was to admit most gray market goods into the United States, thereby providing substantial price competition, but uncertain coverage under manufacturers' warranty, service and rebate programs. Some firms, like K Mart, excel at gray market importing and may provide independent warranty and repair service contracts. Since 1986, New York and California require disclosure by sellers of gray market goods that manufacturers' programs may not apply.

A split in the federal courts of appeal as to the legitimacy in light of the Genuine Goods Exclusion Act of the Customs Service position on gray market imports resulted in a U.S. Supreme Court ruling. In an extremely technical, not very policy oriented decision, the Supreme Court in *K Mart Corp. v. Cartier, Inc.*, 486 U.S. 281 (1988) arrived at a compromise. The Customs Service can continue to permit entry of genuine goods when common ownership of the trademarks exists. The Service must seize such goods only when they were authorized (licensed), but the marks are not subject to common ownership. Many believe that the bulk of U.S. imports of gray market goods have continued under this ruling.

Other Gray Market Remedies

An attempt in 1985 by Duracell to exclude gray market batteries under Section 337 of the Tariff Act of 1930 as an unfair import practice was upheld by the U.S. International Trade Commission, but denied relief by President Reagan in deference to the Customs Service position.

Injunctive relief under trademark or copyright law is sometimes available against gray market importers and distributors. In *Quality King Distributors, Inc. v. L'anza Research Intern., Inc.*, 523 U.S. 135 (1998),however, the U.S. Supreme Court held that the "first sale doctrine" bars injunctive relief under the Copyright Act against gray market re-importation of U.S. exports. But in *Costco Wholesale Corp. v. Omega S.A., _U.S._(2010) affirming by tie vote 541 F.3d 982 (9th Cir. 2008),* the Supreme Court allowed copyright injunctive relief against foreign-made gray market goods. In *Lever Bros.*, the D.C. Circuit allowed Trademark Act injunctive relief against materially different gray market goods where those differences had not been disclosed in labeling. When available, injunctive relief applies only to the parties and does not prohibit gray market imports or sales by others. This remedy is thus useful, but normally insufficient.

Most foreign jurisdictions permit entry of gray market goods. The use of intellectual property rights to block trade in gray market ("parallel") goods within the Common Market has been repeatedly denied by the European Court of Justice in its competition and customs law rulings. Once authorized goods reach the market and title has passed to others, intellectual property rights in them are said as a matter of European law to be "exhausted." But under the *Silhouette v. Hartlauer* opinion of the European Court of Justice intellectual property rights can be used to block the importation of gray market goods from outside the Common Market. In other words, the exhaustion doctrine does not apply externally. Levi Strauss, for example, has seized upon this distinction to actively pursue EU importers of blue jeans from non-EU sources.

TRANSBORDER DATA FLOWS

Because information transfers are linked with employment and trade patterns, many countries have taken a keen interest in regulating trans-border data flows (TBDFs). Technical strides in satellite communications and the digital age make regulation a challenge. In 1981, the OECD approved fourteen principles as Guidelines on the Protection of Privacy and TransBorder Flow of Personal Data. In 1998, Europe finalized a data privacy directive that is noticeably more protective of individual privacy than U.S. law. Any information relating to natural persons must be secure, current, relevant and not excessive in content. In most cases, personal data may be processed only with individual consent. Individuals have broad rights of disclosure, access, correction and erasure of data, particularly before it is used in direct marketing.

Transfers of data to non-EU countries are prohibited unless the recipient jurisdiction provides an "adequate level of protection." Whether the United States does so is hotly debated. To remove risks of liability under the European law, "safe harbors" have been created by EU-USA agreement for firms willing to abide by the EU rules on data privacy. The primary safe harbor involves participation in self-regulating privacy groups (e.g., BBB Online) supervised by the U.S. Federal Trade Commission. EU law on data privacy has thus become a global industry standard.

SPECIAL 301 PROCEDURES

Extensive negotiations were conducted within the GATT under the Uruguay Round on trade-related intellectual property rights (TRIPs). The developed nations sought an Anti-Counterfeiting Code and greater patent, copyright and trademark protection in the third world. The developing nations resisted on nearly all fronts. The TRIPs negotiations failed to reach a conclusion as scheduled in December of 1990. Meanwhile, faced with massive technology transfer losses, "Special 301" procedures were established unilaterally by the United States in the 1988 Omnibus Trade and Competitiveness Act. These procedures are located in Section 182 of the Trade Act of 1974. They can lead to initiation of Section 301 proceedings under that Act. Section 301 proceedings are generally used to obtain market access for U.S. exporters of goods and services, but are also capable of being used to pressure and perhaps sanction other nations whose intellectual property policies diverge from U.S. standards.

Special 301 requires the U.S. Trade Representative (USTR) to identify those countries that deny "adequate and effective protection of intellectual property rights" or deny "fair and equitable market access to U.S. persons who rely upon intellectual property protection." The USTR must also identify "priority foreign countries" whose practices are the most "onerous or egregious" and have the greatest adverse impact on the United States, and who are not entering into good faith negotiations or making significant progress in negotiations towards provision of adequate and effective protection of intellectual property rights.

The USTR developed "watch lists" and "priority watch lists" under Special 301 while pursuing negotiations with the many nations on those lists. These negotiations had some success. Argentina agreed, as a result of Special 301 negotiations, to modify registration procedures for and improve protection of pharmaceuticals under its patent law. Mexico was removed from priority status on the Special 301 watch list after it announced new patent legislation. This legislation increased the term of Mexican patents to 20 years, offered protection for chemical and pharmaceutical products as well as biotechnology processes, restricted use of compulsory licenses and made improvements to the Mexican law of trademarks and trade secrets. Intellectual property reforms in Korea, Taiwan and Saudi Arabia also removed them from the USTR's priority watch list.

India, Thailand and the People's Republic of China were formally named the first priority Special 301 countries. Naming any country under Special 301 triggers the possibility of unilateral U.S. trade sanctions under Section 301 of the Trade Act of 1974. Early in 1992, the United States and the PRC reached a last minute agreement on intellectual reforms in the PRC. This agreement avoided trade sanctions. In recent years, China and Russia were priority watch listed, again with a focus on protection of intellectual property rights. China has been repeatedly cited on a new "Notorious Markets List".

To a large degree, the potential for Special 301 trade sanctions has been diluted by U.S. participation in the World Trade Organization Agreement on TRIPs. Since 1995, nearly all U.S. intellectual property complaints have gone to WTO dispute settlement, a subject covered in our *International Trade and Economic Relations* Nutshell. The Special 301 "naming" and "watching" process, however, continues in full force.

CHAPTER 5

FOREIGN INVESTMENT
TRANSACTIONS

DEFINING THE FOREIGN INVESTMENT

Investment commonly involves the *ownership* of some of the equity in a business. Depending on the amount of ownership, it may also involve *control*. Ownership and control issues are often complex, especially in cross-border situations, as, for example, when a corporation chartered in one nation has its center of management in a second nation and its owners (shareholders) are citizens of a third nation. While identifying the nation of the corporation's articles of incorporation (charter) is usually easy, it may not be easy to determine who owns or controls the entity, or even where that control occurs. Where an investor owns all the equity in the foreign investment, there is usually little question regarding who has ownership and control. But as the equity percentage owned by the foreign investor diminishes, who has control may be less certain. Ownership of a majority of the voting equity of the foreign entity *usually* means the entity is a subsidiary under the control of the investor.

If an investor from abroad has exactly half the equity, who has control may be quite uncertain. No one has control solely by virtue of ownership of 50 percent, but one of the 50 percent owners may be able to exert control. It may depend on the ability to control proxies, if such method of voting is permitted. Where the ownership is less than 50 percent, often true of a joint venture where the foreign owner is limited to 49 percent equity, control is quite likely to be the result not of the equity split, but due to some form of management agreement. Few multinational corporations having foreign investments in many nations are willing to hold 49 percent equity without very substantial participation in management, if not assurance of absolute control.

Restrictions on control and ownership are most likely to be part of a developing or nonmarket economy nation's foreign investment legal and policy framework. As developing and transitional nations join international trade organizations and regional economic groups, such as the WTO, EU or NAFTA, they are required to reduce or abolish restrictions on foreign investment. But often they are permitted to retain reservations that allow such mandated reductions or abolition to occur over long periods of time, or are even allowed to permanently retain limited restrictions.

BEYOND OWNERSHIP AND CONTROL

Ownership and control may define investment whether it is domestic or foreign. *Foreign* investment usually involves the ownership and control of some form of service or manufacturing industry that is located in another country. That country may be close geographically and similar in many ways, such as

Canada, or far away and different in many ways, such as Indonesia. The foreign investment may confront many new methods of living and working. Different legal systems may be involved, as may different languages, currencies, cultures, forms of doing business, concepts of legal practice, forms of labor participation and workers' rights, levels and forms of officer compensation, risks of expropriation, intrusiveness of government participation, attitudes towards democracy and socialism, standards of business dress and decorum, methods of finance and rules governing discrimination in the workplace. These differences, not merely the concepts of ownership and control, must be understood and dealt with for the foreign investment to succeed. A successful international business lawyer knows how to give advice on more than the different legal systems; non-legal advice may extend to any of the above areas, and more.

REASONS FOR ESTABLISHING A FOREIGN INVESTMENT

Foreign investments are initiated for many different reasons. Sometimes it is the natural succession to a successful period of increasing export sales to a foreign nation, when the company believes the foreign market is sufficiently large to justify foreign production. Local, foreign production will reduce transportation costs of finished products sold in the domestic market of the foreign nation, and will allow the use of local resources available at lower costs, especially labor. Foreign investment may follow immediately after a successful period of export sales, or follow a period of foreign production not by means of a direct equity investment, but by licensing the technology for foreign production to a domestic firm in the foreign nation. An example is the aircraft manufacturing industry. In order to assure participation in sales in the increasing Asian market, especially China, U.S. and European aircraft manufacturing companies have moved the manufacture of some parts to Asia, both by licensing and by new direct foreign investment. Sometimes it has involved countertrade.

The multinational company may dislike transferring technology to a company owned by a host nation party, whether due to a fear of loss of that technology, or an inability to control production quality. The fear of loss of the technology is of special concern when the technology consists of knowhow, which often lacks the more specific protection provided patents, trademarks and copyrights. Such fear is particularly well founded with respect to nations which do not afford very strong protection to intellectual property rights. Even if a transfer of technology license to an unrelated company in another nation has resulted in a profitable relationship, the technology owning multinational may prefer to establish a wholly or majority owned subsidiary to take over the production of the goods or services. The multinational may not wish to share in the profits with the licensee when it could do the production itself, and keep better control over production quality.

The foreign investment that follows export sales or a transfer of technology tends to be *voluntary* in the sense that the company makes the decision for business reasons, not because the framework of laws and policies of the foreign government require local production. In some cases, however, especially in developing nations with balance of payments problems, the government may make it very difficult, if not impossible, for other nations' businesses to export to the country. Tariffs, quotas and other nontariff barriers may be used both to reduce imports and the consequent demand for scarce foreign currency to pay for the imports, and also to offer considerable protection to domestic industries. The answer may be to establish a direct foreign investment. This would be to some degree an *involuntary* investment, in that it is not one of several alternatives available, but the only allowable form of doing business.

WHERE TO ESTABLISH THE FOREIGN INVESTMENT

Lawyers are not usually asked this question, but they may be asked if they can undertake a risk analysis of investing in several possible foreign locations. The legal climate may be the deciding factor in location. For example, a company may be interested in starting an investment in the European Union. One of the newer members may have attractive incentives such as lower labor costs. But what is the legal climate in such nations? Are there vestiges of the old socialism that will be hard to deal with? Are incentives likely to short-lived? Might the nation return to socialism? Or borrow so extensively that it cannot pay its debts and is in risk of collapse? If the investment is proposed for a market economy, will the nation retain that form? Can you predict the future for Venezuela better than for Hungary? Is there an unwritten law, or "operational code", that governs investment and differs from the written law? If so, does it differ very much, and is it more or less restrictive?

WHO GOVERNS FOREIGN INVESTMENT?

The expected source of governance is by the host nation where the affiliate or subsidiary is located. There may or may not be an express foreign investment law, but there will be many rules of governance such as the corporation or company law, labor law, environmental rules, bankruptcy laws and perhaps investment incentive programs. There are other sources of governance. The home nation may govern its multinationals' activities abroad, in such areas as antitrust, securities regulation, prohibitions of payments to foreign officials, export restrictions, and boycott or antiboycott rules. Additional regulation may be by multi-nation organizations, such as the United Nations, the EU, the NAFTA or the WTO, and also by international law. Foreign investment thus differs from domestic investment by the broader scope of sources of governance, as well as the diversity of approaches to different rules (e.g., mandatory joint ventures), and the uncertain status of alleged customary rules of international law (e.g., standards of compensation for expropriation).

RESTRICTIONS ON FOREIGN INVESTMENT AT VARIOUS STAGES

Some nations place numerous obstacles to approval of the establishment of a foreign investment. They occur at the stage of formation, during the operation of the business, and or during withdrawal. Restrictions may include mandatory joint ventures, export mandates, import substitution, use of a subsidiary rather than a branch, limits on the number of foreign employees or directors, and many other areas. Often once established there is little further restriction either during the operation or withdrawal of the investment that would not be expected of a domestic investment in the United States. Some nations make it easy to establish an investment but not easy to operate. Currency controls, increasingly shorter work weeks, workers' participation in management, and limits on profit transfers and payment for technology may reduce profit expectations. Finally, there may be severe restrictions on withdrawal, from inability to repatriate capital to difficult insolvency laws. Many of the "laws" may actually be unwritten policies that are difficult to know about in advance of actual application. Such issues are merely further examples of the challenges and risks of a foreign investment.

RESTRICTION ON FOREIGN INVESTMENT— DEVELOPING NATIONS

Until the early 1970s, there were comparatively few restrictions on foreign ownership in market economy developing nations. During the 1960s, many large multinationals expanded abroad by opening new plants or by acquiring locally owned enterprises. The acquisition of existing enterprises in developing nations generated concern and often hostility, and led to the adoption of laws in many developing nations regulating foreign investment. Those laws tended to have fairly common approaches to foreign investment. First, the acquisition of host nation enterprises was either limited or prohibited. Second, new investment was required to allow certain percentages of local equity participation. Some areas of investment, such as export oriented extractive industries, communications, transportation, banking, insurance and electricity, often were reserved for either exclusively state owned enterprises, or enterprises owned by nationals to the exclusion of all foreign participation. Other areas of business, those not expressly designated for the above limits, could have specific levels of participation by foreign investors. As in the case of the transfer of technology, a government agency had to approve acquisitions or new investment. The agency usually was allowed discretion in granting exceptions, and frequently the governing statutes provided a list of criteria for approving or disapproving the proposed investment. Common criteria, whether in those lists or in the unwritten policy of the approving agency, would include (1) assisting in generating economic development, (2) agreeing on the number of workers to be employed, (3) considering the effect on existing national businesses, (4) considering the effect on balance of payments, (5) mandating the use of domestic materials and parts, (6) requiring financing be obtained from abroad, (7) contributing to host nation acquisition of advanced technology, (8) locating the plant in designated development zones, and (9) establishing research and development facilities in the nation.

Investment laws were often supplemented by regulations, guidelines and decisions of foreign investment registration and review agencies. Frequently the decisions of review agencies were not made available to the public. But attorneys occasionally gained access to these decisions through personal contacts in the government, and counsel with such access were better able to assist in predicting how the agencies were likely to respond to applications for exceptions to the restrictive investment laws. What thus confronted potential investors in developing nations were not only the restrictive investment laws on the books, but written and unwritten guidelines and policies that generally moderated many of the restrictions.

Developing nation joint venture laws were quite different from joint venture laws in nonmarket economy nations. The latter were passed by nations which had long prohibited any foreign investment; new investment laws were intended to "attract" foreign investment, but initially only to a maximum level of 49 percent foreign ownership. Foreign equity was sometimes limited by constitutional provisions that placed the ownership of the means of production and distribution in the state. Developing nation joint venture laws, contrastingly, were intended to "restrict" new investment, and also to encourage, or coerce, existing wholly foreign owned investment to sell majority ownership to local individuals or entities owned by local investors or the state.

The laws were rarely retroactive by their terms, but they often contained features that made them retroactive in application. Sometimes the foreign investment law did not apply to existing companies, but a company could neither expand into new lines of products nor open new locations without converting the entire company to a joint venture. That meant reducing the foreign equity to no more than 49 percent. Devices were created by the foreign investors to avoid this impact, such as fragmenting the manufacturing of products, by adopting the joint venture for new subsidiaries producing new products, but keeping the old enterprise wholly foreign owned.

Accompanying the mandates for local ownership were similar requirements for local management. Where foreign equity was limited to 49 percent, that same percentage would apply to the number of foreigners allowed on the board. But a minority in *numbers* did not necessarily mean a minority in *influence*, and the local board members usually were motivated by the same profit goals as the foreign parent appointees. Nationalism might arise among the board members, however, if the parent wanted the foreign affiliate to shift production to another nation, or take any action that appeared to benefit the company's activities in another nation at the expense of the entity in the host nation.

Some developing countries, after several years of reasonable compliance with the host nation's restrictive rules by multinational enterprises, began to wonder why their nations had not increased their rates of development. No one gave much thought to the fact that developing nation private shareholders had the same aspirations to earn profit as developed nation shareholders, and developing nation directors acted in much the same way as their counterparts in developed nations. Shifting ownership from foreign to domestic was no guarantee of economic development in the nation as a whole. To encourage more investment, many nations with restrictive laws began to allow total foreign ownership under written or unwritten "exception" provisions. The foreign investor was allowed to retain total ownership if it transferred its most modern technology to the host nation, or located the proposed plant in an area of high unemployment or a zone designated for economic development, or exported a high percentage of its output, or located research and development facilities in the nation.

IBM is a good example of a company with a pragmatic approach to investment but with a firm *no equity joint venture* policy. In Mexico, IBM expanded production considerably even after the enactment of the strict Mexican foreign investment law in 1973, by agreeing to produce the most recent models and by exporting a high percentage of production. Contrastingly, when uncompromisingly told by the Indian government in the 1980s that it had to alter its Indian investment structure to an equity joint venture, with a majority Indian owned, IBM withdrew its investment. It later returned when the restrictive Indian rules were altered.

After (1) the debt crisis in the early 1980s, (2) the opening to investment by many *non*market economies in transition to market economies, and (3) the election of less "populist" governments in many developing nations, the rules of the game began to change dramatically in the 1980s and 1990s. Developing nations as well as nonmarket economies pushed aside the "myth of privatization" and began to take it seriously, selling off many state owned industries. Restrictive investment laws were interpreted in favor of foreign investors' wishes, and subsequently replaced by laws more encouraging than restrictive of investment. Even India seems determined to attract more foreign investment by relaxing its restrictions as the new century unfolded.

Foreign investment laws adopted since the 1980s usually allow total foreign ownership, but often restrict some areas for continued state ownership. Joint ventures are still encouraged, but when formed they tend to be more voluntary (e.g., tax motivated) than involuntary. Sometimes continuing restrictions on foreign ownership of land induces a joint venture, as might risk analysis which suggests limiting equity participation, even though market studies encourage entering the market.

The ability under local law to form a foreign investment is now less the issue than the method chosen. For the host nation, the initiation of a new investment ("greenfields" investing) may be preferred over the acquisition of an existing company, and a joint venture is sometimes preferred over total foreign ownership, although the foreign investor often is the one making the final choice. Many nations, including some developed nations (Canada, the United States, etc.), have some method of reviewing acquisitions, for such various reasons as national security or national economic interests.

Most developing nations encourage foreign investment to a greater degree than three-four decades ago, especially during the often hostile North-South dialogue era of the late 1960s and 1970s. A few nations have returned to restrictive policies, including Venezuela and Bolivia, resulting in a lessening of foreign investment. Most nations that were formerly hostile to foreign investment have become more receptive to investment than during that earlier troubled era. Essential to understand is that there is a *dynamic* process to investment attitudes among nations. The laws of a host nation in place at one time ought not to be viewed as representative of the legal framework likely to exist a decade or two in the future. Investors must be prophets *not* in their own land, and be aware than the dynamic process of economic and political development and change is the engine that pulls the train of rules regulating trade and investment.

RESTRICTIONS ON FOREIGH INVESTMENT—NONMARKET AND TRANSITION ECONOMY NATIONS

Nonmarket economy nations in many cases have also been developing nations. Thus nonmarket economy nations often have imposed limitations on the initiation of foreign investment that parallel those in developing nations. But there are differences in the restrictions due to the nature of a nonmarket economy. The restrictive rules on foreign investment were part of the political-economic Marxist philosophy adopted by most nonmarket economies, and expressed by the term *nonmarket economy*. But as those nations failed to achieve the levels of growth occurring in market economies, and failed to produce internally or acquire from abroad advanced technology, they began to trade with and then admit some limited foreign investment. When the wall between the market and nonmarket economies came down in the late 1980s, the rush to become market economies began in earnest.

Earlier, many nonmarket economies had attempted to obtain technology through transfers to local, state owned productive facilities. But they failed, usually because of inadequate legal protection of intellectual property. The lack of adequate protection was sometimes due to a stated belief that intellectual property was not subject to private ownership, but was the patrimony of mankind. Philosophical differences about ownership of the means of production and distribution persist even as nonmarket economies enter the transition to market economies. Often there are poor links of communication between foreign investors and the newly developing local business community. Labor has been vocal and sometimes well organized, and government ministries sometimes continue to be the negotiators or lobbyists for local, private business. Political interference is a continuing characteristic of investment in nonmarket economies. But it is a frustrating and elusive interference—the one who has the final say in the government is often "everyone and no-one".

Market economy nation companies do not wish to risk valuable technology and other intellectual property to Marxist principles of the patrimony of mankind. They would thus license technology only to wholly or majority owned subsidiaries, which local law often did not permit. Consequently, nonmarket economies were unable to gain access to very much advanced technology, because of their refusal to admit direct foreign equity investments, or provide protection to licensed technology. In the early 1970s, however, the desire for better technology pushed some of the rigid Marxist theory to the back burner in an ever increasing number of nonmarket economy nations.

Poland, Yugoslavia, Hungary and Romania each adopted joint venture laws, nevertheless limiting the foreign equity participation to 49 percent. Since the nonmarket economies did not have equity share corporations, nor corporation or company laws governing the formation and operation of such entities, the two principal incidents of share ownership, management participation and profits, necessarily had to be creations of the joint venture *contract* rather than share certificates. Profits often would be taken in the form of some percentage of the production, to be sold in Western markets. Called *compensation* or *buy-back* agreements, they are included under the umbrella of *countertrade.* These arrangements were not without difficulties, however, because the quality of nonmarket economy production was often poor, with high percentages of returns of unacceptable products. Furthermore, unless the parent company expanded its markets in the West, the nonmarket economy entity production taken as profit and sold in the West, would necessarily displace some Western production. What goodwill might have been created in the nonmarket economy could be lost in the Western nation affected by a loss of its production.

The second element of direct investment, participation in *control,* creates more philosophical problems than the problems of profit sharing, which are often related to currency shortages. In the nonmarket economies, management was in the hands of the state or, as in Yugoslavia under "workers' social property" theory, directly in the hands of a plant's workers. Joint venture contracts sometimes provided for sharing major management decisions, but did not allow management to be dominated in numbers by foreign participants. A minority of a managing board, however, might be accepted by the majority as the influential management group. The participation of workers in ownership and control has influenced the role of unions as nonmarket nations have entered the transition phase. Governments often are not certain how to deal with their work force, but have tended to attempt to allow them to participate in ownership, and sometimes management representation, when state owned entities are privatized, and to allow them to organize in what in some countries are very strong unions. But these unions often lack direction.

Joint venture laws varied significantly throughout the nonmarket economy world. The Eastern European laws developed over nearly two decades of experience, and were occasionally amended to accommodate new problems. China enacted a joint venture law in 1979, which was brief and unclear, but underwent modifications in fact and in interpretation as the Chinese economy moved to adopt more market economy characteristics. By 1986, the Chinese were even allowing wholly owned subsidiaries. Contrastingly, the 1982 Cuban joint venture law generated little response from foreign investors (U.S. investors are not permitted to invest in Cuba), for reasons that were obvious to all but the Cuban government. The 1982 law was outmoded when it was enacted in comparison to the amendments occurring in

Eastern European joint venture laws. Cuba wanted the benefits of foreign investment, without assuming any obligations of a host nation. In 1995 a new law replaced the old, offering new concessions, but still a decade or more behind developments in those nations already well into the period of transition towards market economies. It has not changed a dozen years into the new century, but the cracks in Cuba's socialism have widened. When a nation's investment law is as unrealistic as that of Cuba, new foreign investment usually focuses on a contract with the government that often ignores some of the restrictive rules of the investment law.

If any label is merited by the nonmarket economies regarding the acceptance of foreign investment, it is that of "pragmatic accommodation." Of course some nations are more pragmatic than others. The most significant changes in the rules regarding foreign investment have occurred in those NME nations where there have been similarly meaningful changes in allowing free market elements to penetrate domestic trade. These changes are usually frustratingly slow and sometimes subject to periodic suspension, but they represent extraordinary alterations in the fundamental economic structures and attitudes of nations long satisfied with a place in the obscure recesses of the international trading community. Many of the nations in transition have moved well into the next phase, ridding the state of significant involvement of ownership of the nation's means of production and distribution. It is the era of privatization.

PRIVATIZATION: THE FOCUS
OF THE 1990s

The lessening of state ownership of the means of production and distribution has been carried out principally by the process of privatization. While such conversion is a critical aspect of the transition of nonmarket economies to market economies, privatization is also occurring with vigor in many developing, *market* economy nations. The reason is partly shared by both forms of economy. State ownership of the means of production and distribution of goods and services is increasingly viewed as philosophically inappropriate as an activity for the government. More practically, most state enterprises have been unable to operate at a profit, causing a drain on state resources. Privatization is viewed as a means of reducing the drain on national revenue used to subsidize state owned enterprises, a way to raise revenue to improve national infrastructure, and a possible future source of tax revenue if private ownership means improving the efficiency of manufacture to the point of competing in world markets and increasing export revenue.

Additionally, privatization is thought to be a better way to provide goods and services demanded by a nation's population. This view extends to the largest developed nations. Britain, Italy, France and Germany have all privatized large state owned industries. U.S. privatization ideology has extended to highways, ports, waste-water facilities, gas utilities, and many local government services such as parking garages, prisons, and even recreational facilities including golf courses and tennis courts.

Not all enterprises have been placed on the market, but the NMEs often express a willingness to sell more large companies than some market economy developing nations in their own process of privatization. For example, Hungary sold the telecommunications company, MATAV, the airline MALEV, and a large lighting products company, Tungsram. But developing market economy nations were not far behind. Argentina sold 45% of the oil and gas company YPF, its airlines Aerolineas Argentinas, and the Telecom company. But new socialism within Argentina has reversed the process, as the government struggles to increase revenue for unsustainable social programs. Some national companies are referred to as "untouchables". But even they are having parts sold. Mexico's previously untouchable oil enterprise, PEMEX, has sold retail outlets, and its petrochemical production. Foreign investment is now allowed in gas production. Only oil production remains for the time-being "untouchable". Mexico's privatization of parts of PEMEX has not been without challenge and criticism, however, the process of privatization was at one time so sensitive in Mexico that it was referred to as "disincorporation."

As a comparatively new phenomenon, privatization has raised new issues for foreign investors. Privatization has become a process based on a mix of law and policy. The policy may be very pro-privatization, but backed by weak laws that do not answer many important questions. Most NMEs have adopted privatization laws that are periodically amended to govern such major issues as determining what to sell, the role of workers in approving the sale, valuation of the business, the level of foreign participation allowed in a sale, rights of nationals and/or employees to ownership preferences, method of financing, and the creation of an adequate legal infrastructure (corporation laws, securities laws, bankruptcy laws, etc.)to support the process. In many cases these questions are not resolved in the written privatization laws of the nations. They must be dealt with in negotiations with the government.

One of the most difficult issues in privatization is how to value the business. Many nonmarket economy enterprises possess little of value for the new owner except the right to function as the business. Obsolete equipment must be replaced. New markets must be sought. Modern technology must be introduced. Work forces often must be reduced and the remaining workers trained in more efficient methods of production and the use of new technology. Accounting methods of the NMEs gave little attention to market economy concepts, and thus book value is generally useless. Since there was no share ownership there was no market value of ownership interests. The value issue in a privatization usually must be negotiated.

Even when a value has been established which seems generally acceptable, the absence of savings in the nonmarket economies probably means that foreign capital will be necessary to carry out the privatization. But there may be reservations about selling majority ownership and control to foreign investors. Additionally, the NMEs may offer their own nationals some preference in the way of certificates that may be exchanged for shares in privatized companies. This means that a foreign purchaser may obtain 80 percent of the equity of the enterprise, but be expected to pay for 100 percent of its value. At the head of the line of nationals seeking preferential treatment may be workers in the enterprise to be sold, holding some form of scrip exchangeable for shares.

The process of privatization is only partly completed. It is a necessary concomitant to becoming a market economy, and has continued into the new century. If there is any doubt about the seriousness of nations to privatize, the figures speak loudly. The IFC of the World Bank reported that some 2,700 state owned enterprises were privatized between 1988 and 1993 in more than 95 countries, raising about $271 billion in revenue. A later 2010 report indicated that 2008 privatizations fell to about $38 billion, a 71% drop from 2007. The least declines were in South Asia, and the most significant activity was in Russia and China.

POLICY VERSUS LAW: DEALING WITH THE OPERATIONAL CODE OF THE WAY THINGS WORK

The written laws of the developing nations are the principal framework for regulating the foreign investor. Many developing and nonmarket economies have specific laws governing foreign investment. These laws are what the public (and too often the foreign investor) believes comprise the *exclusive* framework for investment. But each nation has another level of law, that which is unwritten. It is the "way things work," an operational code. It consists of unpublished regulations and rulings that are applied in some cases, but not even mentioned in others. The Brazilians call them "drawer regulations." Investors in China are sometimes confronted with laws they have never heard of, and which they are told may not even be read by foreigners. This operational code allows the government to give different treatment to different investors. Fortunately, many local attorneys know what they are and how to use them. They are a reason for choosing local counsel wisely.

RESTRICTIONS ON FOREIGN INVESTMENT IN DEVELOPED, MARKET ECONOMY NATIONS

The enactment of laws affecting foreign investment is not limited to the developing nations and nonmarket economy nations. Investors attempting to establish equity investments in Japan confront numerous obstacles, although no written, restrictive foreign investment law exists. Many new foreign investors began to establish a base in the European Union for fear that a "Fortress Europe" would develop (the consequence of the achievement of a "Europe Without *Internal* Frontiers") that would restrict foreign investment. Canada adopted a fairly restrictive foreign investment law in 1973, but following much criticism from abroad and debate within, the law was replaced with the far less restrictive Investment Canada Act in 1985. The 1985 law, which required review of large proposed investments, was incorporated into the 1989 Canada-United States Free Trade Agreement (CFTA), but with major exceptions for U.S. investors. The North American Free Trade Agreement (NAFTA) Chapter 11 establishes investment rules, reflecting to some extent the provisions in the earlier CFTA. France, Korea and other developed nations additionally review some foreign investment on national interest grounds. One ought not assume that control of foreign investment is limited to developing and nonmarket economy nations. Or assume that the United States does not control foreign investment in the United States.

The United States has long promoted an image of an investment encouraging nation, where only a few areas are subject to ownership and control limitations, such as national defense, nuclear energy and domestic air transportation. Upon occasion (e.g., fear of Japanese trade domination in the 1980s) proposals have been introduced in the Congress to require some level of registration of foreign investment, but invariably they have been defeated as restrictive and discouraging of desirable job-creating foreign investment. A Committee on Foreign Investment in the United States (CFIUS), was created in 1975 to monitor foreign investment (www.treas.gov/oii). CFIUS became the presidential designee to monitor and review foreign investment when Congress in 1988 enacted the Exon-Florio Amendment of the 1950 Defense Production Act (DPA), as part of the Omnibus Trade and Competitiveness Act. The Exon-Florio law was partly the response to the proposed acquisition of Fairchild Semiconductor Corporation by the Japanese company Fujitsu, Ltd. Fairchild was engaged in defense manufacturing. CFIUS had reviewed this proposed acquisition (before the enactment of Exon-Florio) and determined that national security interests were at risk, but CFIUS had no authority to stop the acquisition. Fujitsu nevertheless terminated its proposed acquisition in the face of government pressure.

The first major amendment to Exon-Florio came in 1992, after Congressional dissatisfaction with the way the President and CFIUS handled the proposed takeover of part of LTV by Thomson-CSF, a conglomerate with majority ownership by the French government. The expected purchase by Thomson of LTV's missile division was terminated by Thomson when it believed it could not expect to gain approval under Exon-Florio from the Department of Defense. Congress had intervened because members were upset with the failure of the administration to act more strictly. Thomson's withdrawal led to litigation as well as to the 1992 amendments.

The Foreign Investment and National Security Act (FINSA) of 2007 reformed and codified the responsibilities of the CFIUS. As in the case of both the original CIFUS and the 1992 amendments, proposed investment in the United States drove the changes. This time it was the 2006 proposed sale to Dubai Ports World International of a British company that held leases to operate six major U.S. ports. Of additional concern was the 2005 proposal by China National Offshore Oil Corporation to purchase shares of Unocal, outbidding Chevron. These two experiences caused CFIUS review filings to increase some 75%. Between 2008 and 2010, companies filed 313 notices that CFIUS determined to be covered under section 721. None resulted in a Presidential decision. The global downturn may have caused some decline in significant transactions.

The FINSA continues Presidential authority (essentially exercised by his designee—the CFIUS) to investigate effects on national security from mergers, acquisitions and takeovers which might result in foreign control. If national security is threatened, the President may prohibit the action. The review, which is essentially voluntary by parties filing a notification with CFIUS, allows a safe harbor for the transaction if it receives CFIUS approval. Review *must* occur if the purchasing foreigner is controlled by or acting on behalf of a foreign government. The law additionally prohibits the sale of some U.S. companies to certain foreign investors, principally those entities involved with foreign governments. FINSA will cause a significant increase in the proposed transactions subject to review. The Department of Homeland Security is now an important player within CFIUS. It may be tempted to use CFIUS to gain control over actions of the parties, regardless of the presence or absence of any serious national security link, especially in the area of cyber security.

Exon-Florio gives the President authority to block an acquisition within statutory guidelines. He must find (1) "credible evidence" that foreign "control" might "impair the national security," and (2) that U.S. law (other than Exon-Florio and the IEEPA) does not provide adequate and appropriate authority for the President to protect national security. It is unclear what industries affect national security, although the law suggests (1) "domestic production needed for projected national defense requirements," (2) "capability and capacity of domestic industries to meet national defense requirements," and (3) "control . . . by foreign citizens as it affects the capability and capacity of the United States to meet the requirements of national security." Certainly the defense industry, to the extent it may be defined, is included. Also included are nondefense industries which manufacture products which have strategic significance, particularly when they have a large share of the U.S. market and there are no easily located substitutes. What action the President may take is not included in the statute, which refers to "appropriate relief." The presidential findings are not reviewable. Important language added by the FINSA, and yet undefined, is when a transaction would result in foreign control of "critical infrastructure." Other issues to be resolved include the determination of which energy assets are "major," and which technologies are "critical."

Of the almost one thousand notifications presented to the executive under the voluntary reporting system, only a little more than a dozen have proceeded to a formal investigation, causing critics to charge that the law is not being used to block investment as allegedly intended. European owned companies have not considered Exon-Florio to be a block to investment in the United States, but more an administrative annoyance. The Department of Defense, as might be expected, has become a major participant in requesting investigations. One example is where Defense joined the Departments of Energy, Treasury and Commerce to challenge the proposed acquisition of General Ceramics by the Japanese company, Tokuyama Soda Co., Ltd. General Ceramics manufactured ceramics used in nuclear weapon electronic circuits. There was evidence that Japan was urging its businesses to manipulate their acquisitions to avoid Exon-Florio challenges. It appeared likely that the acquisition would be blocked, and General Ceramics sold its defense related business to another company, leading CFIUS to find no objection to the acquisition.

The one case where a proposed acquisition led to a presidential order blocking the acquisition involved China's National Aero-Technology Import and Export Corp.'s (CATIC) proposed acquisition of MAMCO Mfg, a Seattle aircraft parts manufacturer. The investigation disclosed that the buyer CATIC had previously violated U.S. export control laws in purchases of General Electric aircraft engines. There were also concerns about CATIC's attempts to gain technology to build jet fighters able to refuel during flight, and carrying on some covert operations in the United States for the Chinese government. The Executive Order calling for divestment referred only to the threat to national security, providing no detailed supporting reasons.

Exon-Florio has been used by U.S. target corporations whose management is hostile to a proposed takeover. It was an unanticipated consequence of the enactment of Exon-Florio. The target company may use the post-notification review period to try to delay the takeover, even to the extent of providing misleading information to CFIUS. The intention would be to cause CFIUS to undertake an investigation. Such delay may be enough to discourage the foreign would-be acquirer, even though there are no legitimate national security grounds to expect an ultimate presidential blockage. There are no clear sanctions for use of Exon-Florio to block a hostile takeover, but providing false or misleading information to CFIUS would seem to violate federal criminal statutes. If the U.S. government intends to be receptive to foreign investment, including investment by way of acquisition, the misuse of Exon-Florio is counterproductive to that policy of openness.

Exon-Florio is viewed by many in Congress as the means by which Congress might increase control over foreign investment. The 1992 amendments and the 2007 FINSA did not solve all Congressional concerns. Remaining open to further consideration, in addition to clearer definitions and a time limit for filing notifications as noted above, are coverage of the acquisition of "critical" technologies with the test constituting the effect on "economic" versus "national" security; consideration of the concentration in the industry (it can be under antitrust laws), including as a factor whether the target company has received U.S. government funds; and transferring the chairmanship of CFIUS from Treasury to Commerce.

FINANCING THE FOREIGN INVESTMENT

Some investment is done using the parent corporation's retained earnings. Or using its traditional borrowing sources for investments in the United States. The foreign investment opens new possible sources, including the same kind of lending institutions in the foreign host nation as are used in the United States. But additional possible sources exist, such as international development banks and agencies, including the World Bank's International Finance Corporation (IFC), or the U.S. Overseas Private Investment Corporation (OPIC). Some international lending authorities invest primarily in infrastructure, which may not benefit many production companies but may be of interest to a U.S. construction business.

THE EFFECT OF A DIFFERENT CURRENCY ON THE FOREIGN INVESTMENT

Imagine that every state within the United States had a different currency. A New York corporation wishing to open a subsidiary in New Mexico might encounter currency controls in New Mexico, or a currency artificially fixed to that of another state, perhaps Texas. This is partly why most of the members of the European Union have abandoned centuries old currencies for adoption of a common EU currency, the Euro. When a business invests in a nation with a different currency, many issues arise. Can or may the foreign currency be readily converted into dollars? What foreign hotel investment in Havana wants its earnings restricted to Cuban pesos? They are not convertible in any other nation. What happens when a convertible currency in, for example, Mexico, suddenly collapses just before the foreign investor planned to convert and repatriate it to the U.S. parent? How much local currency should be retained for business needs? The investor must learn about hedging, buying contracts that assure later conversion at a determined rate. All of this attention to a different currency costs money, and that usually means transferring such costs on to the ultimate consumer.

TRANSFER PRICING

If the U.S. investment in another nation faces restrictions on repatriating profits to the parent, but
allows transfers to pay for technology, perhaps the
parent will simply raise the price charged the foreign
subsidiary for technology and thus operate without
showing any profits that if existed would be frozen in
the non-transferrable foreign currency. That would
also mean no taxes because there were no profits,
even though there were actually disguised profits.
Transfer pricing is used for many reasons, usually to
avoid what are considered onerous and unfair rule
changes in the host nation. They obviously are disliked by the host government that may lose needed
tax revenue. And they may be very much disliked by
any host nation joint venture equity partners that
lose dividends because the profits (in which they
would share) were renamed technology payments (in
which they do not share). Transfer pricing is not only
a problem for developing nations, any nation that is
host to foreign investment worries about and tries to
prevent such transfer pricing. California was concerned that some foreign investors in California were
not paying proper California state income taxes and
in the 1990s adopted a unitary tax. It required taxa-
ble profits to be roughly equal to the percent of the
company's assets, employees and sales existing in
California.

THE ROLE OF BILATERAL INVESTMENT TREATIES

International law has been slow to establish standards regarding how nations ought to treat foreign investment. The U.N.'s efforts in the 1970s to draft a code of conduct for multinational enterprises did not include provisions regulating the conduct of host nations. The one-sided efforts of the U.N. were thus quite unsatisfactory to foreign investors, who sought assistance from their home nations. Bilateral investment treaties (BITs) have provided some help. To promote national treatment and protect U.S. investors abroad, the United States embarked on the BIT program in the early 1980s. The BIT program followed earlier extensive use of Friendship, Commerce, and Navigation (FCN) treaties. Unlike the FCNs, the model BIT focuses more exclusively on investment related issues, such as employment of one's nationals in a foreign subsidiary. As a result of a 1982 U.S. Supreme Court ruling, the earlier used FCN treaty afforded no protection to a foreign company wanting to nearly exclusively hire its own nationals. Under the typical BIT, explicit freedom to hire foreign nationals exists in a narrow range of management provisions. But investment screening mechanisms and key sectors often remain exempt from BIT protection, typically listed in a BIT Annex. While elimination of foreign investment screening and imposition of performance requirements has been an object of the BIT program, these provisions of the model BIT have been weakened in the treaties currently in force.

It is not only the United States which has emphasized the BIT, they are common features of most developed nations in their relations with host nations for foreign investment. For example, China has investment protection agreements with such nations as Australia, Austria, Belgium-Luxembourg, Denmark, France, Germany, Japan, the Netherlands, and the United Kingdom. A benefit of such an agreement is that its provisions prevail over domestic law, although the agreements usually allow for exceptions to investment protection when in the interests of national security.

The United States has entered into a number of bilateral *investment* treaties, as well as a number of less formal bilateral *trade* agreements. But many of the earlier trade agreements merely referred to investment as an area for further discussion, tending to deal only with tariff and nontariff barriers to trade. The bilateral *investment* treaties by their nature do address investment issues. They generally replace earlier FCN treaties, to the extent that they apply to investments. Most of the BITs negotiated by the United States have been with small developing countries, such as Albania, Latvia, Ruwanda, and Uruguay. But the United States has signed BITs with such important trading nations as Argentina and Russia. The Argentina-United States BIT follows the U.S. BIT prototype of addressing both investment protection and investor access to each other's markets. The Russia agreement awaits Russian approval. The provisions of the BITs are perhaps fairly compared to the investor protection contained in Chapter 11 of the NAFTA with Canada and Mexico.

The BITs do not prohibit nations from enacting investment laws, but provide that any such laws should not interfere with any rights in the treaty. The free access aspect of some BITs may not be perceived as a right. Thus investment laws might be enacted that limit access to certain areas, but would not create a right of the other party to challenge the law under the BIT.

One important provision the United States seeks to include in its BITs is the "prompt, adequate and effective" concept (if not always the language) of compensation following expropriation. Many of the nations which have recently agreed to this language disputed its appropriateness during the nationalistic North-South dialogue years of the 1960s and 1970s. But as they began to promote rather than restrict investment, these nations had to accept the idea that expropriated investment should be compensated reasonably soon after the taking ("prompt"), based on a fair valuation ("adequate"), and in a realistic form ("effective"). The Argentina-United States BIT uses language referring to the "fair market value ... immediately before the expropriatory action."

Most BITs do not include provisions for consultations when differences arise in the interpretation of the treaty. The Argentina-United States BIT is one of a few exceptions. BITs do often provide for arbitration, sometimes with no necessary recourse to prior exhaustion of local remedies.

The BIT process is quite dynamic. Each successive agreement with a new country may include some new provisions. The United States has a prototype agreement, but it has been modified as host nations have sought new foreign investment and have been willing to sign a BIT to establish the most attractive conditions for that investment. It is certain that the BITs in existence today will not be identical to BITs executed in years ahead. BITs are an important contribution of the developed home nation to lessening the risk for their multinationals investing abroad. A BIT establishes some ground rules for investment on a bilateral, treaty basis which should not be unilaterally altered by the host nation to impose restrictions on the investments which are inconsistent with the BIT. Certainly, revolutionary governments have ignored similar agreements in the past and may in the future. But the BITs do provide some investment security, at least as long as the host governments remain relatively stable, and receptive to foreign investment. BITs have not disappeared following the creation of the WTO and its Agreement on Trade-Related Investment Measures (TRIMs). The GATT/WTO rules regarding investment are a step in the right direction, but remain less specific than agreements among smaller groups of nations (such as the NAFTA), or bilateral agreements.

FOREIGN INVESTMENT UNDER THE NORTH AMERICAN FREE TRADE AGREEMENT

U.S. foreign investors in Canada and Mexico benefit from the provisions of the North American Free Trade Agreement (NAFTA). Chapter 11 covers foreign investment. Section A includes provisions affecting Investment, while Section B addresses the Settlement of Disputes between a Party and an Investor of another Party. The investment provisions in Chapter 11 to some extent reflect provisions in the earlier Canada-United States FTA, but there are some provisions unique to the NAFTA. For example, provisions for local management and control were important provisions in the 1973 Mexican Investment Law. NAFTA, as well as the newer 1993 Mexican Investment Law, prohibit mandating the nationality of senior management. But NAFTA does allow for requirements that the majority of the board of an enterprise that is a foreign investment be of a particular nationality, or be resident in the territory, provided that such a requirement does not materially impair the investor's control over the investment. The provisions attempt to balance eliminating the distortions associated with mandating local management, with ensuring that host nation input is provided.

NAFTA investment rules are based on the concepts of national treatment and most-favored-nation status. Thus, each Party must grant investors of the other NAFTA Parties treatment no less favorable than is granted to domestic investors. Also, each Party must grant investors of the other Parties treatment no less favorable than it grants to any other nation outside NAFTA. Performance requirements are prohibited under NAFTA, under provisions that specifically list seven areas of prohibited performance requirements. But a nation may impose measures to protect life or health, safety, or the environmental. Incentives to invest may not be conditioned on most performance requirements, but may be conditioned on location, provision of services, training or employing workers, constructing or expanding facilities, or undertaking research.

NAFTA allows investors to freely transfer profits, dividends, interest, capital, royalties, management and technical advice fees, and other fees, as well as proceeds from the sale of the investment and various payments (such as loan repayments). But limitations on transfers may be made involving certain bankruptcy actions, securities dealings, criminal acts, issues involving property, reporting of transfers, and to ensure satisfaction of judgments.

Each of the member nations of NAFTA listed exceptions to the investment rules, thus deviating from the basic principle of national treatment. Some exceptions were mandated by the nation's constitution, others by federal law. Where a nation has made exceptions which disallow foreign participation, it may either reserve the area for national ownership or exclusively for private domestic ownership. But it may also allow some foreign participation. Thus, some of the restrictive nature of earlier investment laws is preserved, but in a considerably more limited form.

FOREIGN INVESTMENT UNDER THE GATT/WORLD TRADE ORGANIZATION

Previous to the Uruguay Round the GATT did not address issues of foreign investment. But the Uruguay Round produced rules on foreign investment, referred to as the Agreement on Trade-Related Investment Measures, (TRIMs). As must be expected with any large organization with divergent views, its negotiated provisions are not likely to be as comprehensive as those in smaller trade agreements, such as discussed above in the NAFTA. The WTO TRIMs provisions are considerably briefer than those in the NAFTA, and only one provision relates to dispute settlement. That article states that the provisions of the General Agreement relating to Consultation (XXII), and Nullification and Impairment (XXIII), and the Understanding on Rules and Procedures Governing the Settlement of Disputes, apply to consultations and dispute settlement under the TRIM provisions. Thus, there are no separate provisions directed to the uniqueness of investment disputes, as in the NAFTA Chapter 11. It will take time to determine how effective the WTO provisions are to resolving investment disputes. While the investment dispute provisions of the NAFTA have been extensively used to date, the WTO TRIMs have received little attention.

The WTO investment rules or TRIMs first set forth a national treatment principal. TRIMs which are considered inconsistent with WTO obligations are listed in an annex, and include such performance requirements as minimum domestic content, imports limited or linked to exports, restrictions on access to foreign exchange to limit imports for use in the investment, etc. Developing countries are allowed to "deviate temporarily" from the national treatment concept, thus diminishing in value the effectiveness of the WTO investment provisions, and obviously discouraging investment in nations which have a history of imposing investment restrictions, and making such agreements as the NAFTA all the more useful and likely to spread.

The essence of the TRIMs is to establish the same principle of national treatment for investments as has been in effect for trade. TRIMs are incorporated in the overall structure of the WTO, alongside trade measures, rather than being treated as a quite distinct area. Because all the deficiencies of the WTO with regard to trade measures may apply to TRIMs, it remains to be seen how effective these measures will be in governing foreign investment. Because the measures are much less certain than those included in bilateral investment treaties, and small area free trade agreements, it is likely that much of the regulation of foreign investment will develop in the context of the latter rather than within the WTO.

THE OECD AND THE MULTILATERAL AGREEMENT ON INVESTMENT

Bilateral investment treaties have been present for several decades, but have been quite limited in scope. Regional agreements such as the NAFTA and the WTO are both more recent and more extensive in addressing foreign investment issues. The next development was thought to be the adoption of the Multilateral Agreement on Investment (MAI) by the Organization for Economic Cooperation and Development (OECD). The nature of the OECD, dominated by developed nations, although less so than in its earlier years, means the MAI is more likely to focus on concerns of the multinational corporations of developed nations than the aspirations of the developing nations that host investment. But there were insurmountable disagreements in the negotiations, and hope for an early settlement of differences ended. Most of the OECD members wished to include limits on the extraterritorial application of laws, such as attempts to impose a nation's boycott on third nations, or govern the acts of foreign subsidiaries. The United States generally opposes such limitations on its use of extraterritorial application of laws. Conclusion of the MAI is now unlikely. At the very best it may be said to be on the "back burner."

PROJECT FINANCING

"Project financing" is a specialized form of financing that is typically used for large industrial projects. Large enterprises may, and commonly do, finance projects on the basis of their own credit. They may use their accrued cash reserves, borrow from a bank or other financial institution, or raise capital through equity (stock) and debt (bond) offerings. But for particularly large industrial projects, even quite substantial enterprises may not have the ability or desire to assume the corresponding debt burdens (often, many billions of dollars). Also, agreements with existing lenders may disallow additional borrowing if it would exceed defined levels or ratios (such as assets to debts)

The innovation of project financing is that the project itself represents the source for repayment of the project debt. The enterprise that initiates the project (the "sponsor") will create the legal structures for the project, secure the financing, and otherwise arrange the myriad related contracts—but lenders and other creditors must look to the revenues and assets of the *project* for payment. Often, the sponsor will establish a separate legal entity (a "special purpose vehicle") as a wholly or partially owned subsidiary to construct, own, and operate the project. The separate legal entity, and not the sponsor, will then serve as the borrower for project loans.

This arrangement ultimately implies two significant elements: First, the project debt is "off balance sheet" for and "nonrecourse" to the sponsor. That is, the project sponsor does not include the debt on its own books and has no direct legal obligation to repay the debt if the project fails. Second, and closely related, the viability of the project financing—the ability to attract lenders and other investors—will depend on the merits of the project and not on the credit of the sponsor. This means that the sponsor will need to convince the project finance lenders that the project will generate sufficient revenue to repay the loans, with interest, as well as satisfy any priority claims of other investors. Thus, secure and sufficient revenue from the project represents the foundation of project financing. The project also will need to provide collateral to protect the lenders upon default, and the lenders will need to be assured that they will have secure, first-priority access to that collateral under applicable legal rules.

All project financings involve the same essential elements. The project sponsor or other project participants will arrange for the issuance of nonrecourse debt (whether short- or long-term notes or bonds). The nonrecourse aspect of such loans is worthy of emphasis. The project sponsor (and any affiliates) will require that they have no liability to the lender in the event of any default in payment or breach of any other provisions of the loan contracts. The lenders thus must agree to have recourse only to the project assets in enforcing their rights arising out of the project finance loans. This fact also reinforces the central role of the viability of the project. To convince the lenders, the project sponsor will undertake and present a feasibility study for the project. The feasibility study will prepare and analyze the business plan and address all of the significant commercial, economic, political, and legal risks of the project. It will contain an analysis of the market for the product the project will generate, the sources and strength of competition in the field, expected future market conditions, as well as all of the related risks for each of these issues. The lenders likely will commission experts to analyze these matters on an independent basis as well.

In addition, project lenders will demand collateral rights—which decrease the risk and thus the interest rate on loans—in a variety of forms. Principal among these will be an assignment of the project revenues in the event any default. That is, the lenders will demand that, should the project fall short in its payments, they will have a direct right to the future revenues of the project, and especially that they may assert valid claims against any third-parties buyers of the project's output. Thus, the sponsor will need to convince the lenders that the assignment is both economically valuable and legally enforceable against third-parties in the future. As explained in more detail below, however, a variety of legal issues may create significant uncertainty on this subject.

If all proceeds perfectly, the sponsor will be able to structure a project financing to address all noteworthy risks and convince the lenders to rely solely upon their rights against the project and its future revenues as security for their loans. Unfortunately, it is the rare case that all things proceed perfectly, and the lenders will typically seek as much security as possible in any event. Thus, the lenders often will demand further protection in the form of "credit enhancements," which provide financial support for the project. Such credit enhancements come essentially from two sources: The first and most common is some form of a guarantee from the sponsor. The sponsor will, of course, resist this as contrary to the nonrecourse nature of project financing; thus, even if forced to give one, it will seek to carefully circumscribe the nature, extent, and triggering events for any guarantee.

The second form of credit enhancement comes from creditworthy third parties. These may include, among others, letters of credit from banks, capital contributions from investors, and third-party guarantees or insurance. The structure and details of these arrangements will differ greatly depending on the nature of the project, the goals of the project sponsor, the legal and political stability in the project's region, and, most important, the economic viability of the project. Where political or economic development considerations are more prominent, governmental or quasi-governmental institutions also may become involved. That is, where political or market instability is high or economic development support is needed, a credit enhancement may take the form of a guarantee by a "Multilateral Investment Guarantee Agency" ("MIGA"). Significant among such institutions are the International Finance Corporation ("IFC"), the World Bank more generally, the Inter-American Development Bank ("IDB"), the European Bank for Reconstruction and Development ("EBRD"), and the Asian Development Bank ("ADB"). The host country (or a political subdivision such as a state or province) also may provide credit enhancements of various types.

As should be clear from this discussion, project financing commonly is a quite complicated endeavor. The project sponsor and its lawyers will need to negotiate and conclude a dizzying array of interrelated contracts. Contracts will be needed, among others, with the lenders; with third-party investors; with issuers of letters of credit, guarantors, or similar third-party providers of credit enhancements; with project developers; with construction contractors; and with project operators. As well, the sponsor and its lawyers will need to conclude security agreements or assignments of rights governing the lenders' access to collateral, especially future project revenues. This likely will involve negotiations with third-party buyers of the project's output, the goal of which will be to secure binding purchase commitments into the future (*see also* below).

An essential aspect of the negotiations on all of these contracts will be the allocation of the myriad risks involved in the construction and financing of a large industrial project. The specifics of this allocation vary significantly depending on the transaction, and will depend decisively on the bargaining position of the participants and the overall viability of the project; but as a general norm, the sponsor will seek an arrangement that allocates each of the risks to the party best able to control it. Thus, for example, the sponsor will seek to have the construction contractor assume risks relating to subsurface conditions at the project site, construction delays arising from known risks, and material and labor shortages.

The project also will have unique risks at each of its three principal stages: design engineering and construction; start-up; and operation. As the project unfolds, new risks will arise and others will diminish. Principally for this reason, project financing typically involves at least two types of lenders (or lender groups). The first are those that extend the construction loan, which is of a relatively short-term nature. The second are those that make the long-term, or "take-out" loan, for the operation of the project throughout its life. Both groups, however, will be very interested in the construction phase, and each will seek assurances concerning the cost and timing of project construction. That is, each will be concerned about whether the project will be completed on time and for the price included in the financial projections for the project loans. Before concluding the loan contracts, therefore, the lenders will require that the sponsor or the construction contractor present design drawings, land surveys, construction schedules, and resumes on the experience of the contractor and expected subcontractors.

Again, the lenders likely will hire their own experts to examine each of these matters.

As reflected by the two separate phases of lending, the start-up of a project commonly is the most sensitive phase for project financing. For one thing, performance tests for project output may trigger third-party (or sponsor) performance guarantees. This also represents the point at which construction lenders are "taken out" by the long-term lenders, which will want to be assured that all construction risks have been addressed and all conditions for the long-term viability of the project (and thus for the disbursement of the long-term loans) have been satisfied. In specific, at this point the long-term lenders (as well as any third-party investors) will require that the sponsor or construction contractor provide any contractually mandated proof that the project is able to generate the type and level of production necessary to pay the project's operating costs and service the project's debts.

A variety of risks also exist during the operation of the project. It is during this phase that the project must demonstrate that it can consistently meet the benchmarks set in the market viability studies that convinced the lenders to provide financing in the first place. But like all commercial ventures, unlikely events may occur, seen risks may become worse, and unseen risks may arise. Prominent among such risks during the operating phase are problems with the supply of input raw materials; a decrease in demand for project output; currency fluctuations; strikes or other employee unrest; governmental expropriation; regulatory or legal changes; management errors; political instability; and insolvency by suppliers or customers. Unless carefully considered in the design of the project and carefully allocated in the related contracts, any of these risks may cause substantial friction among the project participants. And even with a clearly allocated risk, negative developments may cause severe harm and even compromise a participant's future solvency. All of this increases significantly the importance of carefully negotiated *"force majeure"* clauses—ones that allocate among the participants the various remote risks that may affect the project in the future.

From a legal perspective, the most important of the risks of project financing relate to the availability of security for project loans under applicable legal rules. As noted, the essential nature of project financing is that the lenders must rely on project revenues for repayment. The lenders, therefore, will want assurances that buyers are both available and willing to pay for project output. Ideally, the lenders will want secure buyers that are legally bound to purchase the output. A variety of contractual arrangements are possible in this regard. They range from "take-if-offered" contracts (under which the buyers must pay only if the output is delivered), to "take-or-pay" contracts (under which the buyers must either take or pay for project output, but excess payments may be credited against future deliveries), to "hell-or-high-water" contracts (under which buyers must pay even if the producer is not able to make any deliveries at all).

Even with these types of arrangements, the lenders will want assurance that they have a first-priority claim to any rights the project may have against the obligated buyers. This raises a variety of difficult legal questions, all of which the participants must resolve (as best they can). First, the concept of a registered and enforceable "security interest," including in future payment obligations (so-called "floating" liens or charges), is well established under U.S. law. *See* UCC §§ 9–102(a)(2), 9–203, 9-204, 9–308. But civil law countries generally do not recognize "floating liens" that extend to future assets. The lenders may seek to have the buyers agree that U.S. law will govern the enforcement of security rights, but substantial doubts may exist over whether the buyers' home country or countries will enforce such an agreement. If this option is not available, the lenders will need to rely on another conceptual device that is recognized by local law— such as an "assignment" or a "pledge" of the project's contract rights against the buyers.

Beyond this are issues of priority. Even if applicable local law recognizes and enforces the lenders' rights to the buyers' future payment obligations, does it establish formal registries of creditor interests and will it enforce priority rights as between competing creditors? And even if all of these rights exist, the lenders will need to assess the costs and extent of delays that attend enforcement through litigation in local courts. To address such concerns, the lenders will seek to conclude an international arbitration agreement with the third-party buyers of project output, which may facilitate a more efficient and impartial resolution of any future disputes.

Separately, the lenders likely will seek to secure rights in the fixed assets located at the project site. A common assumption is that such "immoveable" assets are the most secure forms of collateral. But a variety of challenges arise for this form of illiquid collateral which are not present for claims against monetary obligations as discussed immediately above. The first is the most obvious: Does local law even permit the creation of a mortgage or similar right in real property? Second, even if so, the lenders will need to identify and carefully follow the local formalities. Third, some local jurisdictions require that a lender place a formal value on the mortgage, and this will both set the ceiling for recovery and determine the amount of required fees or taxes. The two considerations obviously are in tension. Moreover, local law may require that the value be denominated in the local currency, and this implicates currency fluctuation risks (an especially serious matter if the currency is a "soft" one). Fourth, the lenders will need to determine what their foreclosure rights are and how they are properly exercised. Substantial and idiosyncratic differences exist on this subject. Prominent among these will be the costs and length of foreclosure proceedings. Delays of five and ten years are not uncommon. In light of this, the lenders will need to determine whether they may operate the project during the foreclosure process—or even thereafter. Required governmental permits and foreign ownership controls (especially in the field of natural resources) may impose severe restrictions in this regard. Finally, some local laws give priority to the claims of governmental bodies or other "preferred" creditors. The extent of such preferences obviously can have a significant effect on the value of the lender's mortgage rights in the fixed assets. The complexity of all of these matters will mean that the lenders must engage competent local counsel for careful advice and planning.

The logical solution for these problems is an international treaty. UNIDROIT has proposed one such treaty on the assignment of the claims a debtor has against third parties from the sale of goods or the supply of services ("receivables," also known as "factoring"). *See* UNIDROIT Convention on International Factoring (1988). As of 2012, however, only seven countries have ratified this treaty. A similar treaty from UNCITRAL, the United Nations Convention on the Assignment of Receivables in International Trade (2001), has not entered into force as of 2012. A substantially more successful treaty from UNIDROIT, the Convention on International Interests in Mobile Equipment (2001), has nearly fifty ratifications as of 2012. This is a framework convention that will allow focused protocols for special categories of mobile equipment in the future, such as the already-concluded protocols on "Matters Specific to Aircraft Equipment" (2001), on "Matters Specific to Railway Rolling Stock" (2007), and on "Matters Specific to Space Assets" (2012).

THE SETTLEMENT OF INVESTMENT DISPUTES: GENERAL

Investment disputes often involve claims by the foreign investor that the host nation interfered with the investment to the degree that it constitutes a taking of property. A taking may violate international law, but that area is poorly defined in international law and the subject of continuing and vigorous disputed by different nations. The International Court of Justice has been a disappointment in establishing some rules for expropriation. Investors have thus sought other forums for investment dispute settlement. Host nation domestic law may include how investment disputes are to be resolved. Often the law provides for stages, beginning with a form of mediation, then arbitration, and if not satisfied through use of the courts. This may be unsatisfactory to the foreign investor if the membership of the mediation and arbitration panels, and the rules under which they operate, appear to favor the host nation. A more neutral settlement process is usually preferred.

THE SETTLEMENT OF INVESTMENT
DISPUTES: NAFTA

The NAFTA investment dispute scheme is extensive and complex. It essentially provides a mechanism to settle investment disputes by arbitration where a party to NAFTA has breached an obligation under Section A of Chapter 11 provisions relating to investment, or under provisions in Chapter 15 governing monopolies and state enterprises, and damage or loss has occurred from the breach. Investors of a party are allowed to submit the claim directly, the first such permission in a trade agreement. The process first requires consultation and negotiation. If unsuccessful, it proceeds to arbitration. The rules to be applied are those of ICSID or UNCITRAL, depending upon NAFTA Party participation in the ICSID Convention. The arbitrators are selected by the parties to the dispute and the arbitration is enforceable. The process is to some degree a mini-ICSID procedure, with participation limited to disputants and arbitrators of the three NAFTA parties.

Two important reservations were made by Canada and Mexico to the NAFTA investment dispute resolution provisions. A Canadian decision following a review under the Investment Canada Act regarding an acquisition is not subject to NAFTA dispute settlement provisions, nor is a Mexican National Commission on Foreign Investment decision on an acquisition subject to such provisions.

Dispute settlement activity under Chapter 11 has been extensive, and replete with some unexpected uses. Several Chapter 11 investment disputes have raised doubt about the intended scope of the use of Chapter 11 dispute procedures. Several U.S. challenges by private investors have been made challenging the application of regulations adopted in Canada and Mexico that have allegedly prevented U.S. foreign investment from functioning. There is debate regarding whether the challenged regulatory provisions constitute regulation or expropriation. When the regulation measures challenged have been environmental protection laws, the concern over the use of Chapter 11 has been more serious and vocal. But an even more contentious case, involving a Canadian funeral home chain subjected to a huge punitive damages decision in a Mississippi state court, and facing severe limitations on the ability to appeal the decision, has challenged the fairness of the state legal system itself, rather than traditional expropriatory measures. These decisions may lead to revisiting the Chapter 11 dispute procedure.

THE SETTLEMENT OF INVESTMENT DISPUTES: ICSID

Some 158 nations have signed the 1966 Convention on the Settlement of Investment Disputes between States and Nationals of Other States. However, only 148 have deposited the instrument and activated membership. The Convention provided for the creation of the International Centre for the Settlement of Investment Disputes (ICSID) as part of the

World Bank. The Convention and Centre provide for the arbitration of investment disputes, offering an institutional framework for the proceedings. Jurisdiction under the Convention extends to "any legal dispute arising directly out of an investment, between a Contracting State or . . . any subdivision . . . and a national of another Contracting State." But the parties must consent in writing to the submission of the dispute to the Centre. Once given, the consent may not be withdrawn.

Disputes regarding jurisdiction may be decided by the arbitration panel and appealed to a committee (ad hoc) created from the Panel of Arbitrators by the Administrative Council of the ICSID. The jurisdiction of the tribunal, challenged in a U.S. court, may well lead to a refusal to uphold the decision. Concern regarding the jurisdictional limitations led to the creation of the Additional Facility, which may conduct conciliation and arbitration proceedings for what are rather special disputes. It was not created to deal with the ordinary investment dispute, but with disputes between parties with long-term special economic relationships involving substantial resource commitments. The Additional Facility may be used only with the blessing of the ICSID Secretary General.

CONCLUSION

The regulation of foreign investment is practiced by nearly every nation in the world, both market and nonmarket economies, and developed and developing nations. The motivation for regulation is nearly always the protection of some domestic interest, whether national security, national economic interests or simply national interests. Important to recognize is that such regulation is a dynamic process. The adoption of the joint venture as a mandatory vehicle for foreign investment by developing nations and nonmarket economies on the 1970s proved to be only one stage in the development process. Unfortunately it is not always acknowledged as merely a stage in an evolving process.

Some nations view what is a transitory stage in the development process as a permanent key to success. But the world has witnessed the development of foreign investment regulation move through stages of nationalizations and mandatory joint ventures, from import substitution promotion to export production promotion, an era of privatization, and currently into an era of offering incentives to encourage foreign investment. Those nations which use investment controls carefully and sparingly, such as the Asian Four Tigers or Four Dragons, have achieved greater rates of growth than those nations which have to their losses viewed strict foreign investment controls as a panacea for economic stagnation. Where the world is headed in investment regulation is always hard to predict. But as the new century unfolds, investment protection appears to be gaining a new justification— the protection of a nation's culture.   Whether it proves to be truly a protection of important elements of culture, or another means of protecting inefficient domestic industry, remains to be played out on the international trade stage in the coming years.

CHAPTER 6
PROPERTY TAKINGS AND REMEDIES

Investments in foreign nations create risks that the host governments may "take" property and refuse to provide "proper" compensation. What is a "taking" and what is "proper" compensation have long been debated. The right to take is difficult to challenge; most nations have some form of eminent domain allowing government taking for public purposes. Thus, the issue usually becomes proper compensation. It is likely to be viewed by the investor as improper unless it is (1) paid with sufficient promptness, (2) adequate in amount, and (3) paid in an effective form.

DEFINING THE TAKING

The terms most frequently used when referring to the taking of foreign property are often neither clear in meaning nor consistently applied. The least intrusive act is usually called an *intervention*. That assumes the taking is intended to be temporary, and that the investment will be returned when the problems that motivated the taking are corrected. If the property is not returned in a reasonable period of time, the taking becomes at least a *nationalization*. The words *nationalization* and *expropriation* are often used interchangeably. They are usually intended to mean a taking followed by some form of compensation. But if no payment or inadequate payment fol-

lows the taking, the act may merit the label *confiscation*. The more usual case of a taking occurs when
there is a nationalization or expropriation followed by
an offer of some payment, but disagreement arises
about whether the payment standard should be
"just", "appropriate", "prompt, adequate and effective," or paid under some other label. These payment
terms have never been very clearly defined.

Government interference may alternatively involve
a series of steps that amount to a disguised, constructive, defacto, or "creeping" expropriation. A taking
may occur almost imperceptibly and often over a substantial period of time. It is nevertheless a taking.
Reasonable taxes on an investment might be raised
to become confiscatory; mandatory labor legislation
might attempt to transfer the financial resources of
an investment to nationals of the host country; remit-
tances and repatriations might be blocked or delayed
to where host country inflation effectively consumes
them; necessary government approvals might prove
unobtainable;   and other regulations dealing with
various aspects of the investment might become bur-
densome to the point of constituting an overwhelming justification for abandoning the investment.

Expropriations may take all property of all investors, or be *selective*, or *discriminatory*, or *retaliatory*.
Or all three. The action may be selective by taking
only one industry, or be discriminatory by taking either the property of a particular foreign investor, or
all the property of all the investors of a particular

foreign nation, or be retaliatory by taking property in response to acts of the foreign investor or its government.

When governments take property of *foreign* investors it is difficult to challenge successfully the public purpose of the taking nation, even though many expropriations clearly appear to have been motivated by little more than revolutionary fervor and with no sound economic justification. National courts, however, are not anxious to rule on the validity of the taking nation's satisfaction of the public purpose mandate.

THE "IZATIONS" OF THE PAST CENTURY

Expropriation in the last century effectively began when Russia (after the 1917 revolution), and Eastern European nations (after World War II), eliminated private ownership of the means of production and distribution. Additionally, Mexico expropriated oil in 1938. Indonesia nationalized most Dutch owned property in the 1950s. Egypt expropriated the Suez Canal Company in 1956. Expropriations were frequent in the 1960s, beginning with the extensive takings by Cuba of all foreign owned properties. The most recent extensive nationalizations were those by Iran in the late 1970s when the revolutionary government also seized the U.S. embassy and its staff. This led to the creation of the Iran-United States Claims Tribunal, a nine member arbitration entity which began hearing claims in 1982. By 2012, nearly all the 4,700 private claims filed against Iran had been resolved. More than $2.5 billion in awards were made. (www.iusct.org). The decisions add significantly to the development of expropriation law.

In the 1970s, the pace of nationalization slowed. Many developing nations turned to a new *"ization"* (*e.g.*, Mexicanization or Peruvianization) process, mandating the conversion of wholly foreign owned subsidiaries to joint ventures with majority local ownership. But that process began to diminish in the early 1980s, particularly after the debt shock in 1982 led many developing nations to encourage more foreign investment in the hope that exports would increase and generate hard currency earnings to help pay foreign debts. The next stage was *privatization*, the reduction of state ownership by the sale of state owned enterprises invariably operating with government subsidies. The most significant privatizations of the final decade of the century took place in the former nonmarket economy nations of Eastern Europe. As the new century began to evolve, some sporadic nationalizations occurred, such as in Venezuela and Bolivia, and more recently Argentina. The meaning of expropriation also was being tested in actions brought under the North American Free Trade Agreement (NAFTA), as the concept of expropriation was seemingly being expanded to include *regulatory* practices which impeded a foreign investment.

Nationalization of property has not been limited to acts by socialist or third world nations. The United Kingdom nationalized coal, steel, airline service and production, and other industries after World War II. France nationalized nearly all banks in 1982. (Many of the U.K. and French nationalized properties were later returned to the private sector, through the process of privatization.) But in both the United Kingdom and France, the takings were of property owned nearly exclusively by nationals rather than by foreign investors. The United States is not without its government's hand in the ownership of business. Part of the nation's passenger railway service was transferred to government ownership. But that involved an industry in severe financial distress. National ownership was viewed as a means of saving a dying, vital service sector, rather than displacing ownership successfully operated by the private sector. Nationalizations as an alternative to bankruptcy are a special and separate classification of property takings.

Actions that lead a country to nationalize a foreign owned commercial enterprise are difficult to predict. A taking of property may follow a change in administration, whether that results from revolution (Cuba, Indonesia, Iran, USSR) or election (Chile, Venezuela, Bolivia). Or the taking may occur during a non-threatened administration (Mexico, Great Britain). Nationalism and a sense of exploitation by foreigners may generate a takeover. Or the taking may occur because other methods of ownership are viewed as economically unsound, or politically or socially inappropriate. Most nationalizations are politically motivated; few have occurred within a stable government where a thorough economic study was first undertaken that concluded that certain sectors of industry ought to be state owned, or at least owned by nationals rather than foreigners.

A particular investment's susceptibility to being nationalized increases to the extent that it engages in what are viewed as essential national industries, such as extractive, export oriented natural resources, banking, insurance, international transportation (airlines, shipping), communications, national defense or agriculture. The entity is also more susceptible if it involves the use of people or processes that can be duplicated easily domestically; or if it consumes supplies that can be obtained easily from sources other than the affected investors; or if it does not have an essential value dependent upon the investor's goodwill or good name in the marketing of goods or services produced by the investment, and it has enough overall value to outweigh any bad press or other offsetting loss following a takeover.

INTERNATIONAL LAW

A nationalization may appear to be legal under domestic law, but it may not pass scrutiny under international law. What constitutes the international law of expropriation, however, is not easy to discern, particularly since the Third World in the late 1960s began to demand participation in formulating rules of international law applying to a nation's taking of property. Nations differ about what constitutes a public purpose and what is required compensation. They also differ regarding the legitimacy of discriminatory nationalizations, when the property of only one nation is taken, especially when that one nation is the colonial power formerly ruling the newly independent nation. Furthermore, some nations have presented lists of deductions to be applied to a multinational's valuation of its property, such as the Chilean deduction for what Chile considered to be excess profits for many past years of operation by foreign copper companies. Finally, and quite importantly, taking nations often reject the notion that any law other than *domestic* law should apply to a sovereign act of taking property, whether the property belongs to their own nationals or to foreigners. Different attitudes are sometimes ascribed to differences in colonial/colonialist political postures over the last two centuries, era and rapidity of the country's industrial development, and differing attitudes toward public/private economic enterprise.

The right of a sovereign nation to full and permanent sovereignty over its natural resources and economic activities and the right to take privately owned property are long accepted international legal norms. That is true whether the property belongs to the country's own nationals or to foreigners. Most constitutions express that right. But the taking must be for a public purpose or in the public interest. Sovereignty nevertheless sometimes becomes a shelter for many acts defined no more specifically than "for the social welfare or economic betterment of the nation." The concept persists that a taking is improper if it cannot be justified for some public purpose. The difficulty of measurement, as well as the doubt that such measurement may be undertaken outside the taking nation, have caused the public purpose element of expropriations to be relegated to obscurity in conflicts of the past half-dozen decades. The expropriation issues of importance have not included whether there was justification for the taking, but what is a taking and whether the question of compensation was properly addressed by the taking nation.

The U.S. government has repeatedly stated its position regarding the proper international law rule for compensation. The view stresses "prompt, adequate and effective" elements to justify a nationalization. However challenged, "prompt, adequate and effective" may express what the Department of State believes ought to be the standard. It is a view with only minimal support from other governments, and from many jurists, arbitrators and international law scholars. The more commonly used terms are "just" or "appropriate" compensation. While the United States adherence to a "prompt, adequate and effective" standard may create obstacles in the settlement of an expropriation case, that standard is applied in determining whether certain benefits of U.S. laws may be extended to countries which carry out expropriations. Ironically, when either the "just" or "appropriate" standard is applied, the measurement seems to include elements of the "prompt, adequate and effective" standard.

The conflict regarding the proper standard of compensation, and the debate whether international law or domestic law applies to a taking, has its modern roots for the United States in the 1938 Mexican expropriation of foreign owned petroleum investments. The United States recognized Mexico's sovereign right to take foreign property, but only upon payment of prompt, adequate and effective compensation according to international law. The Mexican response refuted both that alleged "prompt, adequate and effective" standard, and even the fundamental premise that international law rather than domestic law was the proper source of the applicable law. Mexico said it would pay because the Mexican constitution required payment, and it would pay according to Mexican standards of compensation. A settlement was ultimately reached regarding payment, but no settlement was reached regarding the standard under which the payment ought to be made. The next large scale nationalization of U.S. property was by Cuba in 1960. Like Mexico, Cuba refuted the prompt, adequate and effective standard. But unlike Mexico, Cuba's continued isolation from the United States more than fifty years after the Castro led revolution has prevented any settlement.

Soon after the Cuban expropriations, the U.N. General Assembly passed the Resolution on Permanent Sovereignty Over Natural Resources, affirming the right of nations to exercise permanent sovereignty over their resources and mandating the payment of "appropriate" compensation "in accordance with

the rules in force in the State taking such measures
in the exercise of its sovereignty and in accordance
with international law." Although a U.N. General
Assembly Resolution does not create international
law, this Resolution appeared to be expressive of the
customary international law of the day. A dozen
years later, during which time the United Nations
had expanded with the addition of many newly independent nations, the General Assembly addressed
the issue again in the Declaration on the Establishment of a New International Economic Order, passed
but with reservations by Japan, West Germany,
France, the United Kingdom and the United States.
Their concern was the absence of any reference to the
application of international law in the settlement of
nationalization compensation issues. Later that same
year, the General Assembly passed the Charter of
Economic Rights and Duties of States, with most of
the major developed nations opposed to the article
that stated that nationalization compensation was a
domestic law matter.

The view of the developing nations expressed in
the U.N. resolutions was consistent with how they
justified expropriations in practice. Chile expropriated the Kennecott Copper Company's holdings, offering to pay according to Chilean law, but only after
deducting excess profits that Kennecott allegedly had
withdrawn from its Chilean operation over a number
of years. Similar refusals to compensate were expressed by other developing nations. Unfortunately,
the International Court of Justice has produced no

international standard. The narrow ruling in the *Barcelona Traction* decision did not reach the issue of expropriation. The ICJ's predecessor, the Permanent Court of International Justice, held in 1928 in the often quoted *Chorzów Factory Case*, that there was a duty of "payment of fair compensation", and the *Norwegian Shipowners' Claims* arbitration in 1922 adopted a "just" standard.

Several arbitration and national court rulings have helped determine the path of development of an international rule of compensation. The *TOPCO-Libyan* arbitral award of 1977, declared the state of customary law to require "appropriate compensation". The *Banco Nacional de Cuba v. Chase Manhattan Bank*, 658 F.2d 875 (2nd Cir. 1981) decision in the United States in 1981, suggested that the consensus of nations was "appropriate compensation." The 1982 *Aminoil-Kuwait* arbitral award also approved "appropriate" as the accepted international standard. But the United States continued to argue the standard to be prompt, adequate and effective. The American Law Institute rejected that as the standard in revising the Restatement on Foreign Relations Law, adopting in the Restatement (Third) a standard of "just" compensation. That standard is believed to avoid the possible inclusion of deductions under an "appropriate" standard, but has received little support.

The Iran–United States Claims Tribunal, meeting at The Hague for more than two decades, did not apply a "prompt, adequate and effective" compensation standard in fact. Claims approved by the Tribunal, nevertheless, for the most part have been paid "promptly" from the funds established for such payment, and they have been paid in dollars, thus meeting any "effectiveness" standard. With respect to the "adequacy" element the tribunal has used various measurements of valuation that seem to satisfy any reasonable "adequacy" standard. Although this experience may support the "prompt, adequate and effective" standard espoused by the U.S. government, the Iranian claims process is *sui generis* because of the vast funds that Iran owned on deposit in the United States at the time of the nationalizations. If any conclusions are to be made regarding current international law of compensation, it seems clear that it is not *called* prompt, adequate and effective, but something very close to those terms seems to be included in the definition of appropriate or just compensation.

If the issue of compensation is reached, the value of the expropriated property must be established. That value may be established by direct negotiations with the taking government. Alternatively, valuation might be decided by an arbitral panel, as in the case of the Iranian nationalizations. But if the taking state refuses to pay compensation, the issue of valuation may come before a court outside the taking state. That could be an international forum, or, more likely, a court either in the nation of the expropriated investor or in a third nation where the taking nation has assets. Because of lack of standing in the International Court of Justice, or reasons associated with defenses either of sovereign immunity or the act of state doctrine, of even because of possible obstacles to collecting under an OPIC or MIGA insurance policy, satisfaction of the claim may have to wait until the U.S. government has negotiated a lump sum settlement with the taking nation. The wait may be long; the 1960 Cuban nationalizations remain unresolved as the new century unfolded. Once payment is made to a nation which has negotiated the claims on behalf of its nationals, international law plays no role in how that sum is divided among claimants.

UNITED STATES LAWS AFFECTING THE NATIONALIZATION PROCESS

The U.S. Congress enacted several laws disclosing a national position that expropriation must be accompanied by compensation, or, if not, the United States will use its powers to deny various benefits the nationalizing country otherwise might receive from the United States. Treaty commitments and provisions of other international agreements between the United States and investor hosting nations may serve to narrow expropriation uncertainties, such as provisions in the earlier, frequently negotiated Treaties of Friendship, Commerce and Navigation, or their successor, Bilateral Investment Treaties (BITs). But BITs have not been concluded with many important Third World nations where there is much foreign investment by U.S. nationals (e.g., Mexico, India, Brazil).

In addition to provisions governing expropriation, Bilateral Investment Treaties have three significant provisions dealing with (1) nondiscrimination in establishing and operating investments; (2) rights regarding transfers of investments; and (3) mandatory dispute resolution methods. Where these treaties do exist there is always the threat that a successor government may reject them, however in violation of international law such action may be. They are important treaties, nevertheless, and investors do gain an added challenge if their property is taken by a nation which has signed such a bilateral treaty with the United States.

The North American Free Trade Agreement (NAFTA) has a detailed provision in Chapter 11 governing the taking of property of a foreign investor from a Party. The right to take property is acknowledged, but only where there is a public purpose, a non-discriminatory taking, due process of law and minimum standards of treatment as contained in the NAFTA, and the payment of compensation. The compensation provisions do not refer to the prompt, adequate and effective standard urged by the United States, but quite clearly meet that standard by more specific language. Chapter 11 cases are developing a NAFTA jurisprudence on taking of foreign property that has drawn much criticism from challenged NAFTA Parties and observers, especially environmental law groups. Government regulations, often directed to environmental issues, have been ruled to constitute expropriation in the manner they have been implemented. While the NAFTA covers the compensation side of expropriation in considerable detail, it does not adequately define what constitutes an expropriation. This must be resolved if investment and investment expropriation is to be included in further trade agreements.

The WTO Agreement on Trade-Related Investment Measures (TRIMs) has provisions that are not as encompassing as those in the NAFTA, and do not include provisions governing the taking of investment property. Perhaps as the issues noted above with the NAFTA expropriation provisions are resolved, further revisions to the WTO TRIMs will include this important investment issue.

Other domestic laws of the United States apply to nations which have expropriated property of U.S. nationals and have failed to provide compensation or to illustrate a willingness to negotiate a compensation agreement. Subsequent to the Cuban nationalizations, the Hickenlooper Amendment to the Foreign Assistance Act was enacted and provides, in part, that the:

> President shall suspend assistance to the government of any country to which assistance is provided under this chapter or any other Act when the government of such country. . . (A) has nationalized or expropriated or seized ownership or control of property owned by any United States citizen . . . (C) has imposed or enforced discriminatory taxes or other exactions,

or restrictive maintenance or operational conditions, or has taken other actions, which have the effect of nationalizing, expropriating, or otherwise seizing ownership or control of property so owned, and such country, government agency, or government sub-division fails within a reasonable time . . . to take appropriate steps . . . to discharge its obligations under international law toward such citizen . . . including speedy compensation for such property in convertible foreign exchange, equivalent to the full value thereof, as required by international law, or fails to take steps designed to provide relief from such taxes, exactions, or conditions, as the case may be; and such suspension shall continue until the President is satisfied that appropriate steps are being taken.

The Sabbatino, or Second Hickenlooper, Amendment was passed by an angry Congress soon after the U.S. Supreme Court, in *Banco Nacional de Cuba v. Sabbatino*, 376 U.S. 398 (1964), held that the Act of State doctrine prevented U.S. courts from hearing cases of foreign expropriation, even where there were allegations of violations of international law. The Congressional response reversed the presumption of *Sabbatino*, allowing U.S. courts to proceed unless the President stated that such adjudication would embarrass the conduct of foreign relations. Additional acts prohibit the United States from casting votes in organizations such as the World Bank or InterAmerican Development Bank (IADB) for loans to countries which have expropriated property of U.S. nationals and refused compensation.

The U.S. 1996 Cuban Liberty and Democratic Solidarity (Libertad) Act promoted what could become a massive challenge to U.S. courts to address the Cuban expropriations. Title III of this commonly called Helms-Burton Act provided for expropriation claims against those foreign parties "trafficking" in property once owned by U.S. nationals. But each president has deferred the implementation of that provision and the litigation has been thwarted.

INSURING AGAINST THE RISKS OF FOREIGN INVESTMENT LOSSES

Investments abroad often are subject to risks that are not significant concerns to a domestic investment. An investment in the United States is not at risk from military conflict, or uncompensated expropriation, or losses from a currency that becomes inconvertible. Because these risks are not present in most developed, democratic nations, and because they present extremely complex risk measurement problems for investors entering developing nations, the *domestic* insurance industries generally have not offered insurance to cover such potential losses for investments made in high risk nations. It is thus to individual government and multi-nation organization investment insurance programs that foreign investors often must turn to reduce the consequences of these risks.

INSURANCE FOR FOREIGN INVESTORS—
OPIC

National insurance programs, such as the U.S. Overseas Private Investment Corporation (OPIC), support government policies that encourage domestic industries to engage in investment abroad. But critics of government "backed" insurance of U.S. investment abroad argue that the program encourages and subsidizes the transfer of productive facilities abroad, at the cost of jobs in the United States. Although OPIC has been the preeminent U.S, insurer of foreign investment risks, many members of Congress believe its role should be assumed by the private sector. They reject the concept that the government should engage in private sector support activities, and worry about the potential burden on U.S. taxpayers. While OPIC is supposed to write insurance adhering to private insurance industry principles of risk management, and on a self-sustaining basis, it does not always or even regularly do so, perhaps because OPIC insurance is backed by the full faith and credit of the United States. Because of the absence of significant expropriations over the past few decades, at least since those by Iran, OPIC has been a financial success that has allowed it to build reserves in excess of $4 billion, while claims have been nearly non-existent. As long as insurance claims remain dormant, OPIC is likely to avoid serious criticism from Congress and others about the risk to the general public. OPIC's role is increasing in financing foreign investment, however important its insurance programs remain.

Until the 1969 creation of OPIC, AID was the primary organization through which the U.S. government issued risk insurance to U.S. investors in developing nations. OPIC was established to "mobilize and facilitate the participation of U.S. private capital and skills in the economic and social development of less developed countries and areas, and countries in transition from nonmarket to market economies."

Initially three principal risks were covered by OPIC—risk of loss due to (1) inconvertibility, (2) expropriation or confiscation, or (3) war, revolution, insurrection or civil strife, now referred to as political violence. Expropriation "includes, but is not limited to, any abrogation, repudiation, or impairment by a foreign government of its own contract with an investor with respect to a project, where such abrogation, repudiation, or impairment is not caused by the investor's own fault or misconduct, and materially adversely affects the continued operation of the project." OPIC contracts have followed a more specific and enumerative approach, because the law does not define more specifically what actions constitute expropriation. The third major form of coverage, political violence, covers loss of assets or income due to war, revolution, insurrection or politically motivated civil strife, terrorism or sabotage. The usual OPIC contract provides protection against injury to the "physical condition, destruction, disappearance or seizure and retention of covered property directly caused by war or by revolution or insurrection and includes injury to the physical condition, destruction, disappearance or seizure and retention of covered property as a direct result of actions taken in hindering, combating or defending against a pending or expected hostile act whether in war, revolution, or insurrection." With terrorism becoming the major focus in many parts of the world, this class of OPIC insurance may become the most important. But the terrorism has been in developed nations, not in the nations where the insurance is written.

The investor must exhaust remedies before OPIC becomes obligated to pay any claim. All reasonable action must be taken by the investor, including initiating administrative and judicial claims, to prevent or contest the challenged action by the host government. Prior to the receipt of payment of a claim, the investor usually will be required to transfer to OPIC all right, title and interest in the insured investment, including when the government expropriatory action consists of preventing the investor from exercising effective control over and withdrawing funds received from the foreign entity as dividends, interest or return of capital. The investor has an ongoing obligation to cooperate with the U.S. government in pressing claims against the host government.

Otherwise qualifying countries may be denied OPIC insurance if they do not extend internationally recognized workers' rights to domestic workers, or if they do not respect human rights, but presidential discretion may result in a waiver of this prohibition on national economic interest grounds.

INSURANCE FOR FOREIGN INVESTORS— MIGA

OPIC insurance is limited to U.S. investors. To encourage increased investment in the developing nations, similar insurance has been established on an international level by the World Bank's 1985 Multilateral Investment Guarantee Agency (MIGA). With the expected completion of Mexico's admission process, all the major nations are subscribers to MIGA.

Risks covered by MIGA include inconvertibility, deprivation of ownership or control by governmental actions, breach of contract by the government where there is no recourse to a judicial or arbitral forum, and loss from military action or civil disturbance. The insurance may cover equity investments or loans made or guaranteed by holders of equity (probably including service and management contracts), and also licensing, franchising and production sharing agreements.

Generally, investors must be from a member country, and only foreign investors qualify. There was considerable discussion regarding insuring only in those developing nations which adopted standards for protecting foreign investment, but the final Convention did not include any such conditions. Such standards may nevertheless be a factor in writing insurance, if any measure of risk management principles is to be followed. The highest percentage of MIGA coverage is in sub-Saharan Africa, followed by Asia, and then by Latin America and the Caribbean.

The viability of MIGA is dependent both on its care in selecting risks to insure, and its ability to negotiate settlements after paying claims. Unlike national programs, such as OPIC, MIGA has the backing of a large group of nations when it presses a claim. Only experience will disclose the extent to which politics will enter the claims procedures. The intention is to avoid political interference and consider solely legal issues. MIGA has yet to face claims experience. If over time the risks MIGA insures diminish, the use of such insurance will decrease. If on the other hand the risks become reality, the effectiveness of the claims procedures will become evident.

Creating MIGA within the World Bank structure offers benefits a separate international organization would lack. MIGA has access to World Bank data on nations' economic and social status, thus helping the assessment of risks. The World Bank has considerable credibility that favors MIGA, and encourages broad participation. It is not certain how MIGA will affect national programs, such as OPIC. A U.S. company, for example, might prefer dealing with OPIC because of greater confidence of claims being paid, of maintaining information confidentiality, and benefitting from legal processes established in bilateral investment treaties. MIGA acts to some degree as a gap filler for U.S. investors when OPIC insurance is not available or inadequate for the project. MIGA's success will likely be where it fills gaps rather than competes with established national insurance programs. Its real test will be when significant claims are made (only three have been paid and some fifty disputes have been resolved)—the past two decades have not witnessed the expropriations that tested the viability of OPIC in the 1970s.

CHAPTER 7

EU BUSINESS COMPETITION RULES[1]—EXTRATERRITORIAL ANTITRUST LAWS

The European Common Market has accomplished among other things, an institutionalization of competitive market doctrines. The role of the Court of Justice and General Court in interpreting Articles 101 and 102 of the Treaty on the Functioning of the European Union (TFEU) is one example of the movement toward greater union. In that sense, these articles assume some of the function of the interstate commerce clause of the U.S. Constitution. Articles 101 and 102 have a mandatory effect upon any international trade or investment touched by their reach. The articles evidence the degree of rule-making complexity and detail achieved in one area of law. Recent Court of Justice and General Court rulings about their application to persons, things and events beyond the territorial limits of the Union serve to introduce the larger issue of extraterritorial laws and international business transactions.

In general, Article 101(1) aims to prohibit "arms length" competitors from agreeing between themselves to prevent, restrain or distort competition. Article 101 (1) is roughly analogous to the prohibition

---

[1] For much more extensive coverage, see Folsom's European Union Law in a Nutshell.

against restraints of trade in Section 1 of the U.S. Sherman Antitrust Act. Broadly speaking, Article 102 prohibits dominant enterprises from abusing their position to the prejudice of competitors or consumers. This prohibition is more encompassing than monopolization as an offense under Section 2 of the Sherman Act.

Articles 101 and 102 are complicated and elastic. Although each article lists certain proscribed business practices, much of their specific, substantive content has been generated by Commission and Court interpretations. Numerous treatises (including several multi-volume works) are devoted to European competition law. A notable feature is their applicability to publicly owned enterprises (of which there are many). For example, the European Court affirmed the applicability of Article 102 to RAI, the Italian state broadcasting monopoly, provided that such application would not obstruct its tasks.

ENFORCEMENT

The terms of Articles 101 and 102 are enforced, in the first instance, by the Commission and since 2004 by member state competition law authorities and national courts. The Commission has the power to investigate, *sua sponte* or upon complaint by interested persons or member states, possible violations. The Commission may obtain information from national authorities as part of its investigatory process and it may require those authorities to conduct investigations for it. The Commission may require enterprises to produce records or documents necessary to its investigation. When there is a failure or refusal to comply with a Commission investigation or enforcement decision, the Commission may seek a compliance order from the Court. Several procedural requirements for Commission investigations and hearings have been discussed by the Court of Justice. One notable decision upheld the authority of the Commission to conduct searches of corporate offices *without* notice or warrant when it has reason to believe that pertinent evidence may be lost. Another notable decision permitted a Swiss "whistle blower" who once worked for Hoffman-La Roche (a defendant in competition law proceedings) to sue in tort for disclosure of his identity as an informant.

The subject matter of Articles 101 and 102 is commerce, yet their impact is as political as commercial. Astute observers have noted that a significant number of the leading "test cases" have involved defendants from Japan, the United States, Switzerland and other non-members. It is, of course, politically much more acceptable when these Articles are applied to foreign firms. But they have also been applied extensively to European enterprises. The quantity and significance of competition law is sufficient to have generated a growing number of lawyers who specialize in giving advice about the effects of Articles 101 and 102 on transactions in the Common Market.

Sanctions

A person who ignores the reach of EU competition law may experience severe consequences, but nothing comparable to the felony criminal sanctions and private treble damages actions found in U.S. antitrust law. Article 101(2) renders offending business agreements null and void. Nullity is most often raised as a defense to enforcement of contracts, licenses and joint ventures in national legal proceedings. Fines may be levied by the Commission for supplying false or misleading information or for holding back information in connection with inquiries about the applicability of the articles, and further fines may be levied if persons or activities are found to have contravened Article 101 or 102.

For example, the Belgian and French subsidiary enterprises of the Japanese electrical and electronic group, Matsushita, were fined by the Commission for supplying it with false information about whether Matsushita recommended retail prices for its products. Furthermore, offending activity may be penalized per day until there is compliance with a Commission order. All Commission decisions imposing fines or penalties under competition law are subject to judicial review by the General Court. In early years the Court tended to reduce the amounts involved because of the developmental state of Article 101 and 102 law. In more recent decisions, the Court has upheld substantial fines and penalties imposed by the Commission in competition law proceedings.

Written communications with external EU-licensed lawyers undertaken for defense purposes are confidential and need not be disclosed. Written communications with in-house lawyers are not exempt from disclosure, nor are communications with external non-EU counsel. Thus communications with North American attorneys (who are not also EU-licensed attorneys) are generally discoverable. For example, the Commission obtained in-house counsel documents from John Deere, Inc., a Belgian subsidiary of the U.S. multinational. These documents were drafted as advice to management on how to avoid competition law liability for export prohibition restraints. They were used by the Commission to justify the finding of an intentional Article 101 violation and a fine of 2 million EUROS. U.S. attorneys have followed these developments with amazement and trepidation. Disclaimers of possible nonconfidentiality are one option to consider in dealing with clients. At a minimum, U.S. attorneys ought to advise their clients that the usual rules on attorney-client privilege may not apply.

Article 101 and 102 fines are reducible to judgment in the courts of any member state. Because regional law supercedes only inconsistent laws in any of the members states, violating Article 101 or 102 may not preclude additional sanctions for breach of a member state's business competition laws (e.g., laws which may authorize an aggrieved person to receive damages). Indeed it is possible, as several examples suggest, that multiple liability under British or German competition law (the most vigorous in the Common Market), European Union law and U.S. antitrust law can simultaneously occur. With such a high level of risk, law in this area is ignored only at great peril to international business.

ARTICLE 101—EXEMPTIONS

Not all anticompetitive agreements violate Article 101(1). By operation of Article 101(3) Article 101(1) may not apply to an agreement, decision or concerted practice which contributes to an improvement of production or distribution of goods, or which promotes technical or economic progress (while allowing consumers a fair share of the resulting benefit), *provided* the agreement or concerted practice does not serve to eliminate competition in a substantial part of the products in question. Since 2004, the Commission, member state competition law authorities, and member state courts share decisionmaking power concerning individual exemptions under Article 101(3). Various procedural rules and Guidelines ensure that the Commission can have the final say on individual exemptions should it wish to do so.

Block Exemptions

Council and Commission regulations operate to exclude from Article 101 (1) certain vertical purchasing, distribution and franchise agreements, categories of research and development agreements, specified agreements in the technology transfer area, and horizontal agreements among smaller firms for product specialization. Also exempted by regulation are certain motor vehicle distribution and servicing agreements. These regulations are known as "block exemptions" since they are based upon the legal criteria of Article 101(3). They have the practical effect of dramatically reducing the Commission's workload because it is not necessary to apply for a block exemption. Parties need only conform their conduct to the terms of these regulations, which often detail permitted, permissible and prohibited contract clauses.

Lawyers representing clients doing business in Europe usually prefer to structure contracts and other arrangements in accordance with block exemptions since this preserves confidentiality. Voluntary adherence to block exemptions has become a successful, cost-effective way of implementing Article 101. The meaning of the regulations is better understood by a review of the leading cases previously brought by the Commission to test its authority in each of these fields. Lines drawn in the block exemptions may later be reviewed in private litigation or public enforcement proceedings.

Such agreements and concerted practices are only a partial list of Council, Commission and Court regulatory concerns under Articles 101 and 102. In 1987 the Court of Justice ruled that Article 101 applies to mergers and acquisitions, activities previously thought to fall only under Article 102. This decision is yet another indication of the significance of competition law to those drafting distribution contracts, licensing agreements, joint ventures and other business arrangements. Counsel should be especially circumspect about any contractual or licensing term that may tend to divide up the Common Market by allocating territories or customers. Since great effort has been made to create the Common Market, private market division arrangements inhibiting competition in goods or services are practically "per se" offenses under Articles 101 and 102. This is sometimes true even of intrabrand vertical market division restraints, which are now frequently permitted under the Rule of Reason approach to U.S. restraint of trade law.

COMMISSION REGULATION OF MERGERS

In 1989, the Council of Ministers unanimously adopted a Regulation on the Control of Concentrations Between Undertakings ("Mergers Regulation"). This regulation became effective in 1990 and was significantly amended in 2003. It vests in the Commission the power to oppose large-scale mergers and acquisitions of competitive consequence to the Common Market. The control process established by the Mergers Regulation commences when a concentration must be notified to the Commission. The duty to notify is triggered only when the concentration involves enterprises with a combined worldwide turnover of at least 2.5 billion EUROS *and* two of them have an aggregate region-wide turnover of 100 million EUROS *and* at least two of the enterprises have a minimum of 25 million EUROS turnover in the same three member states.

As a general rule, concentrations meeting these criteria cannot be put into effect and fall exclusively within the Commission's domain. The effort here is to create a "one-stop" regulatory system. However, certain exceptions apply so as to allow national authorities to challenge some mergers. For example, this may occur under national law when two-thirds of the activities of each of the companies involved take place in the same member state. The member states can also oppose mergers when their public security is at stake, to preserve plurality in media ownership, when financial institutions are involved or other legitimate interests are at risk. If the threshold criteria of the Mergers Regulation are not met, member states can ask the Commission to investigate mergers that create or strengthen a dominant position in that state. States that lack national merger controls seem likely to do this. Since 2004, parties to a merger that is subject to notification in three or more member states may request "one-stop" review by the Commission, which will occur provided no member state objects.

Once a concentration is notified to the Commission, it has one month to decide to investigate the merger. If a formal investigation is commenced, the Commission ordinarily then has four months to challenge or approve the merger. During these months, in most cases, the concentration cannot be put into effect. It is on hold.

The Commission evaluates mergers in terms of their "compatibility" with the Common Market. The

1990 Mergers Regulation stated that if the concentration created or strengthened a dominant position such that competition was "significantly impeded," it was incompatible. Effective 2004, this test was replaced by a prohibition against mergers that "significantly impede effective competition" by creating or strengthening dominant positions. Thus the new test focuses on effects not dominance. A set of Guidelines on Horizontal Mergers issued by the Commission in 2004 elaborate upon this approach. It is thought that this change will bring EU and U.S. mergers law closer together (the U.S. test is "substantial lessening of competition").

During a mergers investigation, the Commission can obtain information and records from the parties, and request member states to help with the investigation. Fines and penalties back up the Commission's powers to obtain what it needs from the parties. If the concentration has already taken effect, the Commission can issue a "hold-separate" order. This requires the corporations or assets acquired to be separated and not, operationally speaking, merged. Approval of the merger may involve modifications of its terms or promises by the parties aimed at diminishing its anticompetitive potential. Negotiations with the Commission to obtain such clearances may follow. If the Commission ultimately decides to oppose the merger in a timely manner, it can order its termination by whatever means are appropriate to restore conditions of effective competition. Such decisions can be appealed to the Court of First Instance.

Case Examples

The first merger actually blocked by the Commission on competition law grounds was the attempted acquisition of a Canadian aircraft manufacturer (DeHaviland—owned by Boeing) by two European companies (Aerospatiale SNI of France and Alenia e Selenia Spa of Italy). Prior to this rejection in late 1991, the Commission had approved over 50 mergers, obtaining modifications in a few instances. The Commission, in the DeHaviland case, took the position that the merger would have created an unassailable dominant position in the world and European market for turbo prop or commuter aircraft. If completed, the merged entity would have had 50 percent of the world and 67 percent of the European market for such aircraft.

In 1997, the Commission dramatically demonstrated its extraterritorial jurisdiction over the Boeing-McDonnell Douglas merger. This merger had already been cleared by the U.S. Federal Trade Commission. The European Commission, however, demanded and got (at the risk of a trade war) important concessions from Boeing. These included abandonment of exclusive supply contracts with three U.S. airlines and licensing of technology derived from McDonnell Douglas' military programs at reasonable royalty rates. The Commission's success in this case was widely perceived in the United States as pro-Airbus.

The Commission blocked the MC Worldcom/Sprint merger in 2001, as did the U.S. Dept. of Justice. Both authorities were worried about the merger's adverse effects on Internet access. For the Commission, this was the first block of a merger taking place outside the EU between two firms established outside the EU. Much more controversy arose when in 2001 the Commission blocked the GE/Honeywell merger after it had been approved by U.S. authorities. The Commission was particularly concerned about the potential for bundling engines with avionics and non-avionics to the disadvantage of rivals. On appeal, the General Court rejected the Commission's legal reasoning. Nevertheless, the merger never took place. The United States and the EU in the wake of GE/Honeywell, have agreed to follow a set of "Best Practices" on coordinated timing, evidence gathering, communication and consistency of remedies.

THE EXTRATERRITORIAL REACH OF ARTICLES 101 AND 102

There is a question about the extent to which the competition rules extend to activity anywhere in the world, including activity occurring entirely or in part within the territorial limits of the United States. Decisions by the Commission and the Court of Justice suggest that the territorial reach of Articles 101 and 102 is expanding and may well extend to an international business transaction occurring within the United States.

For an agreement to be incompatible with the Common Market and prohibited under Article 101(1) it must be "likely to affect trade between member states" and have "the object or effect" of impairing "competition within the Common Market". The Court has repeatedly held that the fact that one of the parties to an agreement is domiciled in a third country does not preclude the applicability of Article 101 (1) if the agreement is effective in the territory of the Common Market. Swiss and British companies, for example, argued that the Commission was not competent to impose competition law fines for acts committed in Switzerland and Britain (before joining the EU) by enterprises domiciled outside the Union solely because the acts had effects within the Common Market. Nevertheless, the Court held those companies in violation of Article 101 because they owned subsidiary companies within the Union and controlled their behavior. The foreign parent and its subsidiaries were treated as a "single enterprise" for purposes of service of process, judgment and collection of fines and penalties. In doing so, the Court observed that the fact that a subsidiary company has its own legal personality does not rule out the possibility that its conduct is attributable to the parent company.

The Court has extended its reasoning to the extraterritorial application of Article 102. A U.S. parent company, for example, was held potentially liable for acquisitions by its Italian subsidiary which affected market conditions within Europe. In another case, the Court held that a Maryland company's refusal to sell its product to a competitor of its affiliate company within the Union was a result of united "single enterprise" action. It proceeded to state that extraterritorial conduct merely having "repercussions on competitive structures" in the Common Market fell within the parameters of Article 102. The Court ordered the U.S. company, through its Italian affiliate, to supply the competitor at reasonable prices.

In 1988, the Court of Justice widened the extraterritorial reach of Article 101 in the *Woodpulp* case where pulp producers from the United States, Canada, Sweden and Finland were fined for price fixing activities affecting Common Market trade and competition. These firms did not have substantial operations within the EU. They were primarily exporters to the Common Market. This decision's reliance upon a "place of implementation" effects test is similar to that used under the Sherman Act.

THE EFFECTS TEST IN UNITED STATES AND EUROPEAN LAW

It may be a substantial jump to predict that Articles 101 and 102 bear upon a business transaction done in the United States or another non-EU country which merely inures to the competitive disadvantage of a company located within the Common Market. Yet in one of the *Dyestuffs* cases as early as 1969 the Commission took the position that:

> The rules of competition of the Treaty are therefore applicable to all restrictions on competition

that produce within the Common Market effects to which Article 101, paragraph 1, applies. There is therefore no need to examine whether the enterprises that originated such restraints of competition have their head office within or outside of the Community. Commission v. I.C.I., 8 Common Mkt.L.Rep. 494 (1969).

Although the Court's disposition of the *Dyestuffs* cases did not endorse such reasoning, the Commission has reasserted its "effects test" in subsequent arguments. The Commission's approach merits close consideration if only because the initiation of an Article 101 or 102 inquiry can generate local overhead costs for those involved in European business transactions. That courts in the United States have also used an "effects test" in connection with the question of the extraterritoriality of U.S. antitrust laws increases the potential for uncertainty and costs in international transactions.

U.S. courts have long asserted the right to apply the Sherman Antitrust Act to foreign commerce intended to or affecting the U.S. market. In some cases, this approach has been tempered to allow consideration of the interests of comity and foreign countries in the outcome. Some limits on the extraterritorial reach of the Sherman Act are created by the act of state doctrine and the Foreign Sovereign Immunities Act. But in the main, U.S. antitrust law has been applied to foreigners and overseas activities with a zeal sometimes approaching religious fervor. This fervor has carried over into other areas, such as the failed attempt of the Reagan administration to apply U.S. export control laws to European enterprises involved in the construction of the Soviet-era natural gas pipeline from Siberia to Western Europe.

Amendments to the Sherman Act in 1984 stress the "direct, substantial and reasonably foreseeable" nature of effects on U.S. foreign commerce as a prerequisite to antitrust jurisdiction. Nevertheless, the potential for conflict in this field is enormous. For example, a multinational enterprise headquartered in the United States but doing business in England could be constrained by U.S. antitrust law from fixing prices, yet permitted by European competition law under Article 101 (3) to do exactly that. Assuming that the price fixing in question has effects in both markets, what course of action is to be followed? There is no easy answer. When the firm is located within a country other than one of the member states of the EU or the United States, but engages in activity having effects within those markets, the problem potential of extraterritoriality may be even more acute. Reconciling a conflict of antitrust laws applied extraterritorially by these two jurisdictions could become a flashpoint in international business.

EXTRATERRITORIAL ANTITRUST LAWS, BLOCKING STATUTES AND INTERNATIONAL SOLUTIONS

Business operations that transcend a nation's borders have focused concern about the extent to which the applicability of a nation's laws must stop at its territorial borders. Absent a controlling and readily enforceable international law, it is at least a fair question to ask whether national laws are needed to regulate extraterritorial business enterprises.

Reasons advanced to support an extraterritorial application of U.S. antitrust laws are founded on the idea that some extraterritorial extension is necessary to prevent their circumvention by multinational corporations which have the business sagacity to ensure that anticompetitive transactions are consummated beyond the territorial borders of the United States. An extraterritorial extension of antitrust laws can help to protect the export opportunities of domestic firms. Extraterritorial application of the antitrust laws can also help to ensure that the American consumer receives the benefit of competing imports, which in turn may spur complacent domestic industries. The effect of foreign auto imports on the car manufacturers in the United States may be cited as an example. In an increasingly internationalized world, extraterritorial antitrust may merely reflect economic reality.

On the other hand, the British argue that extraterritoriality permits the United States to unjustifiably "mold the international economic and trading world to its own image." In particular, the U.S. "effects" doctrine creates legal uncertainty for international traders, and U.S. courts pay little attention to the competing policies (interests) of other concerned governments. As the House of Lords stated in *Rio Tinto Zinc*: "It is axiomatic that in anti-trust matters the policy of one state may be to defend what it is the policy of another state to attack."

The British also argue, not without some support, that customary international law does not permit extraterritorial application of national laws. In making this argument, the British have a convenient way of forgetting about the extraterritorial scope of Articles 101 and 102, which are now part of their law. Moreover, in a curious reversal of roles illustrating the extremes of the debate, the British government applied the Protection of Trading Interests Act to block the pursuit of treble damages in *United States* courts by the liquidator of Laker Airways against British Airways and other defendants. A House of Lords decision reversed this ban but retained government restrictions on discovery related to the case.

Extraterritoriality is a matter of balance. The Executive, Legislative, and Judicial branches of government in the United States have reached out extraterritorially in the law of admiralty, antitrust, crime, labor, securities regulation, taxation, torts, trademarks and wildlife management. A balance drawn wrongly by one nation invites retaliatory action by others. In the case of antitrust judgments emanating from courts in the United States, most notably the "Uranium Cartel" treble damages litigation of the late 1970s, many nations consider that the balance has been wrongly drawn. Many nations have taken retaliatory action by enacting "blocking statutes."

Blocking Statutes

The United Kingdom blocking statute is the Protection of Trading Interests Act of 1980. This Act (without specifying U.S. antitrust law) makes it difficult to depose witnesses, obtain documents or enforce multiple liability judgments extraterritorially in the U.K. Violation of the 1980 Act may result in criminal penalties. Furthermore, under the "clawback" provision of the Act, parties with outstanding multiple liabilities in foreign jurisdictions (*e.g.*, U.S. treble damages defendants) may recoup the punitive element of such awards in Britain against assets of the successful plaintiff. The British Act invites other nations to adopt clawback provisions by offering clawback reciprocity. U.S. attorneys confronted with a blocking statute need to understand that multiple liability judgments combined with contingency fee arrangements are virtually unknown elsewhere.

The extensive array of pre-trial discovery mechanisms allowed in U.S. civil litigation rarely, if ever, have a counterpart in foreign law. Discovery subpoenas originating in U.S. litigation are often "shocking" to many foreign defendants. And the U.S. Supreme Court ruled in *Aérospatiale* that use of letters rogatory under the Hague Convention is not obligatory. It is the blocking of discovery that potentially most threatens the extraterritorial application of U.S. laws, especially antitrust. Since U.S. courts may sanction parties who in bad faith fail to respond to discovery requests, foreign defendants requesting help from their home governments under blocking statutes are especially at risk. On the other hand, good faith efforts to modify or work around discovery blockades may favor foreign defendants. Such defendants are often caught in a "no win" situation. Either way they will be penalized.

International Antitrust Cooperation

Some evidence of international antitrust cooperation is contained in a 1967 recommendation of the OECD which provides for notification of antitrust actions, exchanges of information to the extent that the disclosure is domestically permissible, and where practical, coordination of antitrust enforcement. The OECD resolution served as a model for the 1972 "Antitrust Notification and Consultation Procedure" between Canada and the United States. Following the "Uranium Cartel" litigation, Australia and the United States reached an Agreement on Cooperation in Antitrust Matters (1982) to minimize jurisdictional conflicts. Australia has taken the position that U.S. courts are not a proper institution to balance interests of concerned countries within the context of private antitrust litigation.

The Agreement on Cooperation provides that when the Government of Australia is concerned with private antitrust proceedings pending in a United States court, the Government of Australia may request the Government of the United States to participate in the litigation. The United States must report to the court on the substance and outcome of consultations with Australia on the matter concerned. In this way, Australia's views and interests in the litigation and its potential outcome are made known to the court. The court is not required to defer to those views, or even to openly consider them. It merely receives the "report." Australia, in turn, has indicated a willingness to be more receptive to discovery requests in U.S. antitrust litigation and to consult before invoking its blocking statute.

Similar arrangements have been made between the United States and Canada. No such agreement has been reached with the United Kingdom, with whom the extraterritoriality issue remains contentious, a fact which has led some to wonder whether the United States ought to have its own blocking statute against extraterritorial European competition law. An antitrust cooperation agreement seems more appropriate and, indeed, late in 1991 the European Union (of which Britain is still a member) and the United States reached such an agreement. This accord commits the parties to notify each other of imminent enforcement action, to share relevant information and consult on potential policy changes. An innovative feature is the inclusion of "positive comity" principles, each side promising to take the other's interests into account when considering antitrust prosecutions. The agreement has had a significant effect on mergers of firms doing business in North America and Europe (above).

Microsoft

The U.S.-EU Antitrust Cooperation Agreement was prominently used to jointly negotiate a 1994 settlement on restrictive practices of the Microsoft Corporation, a settlement that is being revisited concerning Microsoft's web browser tactics. In the more recent round of public prosecutions focused on Windows as a monopoly, the U.S. settlement reached in 2001 is less demanding than the Commission judgment of 2004 which requires an unbundling of media playback capabilities. This example reaffirms that transatlantic antitrust "cooperation" need not necessarily result in similar outcomes. In 2007, the Court of First Instance broadly confirmed the Commission's 2004 decision. Shortly thereafter, Microsoft settled the prosecution by altering its operating systems' licensing arrangements to favor "open source" software developers (e.g., Linux). Prior to settlement, Microsoft had been fined, including daily noncompliance penalties, in excess of 2 billion Euros. By 2008, the Commission was investigating Microsoft's bundling of its web browser with Windows, and the compatibility of its Office software with rival programs. A quick settlement "unbundled" web browsers on Windows...there are now over a dozen choices. Other U.S. technology firms have also been under the EU competition law microscope: Qualcomm, Intel, Google, IBM and Apple included. In 2009, the Commission fined Intel 1.06 billion Euros for abusing its dominant position in microprocessors for PCs. Intel's price discounts and loyalty rebates are the center of this decision, now on appeal.

CHAPTER 8

RESOLUTION OF INTERNATIONAL DISPUTES: LITIGATION AND ARBITRATION

Although a leitmotif of this book has been that a transactions counsel should try to avoid litigation by means of thorough planning of the transaction, exhaustive assignment of all risks, and careful drafting of all documents, disputes can and will arise which cannot be resolved by the parties themselves. In such instances, the parties to a transaction must seek assistance from outside sources. Faced with such a dispute, parties may seek access to resolve their dispute through the courts in one or more countries, through arbitration or through mediation. This Chapter discusses some considerations associated with litigation in national courts, before briefly discussing the widespread and increasing preference which merchants, investors and host countries have for arbitration.

Dispute settlement should also be dealt with when drafting the initial international business agreements between the parties, so that the dispute resolution process is known and understood before any actual dispute arises. The formal process chosen in the contract is most commonly either litigation or arbitration. Many international contracts require that mediation be used before any formal process is used, and mediation is the process preferred by many parties, especially Asian businesses. Whichever process is chosen, the contract should also choose the forum or tribunal and the governing law.

Not only is the question raised regarding *how* a dispute ought to be resolved, such as arbitration versus litigation, but there are further questions such as *where* the dispute should be resolved, and under *what* rules. These questions may best be addressed well before any dispute arises, and be the subject of provisions in the initial contract or agreement. Such agreements may stipulate that a contract for the sale of goods is to be governed by the ICC INCOTERMS, or the provisions of the applicable state version of the UCC. For substantive contract terms the parties may choose to opt out of the otherwise applicable CISG, instead preferring the UNIDROIT Principles of International Commercial Contracts, or a particular nation's sales law, such as the U.S. Uniform Commercial Code or the Spanish Codigo Comercio. The parties may choose the applicable forum for dispute resolution, although they may not thrust upon a court otherwise inapplicable subject matter jurisdiction. The chosen forum might be the courts of one of the party's nations, or a third nation, or perhaps an international tribunal. There may not be an applicable international court with jurisdiction, but the agreement might provide for international arbitration and determine how the panel should be selected, or defer that to the procedures of a recognized organization such as the Paris based ICC, or the American Arbitration Association. Investors and the host nation may agree to use the World Bank's generally highly regarded International Centre for the Settlement of Investment Disputes (ICSID) for investment dispute resolution.

With regard to contracts, hopefully most will be fulfilled and not lead to any dispute. If they do result in a dispute, however, the parties may view the appropriate method of dispute resolution very differently than at the time of planning the contract or agreement, when neither party could foresee the nature of the forthcoming dispute. It is very unlikely that the parties could have predicted every possible form of dispute, and one of the parties may regret having agreed to arbitrate all matters relating to the contract or agreement, and later discover arbitration is demanded by the other party over a matter that does not seem among those areas contemplated to be arbitrable. If one party feels especially strong about their position, they may be disinclined to consider mediation or arbitration, and wish to move directly to litigation. But that view may change when they realize that the litigation may most likely take place in the other party's courts where the court is inclined to apply its own national law.

Each form of dispute resolution has advantages and disadvantages to the parties from their perspectives at the time of drafting the contract or agreement, or in the absence of making the decisions from their perspectives at such later time when a dispute has arisen. A client will expect to be advised as to the most favorable form of dispute resolution for their own individual interests, not some form of resolution based upon some philosophical value judgment of the "fairest" method of dispute resolution or the "best" legal system.

Every form of dispute resolution may not be available to the parties from which to choose. For example, mandatory laws in some nations may prohibit arbitration outside the country. Or one form of resolution may by law be mandatory, such as where the appropriate jurisdiction for litigation has a rule requiring some attempt at mediation before the filed suit may proceed to trial. One form of dispute resolution may be available, but there may be obstacles to its effective use, such as where civil dockets are not addressing many civil cases in order to deal with crowded criminal dockets. The latter is a problem in some U.S. federal courts, where drug related criminal law cases have overwhelmed the courts and effectively forced parties to turn to the arbitration of civil disputes.

The capacity to make decisions and the inclination (or perception of such inclination) to resolve matters on non-legal grounds will influence parties' choice of form of dispute resolution. Mediation is usually by definition a process where the mediator has relatively little power to force conclusions on the parties - the mediator is rather expected to keep the parties negotiating so that they reach their own conclusions and perhaps narrow the issues. But the dispute may require more, it may require someone to step in and make decisions. Arbitration may or may not be the answer. Sometimes arbitrators are perceived as persons who believe that they must find a resolution which satisfies both parties to some degree, the charge of dividing up the pie rather than awarding it all to the party whose legal arguments are correct. However untrue this perception of arbitration may be, it may cause a party who strongly believes that its position is correct, especially after a dispute has occurred and there is no compulsory arbitration, to reject arbitration and turn to litigation. It is to such litigation that we first turn, although the final part in this chapter will provide an overview of arbitration.

THE PROCESS OF INTERNATIONAL BUSINESS LITIGATION

Notwithstanding the importance of discussing the use of alternate dispute resolution methods at the time of preparing commercial transaction documents, commercial litigation arises both where parties have made such decisions, such as selecting arbitration or selecting a forum and choice of law, and where they have not. That the documents show no evidence of such choices does not mean that they were not considered. The parties may have discussed the use of arbitration or the selection of a forum or choice of law, but been unable to agree and thus left the matter unaddressed, hoping it would never arise. Furthermore, that they were considered and a choice adopted does not mean that a court will respect such decision, although the likelihood is that a selection of arbitration, or of a particular nation's courts, or of a choice of law, will be respected.

While there is a natural sequence to most of the topics to be discussed, a few are not so easy to classify within the time frame of an action. For example, personal jurisdiction might be challenged before or after, or at the same time as, subject matter jurisdiction. Personal jurisdiction may also be challenged prior to or after *forum non conveniens*. Choice of law may be part of the *forum non conveniens* argument, or follow a denial of a *forum non conveniens* challenge. But, clearly, service of process should be addressed before choice of law, and jurisdiction before discovery.

One matter needs to be stressed repeatedly. Every one of these areas should be evaluated separately before making decisions regarding any one of them. For example, bringing suit in a nation favorable to the plaintiff with regard to ease of proof and the availability of substantial damages may prove futile if a favorable verdict is gained but the defendant's assets are all located in another nation that does not enforce any foreign judgments, or specifically any judgments of the chosen forum because that nation does not grant reciprocity. Choosing the best forum for a plaintiff means working through each stage for obstacles and solutions, such as whether that forum has the legal authority to and in practice actually does apply foreign law.

THE CHOICE OF FORUM

Forum selection clauses. In negotiating a contract, the parties should always at least consider the appropriateness of stipulating a chosen forum. They may not be able to agree and do nothing, but at least they considered the issue. If a choice is made and they submit to a specific forum, accepting jurisdiction, it does not mean that jurisdiction may be thrust upon a court that under the rules of the forum does not have jurisdiction. Nor does it mean that a court that has not been selected, but that under its rules could have jurisdiction, will respect the choice of forum. Such a court would not dismiss the case due to the forum selection clause were the matter to be filed there. While U.S. courts generally respect forum selection clauses, many foreign courts follow rules that require the court to go forward if it has jurisdiction, regardless of the party's choice of a different forum.

One of the most difficult issues for a court is to determine whether a forum selection clause was sufficiently freely negotiated and accepted by both parties, and whether it was the consequence of the use of a standard contract with a forum selection clause chosen by one party and imposed upon the other. In such situation it may be more likely that a court will uphold a forum selection clause that requires a Texas party to submit to a clause selecting another state's courts, such as California, than for that same court to uphold a forum selection clause that requires the Texas party to submit to a foreign court, such as Argentina. The international characteristics of the facts leading to the dispute may be the only difference in the court's decision.

At common law, choice of forum clauses were ineffective, since they were perceived as attempts to interfere with judicial administration by depriving a competent court of jurisdiction. The attitudes of U.S. courts have changed because of the U.S. Supreme Court's decision in *M/S Bremen v. Zapata Off-Shore Co.*, 407 U.S. 1 (1972). In that case, the Court upheld a Forum Selection Clause in which the parties had chosen, not the courts of one of their own countries, but the courts of London—a neutral forum which had no other relationship to the transaction. "[I]n the light of present day commercial realities and expanding international trade we conclude that the forum clause should control absent a strong showing that it should be set aside."

Parties often agree to choice of dispute resolution forms (arbitration versus litigation), choice of court clauses (one nation's courts versus another) and choice of law clauses (one nation's law versus another). The first two are essentially forum selection clauses, and along with the third, attempt to inform and persuade courts as to their appropriateness in being the resolving forum, and applying the selected choice of law rules. The forum before which a particular matter comes, whether it is the forum selected or some other forum, in which one party has initiated an action, will have to determine whether it will accept the choice of forum, and also the choice of law. A forum that was not selected might accept the matter and reject the forum selection clause, or the forum which was selected might reject the forum selection clause and refuse to proceed for any of several reasons such as *forum non conveniens*. The forum that was not selected might be more inclined to apply the selected law than the selected forum, such as where the parties chose a U.S. forum and a foreign law that would be difficult to apply in the chosen U.S. forum. The decision of a court not to accept the matter even when the parties have stipulated it as the proper forum, may well look more like a *forum non conveniens* decision than one of choice of forum.

In many if not most cases the parties do not include a forum selection provision in their commercial agreements. That may be because they did not discuss the matter, or because they did discuss the matter at arm's length but could not agree on a forum. They both expect the contract to be carried out or they would not have agreed to it in the first place. Thus they do not expect the issues of the proper dispute resolution forum or choice of law to arise. But if these issues might arise in the unexpected event that a dispute ensues, the parties may be quite willing to defer to the decision of a court applying the court's proper forum and choice law rules. That partly may be because the court might not accept even an arm's length and carefully bargained choice of forum and/or choice of law clause agreed to by the parties.

It had been thought that courts would refuse to enforce Forum Selection Clauses which are found in contracts of adhesion, or in the fine print boiler plate printed clauses in a contract involving parties of unequal bargaining power, especially if counsel has not been consulted. However, in *Carnival Cruise Lines, Inc. v. Shute,* 499 U.S. 585 (1991), the U.S. Supreme Court upheld a Forum Selection Clause which was not bargained for and was contained in the middle of 25 paragraphs of boiler plate on a ticket form which was received after the conclusion of the transaction. The Court found the clause "reasonable" because it saved "judicial resources" and might lead to lower ticket prices, but the court noted that a domestic, not an alien, forum had been selected.

U.S. plaintiff. Where no forum has been chosen by the parties, a U.S. plaintiff will usually assume that a U.S. forum is the best choice. That may not be true. A foreign forum may be the only place where the defendant may be subject to jurisdiction, or where the law is most favorable, or where the defendant has most or all of its assets. If the defendant is also a U.S. party, the dispute is likely to constitute domestic rather than international litigation. But the issue could be the liability of a U.S. hotel operating in a foreign country to a U.S. guest injured while staying in the foreign located hotel. The injured U.S. party has come home to recover and sues the owner of the hotel at home, regardless whether the defendant is only the parent of the foreign subsidiary that operated the hotel abroad. The U.S. plaintiff may assume that the U.S. court will apply U.S. law, but the U.S. defendant may argue successfully in the U.S. court that the law of the place of the injury applies, which would be foreign law. If the defendant is a foreign party, the U.S. plaintiff nevertheless may wish to litigate in the United States, but may have to address complex issues of personal jurisdiction over the foreign defendant in the U.S. court.

Foreign plaintiff. Foreign plaintiffs increasingly seek a favorable U.S. forum to decide matters that often have far more links to their own foreign nation. The reason for such forum shopping, especially where the issue is a tort, is usually the prospect of damages not available in the foreign plaintiff's nation, such as for pain and suffering and punitive damages. But even for commercial litigation the U.S. system may appear the better choice to a foreign plaintiff, with its more extensive discovery, jury system and possible contingent fee arrangement.

Defendant's responses. The response of a defendant may be that the court is an improper forum because it does not have jurisdiction. But it may also be that it is inappropriate to proceed because there is parallel litigation because the defendant has sim-

ultaneously sued the plaintiff in the plaintiff's foreign forum on the same facts, and that comity suggests that one of the forums should dismiss or stay
the matter in respect of the other. The U.S. court
may consider both forums to be proper forums, but
the foreign forum to be a more convenient forum,
and dismiss the matter under the doctrine known as
forum non conveniens. That is a doctrine generally
limited to common law nations; civil law legal systems usually reject *forum non conveniens* in favor of
the position that a court vested of jurisdiction must
go forward with the case. A court alternatively may
believe it is the *only* appropriate forum, and issue
an anti-suit injunction against the defendant, order-
ing withdrawal from the suit it filed abroad.

The fact that there are international dimensions
to these suits makes the resolution of what may be
relatively easy issues in domestic litigation quite
difficult because the court has before it an international case. One has only to consider what U.S. Supreme Court Justice O'Connor meant in the famous
Asahi[1] decision, when she noted that the case involved a foreign defendant, thus differing from the
most important previous jurisdiction case the Court

---

[1] Asahi Metal Indus. Co. v. Superior Court of California, 480 U.S. 102, 107 S.Ct. 1026, 94 L.Ed.2d 92
(1987).

had dealt with, where the defendant was a U.S. entity—*World-Wide Volkswagen*.[2]

JURISDICTION

Jurisdiction in U.S. Courts. While U.S. law distinguished between subject matter and personal jurisdiction, that is not a characteristic of the civil law tradition where the two concepts tend to be fused under the theory of judicial competency of the court. While consideration of personal jurisdiction in the United States turns one's attention to case law and discussions of minimum contacts and due process, subject matter jurisdiction is found in federal and state constitutions and legislation. Some subject matter jurisdiction provisions may be general and others may address foreign litigation exclusively. For example, the federal Foreign Sovereign Immunities Act is the exclusive means for subject matter jurisdiction over foreign states.

Business torts such as the negligent manufacture of a product may come before U.S. courts because of either a territorial link to the United States, such as negligent manufacture, or a nationality link, such as the incorporation or presence of sufficient doing business in the United States, essentially based on nationality of the parties. There is often a dispute over whether the tort occurred at the place of manufacture or the place of the direct injury. The former is often in the United States where a product was

---

[2] World-Wide Volkswagen v. Woodson, 444 U.S. 286, 100 S. Ct. 580, 62 L.Ed.2d 490 (1980).

designed and manufactured, while the latter is often abroad where the manufactured product was used and involved in an alleged injury.

Subject matter jurisdiction in the United States may include a question of jurisdiction in federal or state court, or the existence of jurisdiction in either. If brought in state court there may be an effort by the defendant, in some cases an absolute right, to remove the matter to federal court. Diversity, one basis for federal court jurisdiction, becomes complex in international litigation because diversity is based not on citizenship but on domicile, and domicile, defined as residence-in-fact with intent to remain, was not designed to address many international issues, such as a U.S. citizen temporarily residing abroad. There appears to be general agreement that diversity jurisdiction rules are in need of reevaluation in view of the globalization of business, but no serious movement toward revision has taken place.

Personal jurisdiction, in contrast to subject matter jurisdiction, usually focuses on issues of constitutional origin. While the meaning is continually debated the standard is generally recognized to constitute a two-part test, first whether the defendant's presence in the forum satisfies a *minimum contacts* test and, second, whether the exercise of personal jurisdiction over the defendant is reasonable according to notions of *fair play and substantial justice.* When the defendant is foreign, should the reasonableness part of the test involve consideration of the international dimension of the case? The attempts to answer this question confuse many U.S. law students and lawyers, and leave most foreign lawyers and their clients absolutely baffled. The U.S. Supreme Court has not yet provided clear guidance.

Jurisdiction in foreign courts. The rules of jurisdiction are not contained in due process provisions of foreign constitutions, but in codes of procedure or private international law. But the rules usually seek to achieve much the same result as in the United States, proper links to the court (subject matter) and fairness in bringing the defendant before the court (personal). In civil law nations there is often a rule that a matter should be decided at the location of the defendant's domicile (general jurisdiction), but may also be decided under an often complex framework addressing the location of the performance of a contract or the place of the commission of a tort (special jurisdiction). These rules place an emphasis on the relationship of the court and the claim, as opposed to the U.S. emphasis of the relationship of the court and the defendant. Unlike the U.S. rules, issues of contract and issues of tort occurring in the same case may have to meet separate special jurisdiction tests.

SERVICE OF PROCESS

Plaintiffs must select a method of service of process on the defendants that meets the requirements of the law of the forum. If the defendants are in a foreign country, service in accordance with the law of the forum may offend the nation in which the foreign defendant is located. Service by mail, for example, is not recognized in many nations. It may constitute sufficient notice in the selected forum, but any decision in favor of the plaintiff might not be recognized and enforced in the nation of any defendant who was served by mail. Thus, a plaintiff in international litigation must think of complying with the service of process laws of at least two nations, where the plaintiff has filed suit and where each defendant is located.

In most of the areas that we address in international litigation procedure there is little help from international rules. That includes choice of forum, choice of law, *forum non conveniens,* pretrial protective measures and jurisdiction. A Choice of Court Convention was concluded in July, 2005. Only Mexico had ratified the Convention as of early 2011, although both the EU and the United States have signed the treaty.

In two areas, service of documents abroad and taking evidence abroad, there are conventions that have been adopted in many nations. The Hague Convention on the Service Abroad of Judicial and Extrajudicial Documents in Civil or Commercial Matters of 1965 addresses service of process. It has been signed by some 65 nations. The United States is a party to this Convention and in compliance with a Convention mandate has designated a private company as the Central Authority to receive requests from other participating states to carry out service in the United States. The Convention provides procedural steps that reasonably assure the plaintiff that such compliance will greatly reduce if not eliminate the possibility of a successful challenge to the service of process or other documents. The Convention allows signatories to take reservations and make declarations to modify or limit obligations under certain provisions of the Convention. For example, the United States has made a declaration under Article 16 that an application for service will not be entertained under certain time of filing limitations. Several nations, not including the United States, have made Article 10 declarations or reservations prohibiting service by mail in their jurisdictions. This has a significant effect on the use of substituted or constructive service by U.S. plaintiffs, where documents may have to be transmitted abroad to complete the service process.

An important issue with any convention is whether it provides for a mandatory or optional procedure. As we will see later, the Convention governing the taking of evidence abroad has been held to be optional, while it is quite clear that the procedures of the Service Convention are mandatory. Article 1 provides that the Convention "shall apply in all cases, in civil or commercial matters, where there is occasion to transmit a judicial or extrajudicial document for service abroad."

FORUM NON CONVENIENS

When a U.S. court has jurisdiction it does not mean that no other court may have jurisdiction. That other court may be a foreign court, and under its rules be fully competent to hear the matter. In such case, the U.S. court may dismiss the action for reasons of *forum non conveniens*. *Forum non conveniens* has roots in Scottish case law, and has been most favorably received in the United States. That is because of characteristics of U.S. law that many foreign plaintiffs believe favor their causes. That includes contingent fee arrangements, civil trial juries, extensive discovery and, most importantly, pain and suffering damages and even the pot of gold at the end of the international rainbowpunitive damages. The source of *forum non conveniens* is almost exclusively case law, save a few states that have enacted statutes modifying or eliminating its use. It is essentially unknown outside some common law tradition nations. Recently two significant changes to the acceptability of *forum non conveniens* have occurred. First, English law was modified by judicial decision in 2000 to eliminate the consideration of public interest factors, leaving only private interest factors. But five years later, a decision in the EU court ruled that the UK's use of *forum non conveniens,* even with non-contracting parties (non-EU), was inconsistent with its obligations under the EU jurisdiction regulation. The court believed that *forum non conveniens* use led to needless unpredictability, and that a court vested with jurisdiction under EU rules was obligated to hear the matter if a case were filed. How this will turn out is unclear, especially with regard to those cases involving not the UK and an EU nation, but the UK and a non-EU nation such as the United States. The court did not feel that there should be a distinction. The second challenge to *forum non conveniens* has been by movements in some developing Latin American nations to block U.S. courts from making *forum non conveniens* rulings by legislation that removes local jurisdiction if a national first filed suit in the United States. The theory is apparently that the filing in the United States terminates what would otherwise be valid jurisdiction in the home nation, and therefore the U.S. court could not dismiss the case because there was an available foreign forum. How this will turn out is also unclear, but it seems that U.S. courts that understand the issue are not recognizing these foreign attempts to nullify a U.S. legal theory.

A court considering a motion to dismiss based on *forum non conveniens* usually proceeds to consider several matters. One will be whether the plaintiff is foreign or a U.S. national or legal resident. If foreign the choice will be less respected than if United States, because it assumes the foreign plaintiff forum shopped for reasons expressed above such as high damages. A second consideration will be whether the foreign forum is available and adequate. Availability has traditionally been limited to whether the law of the foreign nation provides jurisdiction over the issue and parties. But, as noted above, it is currently also addressing whether any alleged lack of availability is due to the plaintiff's act of making it unavailable. Adequacy, the second related issue, usually considers whether the foreign forum recognizes theories of action that the United States recognizes, such as strict liability, antitrust, class actions or consumer protection. But adequacy also has become enmeshed with considering whether the foreign forum is so corrupt, inefficient, inadequate and/or intimidating, that it would be unjust to transfer the matter abroad only to meet a certain doom. Courts do not like to classify other nation's courts as incapable of providing justice, but the reality is that there are many nations that are so incapable. The third consideration by the court involves what may be a lengthy review of private and public factors. Private factors include where evidence is located and getting it to the forum; the movement and inconvenience of bringing parties, witnesses and experts to the forum; the need to translate documents and testimony; the ability to implead third-party defendants; and implications from fragmenting the suit if it were dismissed in favor of different nations of different plaintiffs, and non-U.S. defendants. Public factors considered include each nation's interest in being the location of the litigation, the burden on the court system and interest of jurors in serving, and sometimes deterring U.S. companies from producing defective products for export.

Often a court will inquire extensively about the substance of the foreign law. If the motion to dismiss is denied, the court may have to apply foreign law. That alone may be a major factor in the court's decision to grant the motion, especially where the foreign law is that of a civil law tradition nation without a highly developed sector dealing with civil litigation. Whether or not the court considers the foreign law in its *forum non conveniens* determination, it will almost assuredly have to address that if the matter remains in the U.S. court.

Courts almost always condition a dismissal subject to some promises from the defendant. The most prevalent is a promise by the defendant to submit to the jurisdiction of the foreign court. Added may be a waiver of any right to use the foreign statute of limitations, but that may not be subject to waiver under foreign law. The next most common is an agreement to pay any judgment rendered in the foreign court, a promise that may be regretted if the foreign nation renders a very large judgment.

In most *forum non conveniens* cases the litigation has been initiated only in the United States. But there are many instances where the same matter is the subject of litigation in the United States and another nation. The plaintiff and defendant in the U.S. court may be, respectively, the defendant and plaintiff in the foreign nation. This is called parallel litigation. A U.S. court could dismiss the case on *forum non conveniens* grounds, but also might stay the matter for reasons of comity, allowing the other court to proceed without each case separately racing for the first judgment.

DISCOVERY

In a domestic case, discovery in another state is not significantly different than in the forum state. But when the parties are from two different nations, access to witnesses and evidence in a foreign state may be very difficult. Assuming the matter is in a U.S. court the parties may wish to apply local discovery rules. But if that means discovery in a foreign nation, any request to a witness to appear or to an individual to produce certain documents may clash with the foreign nation's permissible access to evidence. Nations have often used letters rogatory to gain such evidence, essentially constituting a request to the foreign nation's court to assist in obtaining the evidence. Such request will have to be crafted carefully so as not to demand what predictably will not be given. Extensive requests from the United States, made directly to persons or entities that are alleged to be under the jurisdiction of the U.S. court, have led many foreign nations to enact "blocking" laws that prohibit nationals from complying with such requests, or even make it a crime merely to ask for documents to be used in foreign proceedings.

Helpful to the gathering of evidence abroad is the Hague Convention on the Taking of Evidence Abroad in Civil or Commercial Matters of 1968, which has been adopted in some 56 nations. The Convention tries to meet the needs of the forum court to obtain evidence that court considers admissible, while not imposing upon the foreign parties or sources of evidence demands that are overly excessive under the rules of their nation. For EU member states, Council Regulation No. 1206/2001 has essentially replaced much of the Hague Convention.

An important early question for U.S. courts was whether the Convention procedures were mandatory or an alternative to the rules of the forum. If optional, a second question asked whether the Convention procedures had to be tried first and only if they proved inadequate could the court use discovery rules of the forum. The U.S. Supreme Court ruled that based on the history and language of the Convention use of the Convention was optional and there was no need to use the Convention first.[3]

One problem faced by the United States is reflected in Article 23 of the Convention. This article allows signatories to restrict pretrial production of documents, which many in the United States believe reflects a lack of understanding by civil law tradition nations of common law trial procedure. Article 23 is often cited as a reason given by foreign nations for rejecting requests for discovery.

---

[3] Societe Nationale Industrielle Aerospatiale v. United States District Court, 482 U.S. 522, 107 S.Ct. 2542, 96 L.Ed.2d 461 (1987).

CHOICE OF LAW

Broadly put, in common law and in European civil law jurisdictions, parties may choose the law which they wish to govern their contract relationship, as long as the law chosen is that of a place which has a substantial relationship to the parties and to the international business transaction, and is not contrary to a strong public policy of the place where suit is brought.

Most international cases involve the presence of at least two different sets of substantive rules. The approaches to deciding a choice of law question may differ depending upon whether the issue is contract or tort. It is an important decision for a court, because a ruling that a foreign law applies that offers very nominal damages is tantamount to a victory for the defendant.

Contract. A sales contract negotiated across borders might reasonably be decided in the nation of the seller or the buyer. Fortunately, international sales of goods rules have been partly harmonized by the United Nations Convention on Contracts for the International Sale of Goods (CISG) of 1980, which has been enacted by more than 70 nations. Major trading nations not participating include Brazil, Hong Kong, India, South Africa, Taiwan, and the United Kingdom. Furthermore, different participating nations may reach different interpretations of the same article, just as may different states in interpreting the Uniform Commercial Code.

A choice of law provision is often included in a contract, and such choices are respected in many nations. Where there is no such choice made in the contract, rules tend to determine the nation most closely connected to the transaction or at least having a significant relationship to the transaction.

Where the validity of the Choice of Law Clauses is determined by statute, there seem to be two different approaches. The Uniform Commercial Code (§ 1–105) permits the parties to choose the law governing the contract, as long as the transaction bears "a reasonable relation" to the jurisdiction providing the governing law. Thus, "party autonomy" is permissible, but only within "reasonable" limits. That is not helpful to the merchants in a U.S.-German transaction who wish to use neither U.S. nor German law, but wish to use the law of some "neutral" country, such as England.

In the EU, the 1980 Convention on the Law Applicable to Contractual Obligations (Article 3) also allows unlimited party autonomy. In sum, the legislative trend may favor fewer limits on party autonomy, and none in international transactions.

Tort. Torts usually occur outside of the framework of a contract that might have an applicable choice of law provision. But there are some such provisions, for example where a person signs an agreement for a stay at a resort or to take a cruise, and the contract has a choice of law (and quite possibly a choice of forum) provision in the event of any injury. But in many tort cases, such as the numerous cases brought against companies for injuries allegedly caused by the company's practices abroad, there is no contract and therefore no choice of law provision. In such case the courts tend to use the long held theory that the law of the place where the injury occurred is the proper choice. But the injury that occurs in one country may be attributable to negligence in another, such as where a product is negligently made in the United States and an injury occurs in a foreign nation after the product is exported. The consequence of the decision may be very important, because damages under U.S. law are likely to be much higher than under the foreign law.

Proving Foreign Law. Part of the analysis of what law should apply may include the problems associated with proving foreign law. While a U.S. court is deemed to know U.S. law, it is not deemed to know foreign law. It must be proved. That means an understanding of Rule 44.1 of the Federal Rules of Civil Procedure, assuming the matter is before a federal court. Rule 44.1 requires a party who plans to request the application of foreign law to give reasonable notice. It also allows the court wide latitude in determining foreign law. That usually includes the use of experts to explain both the nature of the foreign legal system, such as how case law fits into the hierarchy of law, and the substantive characteristics of the applicable law. Experts usually provide affidavits that include translations of the applicable legal provisions.

RECOGNITION AND ENFORCEMENT OF FOREIGN JUDGMENTS

Americans are used to recognition and enforcement of the judgments of one state of the United States by any other state of the United States. Sometimes they forget that this recognition and enforcement is due to the "full faith and credit" clause of the U.S. Constitution, and that the courts of most legal systems do not recognize judgments from other jurisdictions. For example, in nearly two thirds of the countries of the world, judgments of U.S. courts either are not enforceable at all or are enforceable only if certain conditions are met. As to foreign judgments brought to the United States, the "full faith and credit" clause does not apply to make them enforceable—but there is no rule prohibiting enforcement. The result is that the courts have been left to their own analyses to develop policies and rules.

The common law rule in England was that a foreign court's judgment for money was only *prima facie* evidence of the subject matter that it purported to decide—but no more than that. It was not conclusive on the merits of the dispute and did not act as either res judicata or collateral estoppel to actions in English courts by the loser in the foreign court.

The U.S. Supreme Court adopted a different approach in *Hilton v. Guyot*, 159 U.S. 113 (1895). The Court denied enforcement of a French judgment, announcing that it followed a rule of "comity," which required the opportunity for a "fair trial abroad before a court of competent jurisdiction," "regular proceedings," citation or appearance of the defendant, "a system of . . . impartial administration of justice," and without "prejudice" or fraud. The Court did not fault French justice on any of the above grounds, but it found that French courts did not recognize U.S. court judgments. Thus, the French judgment was denied conclusive effect, not because "comity" was lacking, but because "mutuality and reciprocity" were lacking. *Hilton* remains the leading federal law decision on the subject.

However, *Hilton* is rarely controlling, for most attempts to enforce foreign judgments will depend upon state law, not federal law, and state courts have felt free to pursue their own policies and doctrines. For example, the New York Court of Appeals, stating that it was not bound by *Hilton* has given conclusive effect to a French court judgment, despite the known lack of reciprocity.

A state court, in determining its own policies, has several options. It may reject the judgment of the foreign court and accord no effect to it, requiring a *de novo* trial on the merits in its own courts. Alternatively, it may accept the foreign court's judgment as its own and "enforce" it in the same manner as a domestic judgment. Or, it may "recognize" the judgment by deciding that there are issues which do not need to be relitigated, even though the court will only "enforce" domestic judgments. Where courts only "recognize" foreign judgments, the party with a foreign court judgment must use it to obtain a domestic court judgment, which may then be enforced in the jurisdiction. Direct enforcement of foreign judgments is unusual; recognition of such judgments is more common.

Finally, there are courts which grant conditional recognition to foreign judgments. The conditions may relate to reciprocity of recognition between the two judicial systems involved, or to "comity between nations." Where comity is the criterion, U.S. courts have tended to examine (1) the jurisdiction of the foreign court over both the persons and the subject matter involved, (2) the adequacy of the notice given, (3) the possibility of fraud in the decision, and (4) whether any public policy of the United States will be harmed by enforcement of the foreign judgment. Some U.S. courts seem to classify foreign legal systems as either favored or not favored, and judgments from favored systems are not investigated in detail. Common law nations' judgments appear to be more favored.

Many states have little or no case law on this issue, so the National Conference of Commissioners on Uniform State Laws drafted first the 1962 Uniform Foreign Money-Judgments Recognition Act, adopted by more than thirty states, and its successor the 2005 Uniform Foreign-Country Money Judgments Recognition Act. Under these similar acts recognition is given only to foreign judgments which are final and enforceable where rendered. Further, only judgments for sums of money are eligible for recognition, not injunctions or specific performance decrees. The Uniform Acts do not require reciprocity for recognition of foreign judgments, but do require an examination of the criteria and issues generally associated with "comity." Several states have added non-uniform amendments to these acts requiring either reciprocity, or "negative reciprocity." The latter requires proof only that the foreign nation has not refused to enforce a state's judgment, not that it has in fact actually enforced such a judgment. The 2005 Act generally follows the 1962 Act, adding some new grounds for non-recognition, adding a burden of proof rule, imposing a 15 year statute of limitations, adding some rules of procedure, and preferring the use of "foreign country" to "foreign State."

If a foreign judgment is given in a foreign currency, how should a state court design its award? In many states, a court's judgment must be in U.S. dollars. Although this should not induce a court to refuse recognition, it does raise issues of the proper time for computing currency conversion. The Uniform Foreign Money Claims Act, enacted in more than twenty states, allows the court to issue a judgment in a foreign currency, gives three criteria for doing so, and requires any conversion to be computed on the date of payment.

Countries have tried to facilitate the enforcement of judgments by bilateral treaty (e.g., the 1980 draft United Kingdom–United States Convention on Recognition and Enforcement of Judgments). Efforts to facilitate the enforcement of foreign judgments have been also the subject of multilateral treaties, such as the 1968 [EC] Common Market Convention on Jurisdiction and the Enforcement of Judgments (replaced by the EU Regulation on Jurisdiction and the Recognition and Enforcement of Foreign Judgment in Civil and Commercial Matters) and the 1979 Inter–American [OAS] Convention on Extraterritorial Validity of Foreign Judgments and Arbitral Awards. A major effort occurred over more than a decade to conclude an international convention on jurisdiction and foreign judgments, not dissimilar to that with the European Union, the Brussels Regulation. But the effort failed to produce such an agreement, settling for adopting the Hague Convention on the Choice of Court Agreements that to date has been accepted by only one state.

In the European Union, the 2000 Regulation on Jurisdiction of Courts and the Recognition and Enforcement of Judgments in Civil and Commercial Matters (Brussels Regulation) provides in Article 23 that parties to a contract which is either a written agreement or an oral agreement evidenced in writing may confer exclusive jurisdiction upon a court. There does not need to be any objective connection between the legal relationship and the court designated. In varying degrees, Forum Selection Clauses in contracts have been treated as presumptively valid in Austria, England, France, Germany, Italy, Latin America and the Scandinavian countries. In some countries (e.g., Luxembourg) the clause must be signed specifically by the parties; the signing of the contract as a whole does not suffice.

ALTERNATIVES TO LITIGATION

The use of alternatives to litigation to resolve international disputes merits some comment. Many nations may perceive that litigation is the primary means of dispute resolution, but there are other forms that one might wish to consider. That might be viewed as a kind of hub and spoke arrangement, with litigation the hub, and spokes leading to arbitration, mediation and trade agreement dispute panels. But other nations may give more equal status to these latter methods, and view litigation on a more horizontal plane along with the other methods. Japan, China and some other countries tend to share this view. But some nations, including Germany and the United Kingdom, seem to view litigation at the apex of a pyramid that leaves other forms at a very distant bottom, if they are part of the pyramid at all. Perhaps that fairly leads to a sense that the former group is at one end and the latter at the other, with the United States somewhere in between.

Litigation versus arbitration may be viewed by different institutions dealing with specific issues, such as banks dealing with letters of credit. It is important for U.S. lawyers representing clients engaged in a dispute with a foreign party to be able to understand not only the characteristics of the various choices of dispute resolution, but how opposing foreign counsel may view the alternatives.

Arbitration is considered to have many of the same problems as litigation. However, in litigation, a major problem arises with the extensive use of pretrial discovery; on the other hand, a major problem with arbitration is that the limited discovery permitted may hinder fact development. Thus, one major criterion for choosing litigation or arbitration will be the relative need for this type of fact development in your client's case, and in your opponent's case. As a theoretical matter, you may have a mechanism which you inherently prefer (unrelated to the specific dispute, parties, etc.)? Part of your choice will depend upon the attitudes and style of the individual advocate. Are you more comfortable with a formal setting or an informal setting? If "objective criteria" are ambivalent in selecting a mechanism, "subjective criteria" (e.g., in what setting are you as an individual more effective) should not be ignored. On the other hand, there are some disputes in which "objective criteria" should be determinative.

Perhaps we ought not to view alternative forms as associated with different nations, but as associated with different uses by different institutions in different nations. Why is arbitration preferable to banks for the resolution of letter of credit issues? The securities industry has long used arbitration, as Thomas H. Oehmke notes:

In 1897 the United States Supreme Court upheld the arbitration process as a fair, equitable and efficient method for settling disputes in the securities industry.* * * Today, nearly all disputes in the securities industry are arbitrated, rather than litigated. This is due to the federal judiciary's recognition of the FAA's preemptive effect in the field of arbitration and to the industry's pervasive effort to have all public customers, member and associated persons sign arbitration contracts. Arbitration, 89 AmJur Trials 55 (2008).

Remember that both parties must agree if litigation is not to be used and another mechanism substituted. The reception of a suggestion to use an agreed-upon forum will depend upon what the parties believe the most likely forum will be if no agreement is reached. Only a determination as to what court or courts have jurisdiction in the absence of agreement will allow the parties to make a comparison between that forum and other mechanisms and courts located elsewhere. What might be an interesting exercise would be to go back through the problems asking what would be the likely forum in the event of litigation and the absence of a forum selection clause.

INTERNATIONAL COMMERCIAL ARBITRATION

Uncertainty about identity of the country and the court in which a dispute may be heard, about procedural and substantive rules to be applied, about the degree of publicity to be given the proceedings and the judgment, about the time needed to settle a dispute, and about the efficacy which may be given to a resulting court judgment all have combined to make arbitration the preferred mechanism for solving international commercial disputes.

Some Western European countries long have been accustomed to arbitration. For example, the London Court of Arbitration, a private arbitration institution, has existed since 1892. The United States has had a Federal Arbitration Act since 1947. Arbitration in international commercial contracts is favored by the Peoples Republic of China, if mediation and conciliation fails, either through the Chinese Foreign Economic and Trade Arbitration Commission (FETAC) or the Chinese Maritime Arbitration Commission (MAC). Most of the nations of the former Soviet Union also favor arbitration, and have organizations similar to the Chinese FETAC and MAC. The Japan Commercial Arbitration Association has been active since 1953. Virtually all countries in Africa have arbitration statutes.

Latin America, historically disadvantaged in many arbitral awards, increasingly is accepting arbitration. For example, the 1975 Inter-American Convention on International Commercial Arbitration undertaken through the Organization of American States affirms the validity of agreements in which parties agree to submit to arbitral decision any differences with respect to commercial transactions. The 1979 Inter-American Convention on Extraterritorial Validity of Foreign Judgments and Arbitral Awards expands upon the scope of the 1975 Convention. Many of the Latin American nations are members of the U.N. Convention on the Recognition and Enforcement of Foreign Arbitral Awards (The New York Convention).

An increasingly adopted "Forum Selection Clause" is one that chooses no court at all, but selects an alternate dispute resolution mechanism, such as an arbitration tribunal. For a long period of time, the courts resisted validating such clauses, holding that they deprived the parties of due process of law (a reaction one might expect toward a competitor). However, legislatures were far more sympathetic to arbitration, and around the turn of the century began to enact statutes validating arbitration clauses. The issue now is firmly settled. Under the principle of "party autonomy," international contracts containing arbitration clauses will almost always be honored. In addition to arbitration, there are many other even less formal alternative dispute resolution mechanisms in use, such as the "mini-trial" or the use of "conciliation." The mini-trial, for example, comes in a variety of packages, each with a different impact on resolution of the dispute. It can be nonbinding if used with a "neutral advisor"; it can be semi-binding if its results are admissible in later proceedings; or it can be binding before a court appointed master.

Arbitration provisions also appear in Treaties of Friendship, Commerce and Navigation and Bilateral Investment Treaties. The purpose of such treaty provisions is to ensure the enforcement of arbitration clauses in commercial contracts between nationals of the Contracting States to the treaty. The treaty provisions will also require the courts of each Contracting State to enforce the awards of arbitral tribunals rendered under such arbitration clauses. Thus, the treaty provision may require the courts of each Contracting State to enforce such arbitration clauses and subsequent arbitration awards, even though the place of arbitration is not located within the Contracting States and the arbitrators are not nationals of the Contracting States.

WHY ARBITRATE?

The growth of international commercial arbitration (ICA) is in part a retreat from the vicissitudes and uncertainties of international business litigation. More positively, ICA offers predictability and neutrality as a forum (who knows which court you may end up in) and the potential for specialized expertise (most judges know little about international law). ICA also allows the parties to select and shape the procedures and costs of dispute resolution. That said, ICA procedures are relatively informal and not laden with legal rights. To quote Judge Learned Hand:

> Arbitration may or may not be a desirable substitute for trials in courts; as to that the parties must decide in each instance. But when they

have adopted it, they must be content with its informalities; they may not hedge it about with those procedural limitations which it is precisely its purpose to avoid. They must content themselves with looser approximations to the enforcement of their rights than those that the law accords them, when they resort to its machinery. *American Almond Products Co. v. Consolidated Pecan Sales Co., Inc.*, 144 F.2d 448 (2d Cir. 1944).

One of the most attractive attributes of ICA is the enforceability in national courts of arbitral awards under the New York Convention. Approximately 140 nations participate in the New York Convention. There is no comparable convention for the enforcement of court judgments around the world, the recent attempts to conclude a Hague Convention on Jurisdiction and Enforcement of Judgments having failed. The Panama Convention renders arbitral awards enforceable in Latin America.

Another major advantage of ICA is the support of legal regimes that give arbitration agreements dispositive effects. In the United States, for example, the Federal Arbitration Act provides a level of legal security unknown to international business litigation. Many countries have similar statutes, thus avoiding issues of subject matter and personal jurisdiction, *forum non conveniens* and the like. Excepting New York, there are no statutory frameworks supporting court selection clauses at the state or federal level. In worst case scenarios, parties selecting a court to resolve their disputes may end up with a court that refuses to hear the case.

One of the least attractive attributes of ICA is the minimal availability of pre-trial provisional remedies. In addition, many arbitrators focus on splitting the differences between the parties, not the vindication of legal rights which in courts might result in "winner takes all." But such extreme results could permanently disrupt otherwise longstanding and mutually beneficial business relationships. Perhaps, therefore, "splitting the baby" through arbitration really is the optimal outcome.

TYPES OF INTERNATIONAL COMMERCIAL ARBITRATIONS

There are two basic types of international commercial arbitration: ad hoc and institutional. Ad hoc arbitrations involve selection by the parties of the arbitrators and rules governing the arbitration. The classic formula involves each side choosing one arbitrator who in turn choose a third arbitrator. The ad hoc arbitration panel selects its procedural rules (such as the UNCITRAL Arbitration Rules). Ad hoc arbitration can be agreed upon in advance or, quite literally, selected ad hoc as disputes arise.

Institutional arbitration involves selection of a specific arbitration center or "court," often accompanied by its own rules of arbitration. Institutional arbitration is in a sense pre-packaged, and the parties need only "plug in" to the arbitration system of their choice. There are numerous competing centers of arbitration, each busy marketing its desirability to the world business community. Some centers are longstanding and busy, such as the International Chamber of Commerce "Court of Arbitration" in Paris which has its own Rules of Arbitration. Other centers are more recent in time and still struggling for clientele, such as the Commercial Arbitration and Mediation Center for the Americas (CAMCA).

Ad hoc arbitration presupposes a certain amount of goodwill and flexibility between the parties. It can be speedy and less costly than institutional arbitration. The latter, on the other hand, offers ease of incorporation in an international business agreement, supervisory services, a stable of experienced arbitrators and a fixed fee schedule. The institutional environment is professional, a quality that sometimes can get lost in ad hoc arbitrations. Awards from well-established arbitration centers (including default awards) are more likely to be favorably recognized in the courts if enforcement is needed. Many institutional arbitration centers now also offer "fast track" or "mini" services to the international business community.

INTERNATIONAL ARBITRAL RULES: UNCITRAL AND ICSID

Model International Commercial Arbitration Rules were issued in 1976 by the United Nations Commission on International Trade Law (UNCITRAL) following ten years of study. The UNCITRAL Rules are intended to be acceptable in all legal systems and in all parts of the world. Rapidly developing countries favor the Rules because of the care with which they have been drafted, and because UNCITRAL was one forum for developing arbitration rules in which their concerns would be heard. The Arbitral Institute of the Stockholm Chamber of Commerce has been willing to work with the UNCITRAL Rules, as has the London Court of Arbitration. The Iran-United States Claims Tribunal has used the UNCITRAL Rules in dealing with claims arising out of the confrontation between the two countries in 1980. Such trade agreements as the NAFTA provide for the use of UNCITRAL (or ICSID) rules in investment disputes. The UNCITRAL Rules are not identified with any national or international arbitration organization, a factor supporting their use as "neutral" ICA rules.

Among other things, UNCITRAL rules provide that an "appointing authority" shall be chosen by the parties or, if they fail to agree upon that point, shall be chosen by the Secretary-General of the Permanent Court of Arbitration at The Hague (comprised of a body of persons prepared to act as arbitrators if requested). The UNCITRAL rules also cover notice requirements, representation of the parties, challenges of arbitrators, evidence, hearings, the place of arbitration, language, statements of claims and defenses, pleas to the arbitrator's jurisdiction, provisional remedies, experts, default, rule waivers, the form and effect of the award, applicable law, settlement, interpretation of the award and costs.

In addition to its 1976 Model Arbitration Rules, UNCITRAL has also promulgated a 1985 Model Law on International Commercial Arbitration (amended in 2006), a 1996 Notes on Organizing Arbitral Proceedings, and a 2002 Model Law on International Commercial Conciliation. The 1985 Model Law has been enacted in some fifty countries (and the 2006 amendment in a half-dozen). It has also been enacted as state law by California, Connecticut, Georgia, Oregon, Texas and other states. In Model Law jurisdictions, an arbitral award may be set aside by local courts on grounds that virtually track those specified as permissible for denials of recognition and enforcement of awards under the 1958 New York Convention (below). Under the UNCITRAL Model Law, submission to arbitration may be *ad hoc* for a particular dispute, but is accomplished most often in advance of the dispute by a general submission clause within a contract. Under Article 8 of the Model Law, an agreement to arbitrate is specifically enforceable. Although no specific language will guarantee the success of an arbitral submission, UNCITRAL recommends the following model submission clause:

> Any dispute, controversy or claim arising out of or relating to this contract, or the breach, termination or invalidity thereof, shall be settled by arbitration in accordance with the UNCITRAL Arbitration Rules as at present in force.

Over 100 countries have signed the 1966 Convention on the Settlement of Investment Disputes Between States and Nationals of Other States. The

Convention is implemented in the United States. An arbitral money award, rendered pursuant to the Convention, is entitled to the same full faith and credit in the United States as is a final judgment of a court of general jurisdiction in a State of the United States. The Convention provided for the establishment of an International Center for the Settlement of Investment Disputes (ICSID), as a non-financial organ of the World Bank. ICSID is designed to serve as a forum for conciliation and for arbitration of disputes between private investors and host governments. It provides an institutional framework within which arbitrators, selected by the disputing parties from an ICSID Panel of Arbitrators or from elsewhere, conduct an arbitration in accordance with ICSID Rules of Procedure for Arbitration Proceedings. Arbitrations are held in Washington D.C. unless agreed otherwise.

Under the Convention, ICSID's jurisdiction extends only to legal disputes arising directly out of an investment, between a Contracting State or . . . any subdivision . . . and a national of another Contracting State, which the parties to the dispute consent in writing to submit to the Center. No party may withdraw its consent unilaterally. Thus, ICSID is an attempt to institutionalize dispute resolution between States and non-State investors. It therefore always presents a "mixed" arbitration. If one party questions such jurisdiction the issue of "arbitrability" may be decided by the arbitration tribunal. A party may seek annulment of any arbitral award by an appeal to an ad hoc committee of persons drawn by the Administrative Council of ICSID from the Panel of Arbitrators under the Convention. Annulment is available only if the Tribunal was not properly constituted, exceeded its powers, seriously departed from a fundamental procedural rule, failed to state the reasons for its award, or included a member who practiced corruption. ICSID awards may not be reviewed in national courts.

The Convention's jurisdictional limitations prompted the ICSID Administrative Counsel to establish an Additional Facility for conducting conciliations and arbitrations for disputes which do not arise directly out of an investment and for investment disputes in which one party is not a Contracting State to the Convention or the national of a Contracting State. The Additional Facility is intended for use by parties having long-term relationships of special economic importance to the State party to the dispute and which involve the commitment of substantial resources on the part of either party. The Facility is not designed to service disputes which fall within the Convention or which are "ordinary commercial transaction" disputes. ICSID's Secretary General must give advance approval of an agreement contemplating use of the Additional Facility. Because the Additional Facility operates outside the scope of the Convention, the Facility has its own Arbitration Rules and its awards can be reviewed by national courts. Numerous NAFTA investor-state arbitrations have operated under the Additional Facility.

ENFORCEMENT OF ARBITRAL AWARDS:
THE NEW YORK CONVENTION

In over 140 countries, the enforcement of arbitral awards is facilitated by the 1958 United Nations Convention on the Recognition and Enforcement of Foreign Arbitral Awards (the "New York Convention") implemented in the United States in conjunction with the Federal Arbitration Act. As the U.S. Supreme Court observed in *Scherk v. Alberto-Culver Co.*, 417 U.S. 506 (1974): "[T]he principal purpose underlying American . . . implementation . . . was to encourage the recognition and enforcement of commercial arbitration agreements in international contracts and to unify the standards by which agreements to arbitrate are observed and arbitral awards are enforced in the signatory countries." In an abbreviated procedure, federal district courts entertain motions to confirm or to challenge a foreign arbitral award.

The New York Convention commits the courts in each Contracting State to recognize and enforce arbitration clauses and separate arbitration agreements for the resolution of international commercial disputes. Where the court finds an arbitral clause or agreement, it "*shall* . . . refer the parties to arbitration, unless it finds that the said agreement is null and void, inoperative, or incapable of being performed" (emphasis added). The Convention also commits the courts in each Contracting State to recognize and enforce the awards of arbitral tribunals under such clauses or agreements, and also sets forth the limited grounds under which recognition and enforcement may be refused.   Grounds for refusal to enforce include: (1)incapacity or invalidity of the agreement containing the arbitration clause "under the law applicable to" a party to the agreement, (2)lack of proper notice of the arbitration proceedings or the appointment of the arbitrator, (3)failure of the arbitral award to restrict itself to the terms of the submission to arbitration, or decision of matters not within the scope of that subdivision, (4)composition of the arbitral tribunal not according to the arbitration agreement or applicable law, and (5)non-finality of the arbitral award under applicable law.

In addition to these grounds for refusal, recognition or enforcement may also be refused if it would be contrary to the public policy of the country in which enforcement is sought; or if the subject matter of the dispute cannot be settled by arbitration under the law of that country. Courts in the United States have taken the position that the public policy limitation on the Convention is to be construed narrowly and to be applied only where enforcement would violate the forum state's most basic notions of morality and justice. Recourse to other limitations of the Convention, in order to defeat its applicability, has been greeted with judicial caution.

Whether the New York Convention applies generally turns upon where the award was or will be made, not the citizenship of the parties. A growing number of courts in developing nations are issuing injunctions against arbitral proceedings before they commence. Many of these injunctions seem deliberately intended to protect local companies. Parties who proceed to arbitrate after such an injunction has been issued do so at their peril. Subsequent enforcement of the award under the New York Convention in the enjoining nation will almost certainly be voided on grounds of public policy. Hence enforcement can only proceed in non-enjoining jurisdictions, assuming that their public policy permits this.

MANDATORY RULES AND LAW

Majors centers for international arbitration include, among others, Geneva, London, Hong Kong, Singapore, New York, Paris, and Stockholm. Arbitration associations at such places have adopted fairly settled procedural rules for conducting arbitrations. In almost all countries, domestic law provides limitations upon the power of persons to specify for themselves what rules should govern their contractual relationship (including aspects of dispute settlement). As between two contracting parties, many provisions of local law may be excluded (called "jus dispositivum"), but the applicability of certain legal rules may not be excluded (called "jus cogens"). Jus cogens is mandatory; it is public law that private parties cannot avoid by contract.

The "jus cogens"/"jus dispositivum" dichotomy is found in the law of many European countries. It is also found in the Uniform Commercial Code and linked to the "mandatory law" rationales of U.S. cases (below). Any arbitration rules chosen by parties to govern their dispute may not be honored if such rules contravene a "non-excludable" mandatory provision of the local law. For example, notwithstanding that parties may desire otherwise, it has been a "non-excludable" rule that when there are several arbitrators, one of them shall be chairman of the tribunal.

Many lower U.S. federal courts had held that "mandatory laws" could not be the subject matter of arbitration, because of both the public interest indicated by the legislative intent underlying the enactment of mandatory law and the public policy favoring judicial enforcement of such law. However, the Supreme Court has now rejected that doctrine. In *Scherk v. Alberto-Culver Co.*, 417 U.S. 506 (1974) the Court held that Securities and Exchange Commission law issues arising out of an international contract are subject to arbitration under the Federal Arbitration Act despite the public interest in protecting the United States investment climate. In *Mitsubishi Motors Corp. v. Soler Chrysler-Plymouth, Inc.*, 473 U.S. 614 (1985), the Court held that antitrust claims arising out of an international transaction were arbitrable, despite the public interest in a competitive national economy, and the legislative pronouncements favoring enforcement by private parties. In *Vimar Seguros y Reaseguros, S.A. v. M/V Sky Reefer*, 515 U.S. 528 (1995) claims that the foreign arbitrators would not apply the U.S. mandatory Carriage of Goods by Sea Act (COGSA) were similarly rejected.

In both *Mitsubishi Motors* and *M/V Sky Reefer*, the Court determined that issues arising out of international transactions involving U.S. mandatory law were arbitrable. However, in *dictum* at the end of the *Mitsubishi* opinion, the Court stated that U.S. courts would have a second chance at the enforcement stage to examine whether the arbitral tribunal "took cognizance of the antitrust claims and actually decided them." Similar language can be found in *M/V Sky Reefer* regarding COGSA claims. It would seem to be difficult to fit any such examination by the U.S. courts properly into the structure of the New York Convention. It is not clear whether *Mitsubishi* invites the U.S. courts merely to examine whether the arbitrators state that they considered the antitrust issues, or also invites them to examine whether the arbitrators considered these issues *correctly* (review on the merits). The former can be evaded by a mechanical phrase; the latter can harm the arbitral process, especially if the parties have chosen non-U.S. law to govern their agreement.

In either case, arbitrators' enforcement of U.S. antitrust laws may not be to the standards of U.S. courts, and the status of recognition and enforcement of arbitral awards involving antitrust issues is not yet clear. Under the New York Convention, a mere "misunderstanding," or error in interpretation, of a mandatory law by an arbitral tribunal has generally not been held to "contravene public policy." The cases are split as to whether even a "manifest disregard" of U.S. law constitutes such a violation of public policy.

Awards have been upheld which violate the U.S. Vessel Owner's Limitation of Liability Act, previously considered mandatory law. Thus, it is not certain, under the New York Convention, that U.S. courts retain the review powers assumed by the *Mitsubishi* and *M/V Sky Reefer* Courts to be available at the "award-enforcement stage" of the proceedings.

ARBITRATION AGREEMENTS, ARBITRATORS AND AWARDS UNDER U.S. LAW

Arbitration agreements, traditionally called *compromis*, come in a variety of forms. Many arbitration centers sponsor model clauses that can be incorporated into business agreements. The New York Convention obliges courts of participating nations to refer upon request disputes to arbitration unless the agreement is "null and void, inoperative or incapable of being performed." The existence and validity of an arbitration agreement must be proved, and can be litigated before the arbitration takes place.

Article II(2) of the New York Convention requires states to recognize written arbitration agreements *signed* by the parties "or contained in an exchange of letters or telegrams." In most jurisdictions exchanges of fax, e-mail and the like embracing arbitration will also be recognized. However, arbitration clauses in unsigned purchase orders do not amount to a written agreement to arbitrate. Pre-arbitration litigation often revolves around motions to compel arbitration. If no such motion is made, and a court judgment is rendered (even by default), the right to arbitrate may be waived.

Whether a valid agreement to arbitrate exists depends on the specifics of the arbitration clause, not the entire business agreement. The arbitration clause is severable, and issues of validity (such as fraud in the inducement of the arbitration clause and unconscionability) directed to it. Many courts will stretch the limits of the New York Convention in order to uphold an arbitration clause When there is a battle of forms, the same judicial bias towards arbitration is often found. But, in most cases, the disputes must "arise under" the business transaction to be arbitrable and legal claims falling outside the transaction remain in court. The Supreme Court has held that a claim that a contract containing an arbitration provision is void for illegality should be decided by an arbitrator rather than a court (*Buckeye Check Cashing, Inc. v. Cardegna*, 546 U.S. 440 (2006)).

The closure or misdescription of an arbitration center designated in the agreement (e.g., the New York Chamber of Commerce) is no barrier to arbitration. A substitute arbitrator will be appointed by the court if the parties cannot agree. The U.S. Supreme Court held in *Commonwealth Coatings*, 393 U.S. 145 (1968) that arbitrators are subject to "requirements of impartiality" and must "disclose to the parties any dealings that might create an impression of possible bias." That said, most U.S. courts are loathe to intrude in proceedings or vacate an arbitration award on disclosure grounds.

There is a split of opinion as to whether the implied ground of "manifest disregard of the law" bars enforcement of an arbitral award in U.S. courts under the New York Convention. Article V of the New York Convention does not recognize manifest disregard of the law as a basis for denial of enforcement. Another issue concerning the New York Convention is whether to adjourn U.S. enforcement proceedings if parallel proceedings to vacate the award have been commenced in the country of arbitration. Despite the risks of forum shopping and delay, adjournment can be appropriate, depending upon the circumstances. Obtaining compulsory non-party discovery in private commercial arbitrations has been denied.

Cases in the United States have pointed out that parties cannot refer a dispute to a court while an arbitration is in progress or block enforcement of an award in the United States in reliance upon the fact that the award, although binding in the country where rendered, is under appeal there. Interim orders of arbitrators, such as records disclosures, may be enforceable "awards" under the New York Convention. After the arbitration is concluded, a party may not be able to block enforcement of the award in reliance upon the U.S. Foreign Sovereign Immunities Act, but a court may decline to enforce in reliance upon the Act of State Doctrine. One court granted enforcement, under the Convention, of a New York award rendered in favor of a non-citizen claimant against a non-citizen defendant.

When arbitral awards are annulled at their situs, courts in enforcing jurisdictions have taken different positions on the enforceability of the award. French courts enforced an improperly vacated award to the detriment of the claimant who had prevailed in a second arbitration. One U.S. court refused to honor the clearly legitimate annulment of an arbitral award by an Egyptian court because the parties had agreed not to appeal the award. The Second Circuit, on the other hand, recognized the annulment of two arbitral awards vacated by a Nigerian court and refused enforcement. The New York Convention does not address the treatment of annulled arbitral awards.

The U.S. Supreme Court indicated in *First Options of Chicago, Inc. v. Kaplan*, 514 U.S. 938 (1995) that questions of the arbitrability of disputes may be arbitrated, but only if the parties have manifested a *clear* willingness to be bound by arbitration on such issues. Silence or ambiguity should favor judicial review of arbitrability issues. Arbitration clauses that adopt the UNITRAL Rules meet the requirement of clarity to arbitrate arbitrability because Article 21 conveys jurisdictional issues to the tribunal.

INDEX

References are to Pages

-A-

ANTITRUST (BUSINESS COMPETITION) LAW, 366–388

Blocking statutes, 382–388

European Union Law, 373–377, 379–381

Enforcement, 367–371

Exemptions, 371–372

Mergers, 288–292

Extraterritorial application, 377–379

United States law, 379–381

ARBITRATION

See Dispute Settlement

-B-

BILLS OF LADING, 147–177

-S-

SALE OF GOODS

-T-

TECHNOLOGY TRANSFERS, 238–284